Packet Guide to Voice over IP

Bruce Hartpence

O'REILLY®

Beijing · Cambridge · Farnham · Köln · Sebastopol · Tokyo

Packet Guide to Voice over IP

by Bruce Hartpence

Printed in the United States of America.

Published by O'Reilly Media, Inc., 1005 Gravenstein Highway North, Sebastopol, CA 95472.

O'Reilly books may be purchased for educational, business, or sales promotional use. Online editions are also available for most titles (*http://my.safaribooksonline.com*). For more information, contact our corporate/institutional sales department: 800-998-9938 or *corporate@oreilly.com*.

Editors: Andy Oram and Maria Gulick	**Cover Designer:** Karen Montgomery
Production Editor: Rachel Steely	**Interior Designer:** David Futato
Copyeditor: Amnet	**Illustrator:** Rebecca Demarest
Proofreader: Amnet	

February 2013:   First Edition

Revision History for the First Edition:

2013-02-21:   First release

2013-03-15:   Second release

See *http://oreilly.com/catalog/errata.csp?isbn=9781449339678* for release details.

ISBN: 978-1-449-33967-8

[LSI]

Table of Contents

Preface

A short while ago, as network engineers made plans for the future, one of the considerations was the eventuality of Voice over the Internet Protocol, or VoIP. For several years, VoIP was always "on the horizon" or "around the corner," as many believed that it was coming but were unsure about the timing. The question was whether network designers and educational programs should become early adopters, building in capacity and knowledge now or whether they should make it part of the next deployment cycle. Pulling the trigger early might put you at risk of making the wrong decision in terms of vendor or protocol. Adopting late might put you behind the competition or make you rush to deploy a system that is not well understood by the local staff.

Voice over the Internet Protocol, a.k.a. Voice over IP, or VoIP, is a huge topic. Those trying to really understand how VoIP systems operate and the issues associated with their deployment must delve into protocols and architecture requirements such as power over Ethernet, or PoE. New security issues arise because voice is now packetized on the data network and accessible via ubiquitous wireless links. Quality-of-service issues associated with mixing data and voice on the same network cause headaches as network administrators are inundated with real-time data. Interconnecting IP voice connections with the public switched telephone network (PSTN) and unified communications (UC) brings additional concerns and increasing workloads to the beleaguered staff.

This book provides an explanation of VoIP from the perspective of operating networks and the packets caught on those networks. Since the topologies were built for the purpose of developing content for the book, the issues and supporting structures necessary for VoIP are also explored. Thus, readers will get a firsthand under-the-hood view of the protocols and architectures used by VoIP-based systems as we track connections from the time VoIP phones boot, through calls and during subsequent connection teardown. Like the previous Packet Guide books (O'Reilly's *Packet Guide to Core Network Protocols* and the *Packet Guide to Routing and Switching*), the tool of choice for viewing the packets will be Wireshark, which is still available for free out at *wireshark.org*. The author built and configured everything seen in this book.

Most basic packetized voice networks start of with some very similar components; Chapter 1 will begin with these. Components include not only VoIP-specific items such as gateways and phones but also requirements such as Dynamic Host Configuration Protocol (DHCP) and Trivial File Transfer Protocol (TFTP).

The files and website support the lab activities in this book. Simple networking experiences can be accomplished on almost any topology. However, it is not always possible to obtain the resources necessary to build and study voice networks. So, for the lab activities in this book, I have posted capture files posted on the companion website (*http://www.brucehartpence.com*). For additional background, a YouTube channel (*http://www.youtube.com/brucehartpence*) provides another resource.

With the exception of those for Skinny, all of the references used for this book are standards from the ITU-T (International Telecommunications Union-Telecom), the IEEE (Institute of Electrical and Electronics Engineers), Request for Comments (RFC) from the Internet Engineering Task Force, or material obtained from operating networks.

Audience

I had several folks in mind when I wrote the Packet Guide books: instructors, students, professionals, and those seeking information to boost their skill set. While the first two books covered topics that are part of almost every single network and this one focuses on a particular area, the goal and the audience have not changed. My goal in writing these is to provide the background to understand the issues but also take an in-depth look at the protocols and operations that are part of a VoIP architecture. A student who reads this book and completes the exercises will be conversant in this important area and will have obtained valuable practical knowledge. A professional looking to brush up or change jobs will gain the necessary leg up or at least knock the rust off. In either case, I hope you enjoy the read.

Contents of This Book

Chapter 1, *Introduction to Voice over the Internet Protocol*
> This chapter provides the foundation for the book. It includes the requirements for a basic VoIP topology and describes the issues associated with deploying packetized voice and video. Readers will also come to understand critical topics such as codecs and power over Ethernet.

Chapter 2, *Traditional Telephony*

Every data network must eventually connect to the rest of the world via the Internet. For VoIP, this usually means connecting to the global telephony network, the uses of which continue to include traditional connectivity. This chapter will familiarize the reader with traditional telephony concepts that will typically be a part of their lives as VoIP administrators including local loop, tip and ring, T carriers, and the necessary protocol conversations.

Chapter 3, *Session Initiation Protocol*

Most VoIP pundits agree that the Session Initialization Protocol, or SIP, is taking over the VoIP world, and I am no different. As a result, SIP will be the first "signaling protocol" that we will discuss in this book and will form the basis for comparisons made throughout the other chapters. As an Internet Engineering Taskforce request for comments, SIP enjoys wide industry support and shares many characteristics with other common web protocols such as the Hypertext Transfer Protocol, making it easy to understand and read.

Chapter 4, *The Real-Time Transport Protocol and the Real-Time Control Protocol*

VoIP protocols are broken into two categories: signaling and transport. The Real-Time Transport Protocol (RTP) and its sidekick, the Real-Time Control Protocol (RTCP), fall into the latter category. Almost every voice or video stream created via signaling protocols such as SIP or H.323 are carried by RTP. RTCP provides information about the stream. This chapter will cover the operation and fields for both protocols. It will also provide some practical information for their deployment.

Chapter 5, *Codecs*

At the center of all voice and video streams is the need to convert analog data to digital for transmission across the network. A codec or coder/decoder is the tool used for this purpose. The proper choice of codec can make the difference between a successful rollout and one that leaves the users questioning your ability. This chapter will spend time on both voice and video codecs, their operation, and the decision process used in making the correct choice.

Chapter 6, *H.323 ITU-T Recommendation for Packet-Based Multimedia Communications Systems*

H.323 became the de facto standard for Internet Telephony mostly because it was the early standard developed for video conferencing. Actually a protocol suite containing subprotocols, H.323 saw wide deployment, which is the reason for its inclusion here. Even though it is slowly being supplanted by SIP, it is still quite common for practitioners to run into H.323, requiring them to manage integration or conversion.

Chapter 7, *Skinny Client Control Protocol*

A Skinny is a proprietary signaling protocol from Cisco, and normally this would exclude it from a book about standard network protocols. However, there are millions of Cisco VoIP phones installed in networks around the world. Even though Cisco is transitioning away from Skinny in favor of SIP, network administrators should have a good handle on Skinny operation and its idiosyncrasies. This chapter will cover the operation, messages, and requirements of a basic Cisco topology.

Conventions Used in This Book

The following typographical conventions are used in this book:

Italic

> Indicates new terms, URLs, email addresses, filenames, and file extensions.

`Constant width`

> Used for program listings, as well as within paragraphs to refer to program elements such as variable or function names, databases, data types, environment variables, statements, and keywords.

`Constant width bold`

> Shows commands or other text that should be typed literally by the user.

`Constant width italic`

> Shows text that should be replaced with user-supplied values or by values determined by context.

> This icon signifies a tip, suggestion, or general note.

> This icon indicates a warning or caution.

Using Code Examples

This book exists to help you get your job done. In general, if this book includes code examples, you may use the code in your programs and documentation. You do not need to contact us for permission unless you're reproducing a significant portion of the code. For example, writing a program that uses several chunks of code from this book does not require permission. Selling or distributing a CD-ROM of examples from O'Reilly books does require permission. Answering a question by citing this book and quoting example code does not require permission. Incorporating a significant amount of example code from this book into your product's documentation does require permission.

We appreciate, but do not require, attribution. An attribution usually includes the title, author, publisher, and ISBN. For example: "*Packet Guide to Voice over IP* by Bruce Hartpence (O'Reilly). Copyright 2013 Bruce Hartpence, 978-1449-33967-8."

If you feel your use of code examples falls outside fair use or the permission given above, feel free to contact us at *permissions@oreilly.com*.

Safari® Books Online

 Safari Books Online (*www.safaribooksonline.com*) is an on-demand digital library that delivers expert content in both book and video form from the world's leading authors in technology and business.

Technology professionals, software developers, web designers, and business and creative professionals use Safari Books Online as their primary resource for research, problem solving, learning, and certification training.

Safari Books Online offers a range of product mixes and pricing programs for organizations, government agencies, and individuals. Subscribers have access to thousands of books, training videos, and prepublication manuscripts in one fully searchable database from publishers like O'Reilly Media, Prentice Hall Professional, Addison-Wesley Professional, Microsoft Press, Sams, Que, Peachpit Press, Focal Press, Cisco Press, John Wiley & Sons, Syngress, Morgan Kaufmann, IBM Redbooks, Packt, Adobe Press, FT Press, Apress, Manning, New Riders, McGraw-Hill, Jones & Bartlett, Course Technology, and dozens more. For more information about Safari Books Online, please visit us online.

How to Contact Us

Please address comments and questions concerning this book to the publisher:

O'Reilly Media, Inc.
1005 Gravenstein Highway North
Sebastopol, CA 95472
800-998-9938 (in the United States or Canada)
707-829-0515 (international or local)
707-829-0104 (fax)

We have a web page for this book, where we list errata, examples, and any additional information. You can access this page at *http://oreil.ly/Packet_Guide_VoIP*.

To comment or ask technical questions about this book, send email to *bookquestions@oreilly.com*.

For more information about our books, courses, conferences, and news, see our website at *http://www.oreilly.com*.

Find us on Facebook: *http://facebook.com/oreilly*

Follow us on Twitter: *http://twitter.com/oreillymedia*

Watch us on YouTube: *http://www.youtube.com/oreillymedia*

Acknowledgments

Good editors make good books. Thanks to the folks at O'Reilly, especially Andy Oram and Maria Gulick, for helping me through the rough spots; someday I may have a handle on XML and Docbook. And thanks for your patience as we struggled with some other challenges. May the electronic revolution go easy on you.

To Rachel B. Steely and Kristiana Burtness—gratitude for the copyediting from the comma-challenged.

Good books also need good reviewers, and I would like to thank Mark Indelicato and Chris Ward for helping out with some tough chapters. I would especially like to thank Jason Burns for reading every page and providing invaluable input. Your knowledge is impressive and willingness to help very much appreciated.

Dedication

Many thanks to my wife and family for continuing to put up with my writing bug. Big hugs.

And here's to the telecom folks trying to understand data and the data folks trying to understand telecom—may you meet in the middle.

CHAPTER 1

Introduction to Voice over the Internet Protocol

Enter the expansion of Voice over IP with its disruptive transition of voice from the old circuit switched networks to new IP-based networks

—Mark Spencer in the foreword for *Asterisk: The Future of Telephony*

Several years ago, most of the writing about Voice over IP (VoIP) was about how important it was going to be, what protocols were going to dominate, the need for higher education to adopt VoIP course work, and the impact on the industry. VoIP and its companion, Unified Communications, are now here to stay. The decision facing most companies is not if they will deploy VoIP but when. There is a need for graduates of communication programs and network professionals to have an in-depth understanding of IP-based voice topologies and protocols. If you read the introductory portion of this book, then you know it offers a comprehensive look into the architecture and standards used in VoIP deployments. For those not intimately familiar with the concepts and issues associated with this increasingly ubiquitous technology, I present this chapter.

This first look into VoIP will cover most of the issues associated with typical deployment and is designed to give you enough information to have an intelligent conversation. As you read, you will discover that VoIP represents a complete change to the methods used to communicate. This chapter starts with a quote regarding the open source product Asterisk and its start into VoIP. I would argue that the term "disruptive" may have been too soft. VoIP represents a complete change to almost everything in the communications pathway. About the only thing that stays the same is the size and shape of the desktop phone. Most folks involved with VoIP would agree that these are very positive changes —especially for consumers. Businesses also benefit from reduced infrastructure and personnel costs. Modern companies are expected to run VoIP on some portion of the network. Those in industry also point out that even traditional telephony providers use VoIP technologies behind the scenes.

VoIP is also known by terms such as Internet Telephony, Computer Telephony, and even Windows Telephony. Attempts to define VoIP involve explaining how it is essentially running telephone calls over the Internet—like Vonage or Skype. All you need is a high-speed Internet connection and an adapter. But if you are actively working with the protocols or researching what is best for your company, you know that there is a lot more to it. You may also know that a successful transition often entails battling things like interoperability and having to analyze packet captures.

A little reflection recalls a time when Internet Service Providers (ISPs) transitioned to high-speed options such as digital subscriber lines and cable. But your telephone was still provided by the traditional local exchange carrier. With the greater capacity for data connections, someone got the idea that it might be possible to run a telephone call over an Internet Protocol (IP) based network. Our friends at Digium were one of the first to point out that traditional providers would never have moved to improve services or offerings were it not for the open-source community and the VoIP protocols.

Some of the first attempts included point-to-point connections or websites working as the centralized call server. Calls like these were plagued by quality issues and a complete lack of industry support. But the idea was out. And what an idea it was—free telephone calls over the Internet? Sign me up! It was a golden dream for some (consumers) and a nightmare for others; namely, the providers. After all, telephone companies made a lot of money without a whole lot of competition. It wasn't long before services such as Vonage, Skype, and Time Warner voice made their appearance. Some of these services offered calling plans for less than half the price of traditional carriers. Some of them, most notably Skype, had as one of their goals putting telephone companies out of business. Even though price plans have settled out somewhat, wars continue with companies like majicJack and Ooma. The perceived quality can vary quite a bit, but there is no doubt that the monopoly held by traditional telephone companies has been broken and that industry is seeking employees possessing knowledge of VoIP in their skill sets.

This chapter will provide the background necessary to answer fundamental questions about VoIP and provide insight into the operations common to most VoIP deployments. Let's begin with a definition of VoIP, explaining why it became so popular and discussing the issues associated with this growing technology.

What Is VoIP?

To start, VoIP is exactly what the name indicates—sending voice (and video) over an IP-based network. This is completely different than the circuit-switched public telephone network that I grew up with. Circuit switching allocates resources to each individual call. Traditional telephone services are usually described by terms such as

Signaling System 7, T carriers, plain old telephone service (POTS), the public switched telephone network (PSTN), tip and ring connections, dial up, local loops, circuit switching, and anything coming from the International Telecommunications Union. All of these refer to a system that has been used for decades to deliver reliable, low-bandwidth telephone calls with a high level of quality. A simple traditional topology might look like the one shown in Figure 1-1. This traditional operation will be covered in greater detail in Chapter 2.

IP networks are packet switched, and each packet sent is semi-autonomous, has its own IP header, and is forwarded separately by routers. Chapters 3 through 7 will take us through the technical details regarding the operation of a VoIP system, but it turns out that understanding VoIP and its impetus is often a matter of understanding the effects of VoIP, which can be significant.

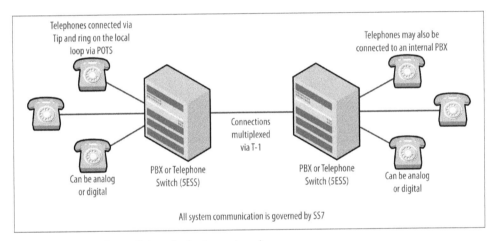

Figure 1-1. Simple traditional telephony topology

Native VoIP systems do away with much of what is considered traditional telephony. Well, almost. A system like the one pictured in Figure 1-1 involves a lot of control signaling to accomplish the various tasks required. For example, telephone numbers are dialed, and those numbers have meaning. Sounds or tones such as busy and off-hook are also messages of a sort. Database lookups for 411 or 800 numbers require additional messages as do services like caller-id, advanced features, and call routing. These signals are sent between the devices like the private branch exchange (PBX) before any human communication can occur.

VoIP takes all of these signaling messages and places them inside IP packets. While traditional telephones can be used in conjunction with a VoIP system, it is often the case that they are not. After a pilot project, companies implementing a VoIP system commonly desire to roll out a single set of equipment in order to simplify support and maintenance. This also reduces cost. After this occurs, endpoints are not referred to as telephones anymore, just VoIP or Ethernet phones. The PBX name is retained, although it is now called an IP PBX, which really means it is a server running on a computer. Redrawing the topology, we might see something like the one shown in Figure 1-2. It is also worth mentioning that since the Internet Protocol can and does run over almost every single type of low-layer communication architecture, Voice over IP can as well.

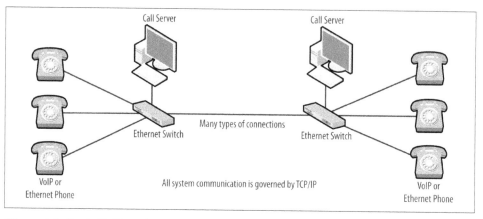

Figure 1-2. Basic VoIP architecture

And this indicates just how big an understatement a simple definition of VoIP can be. The languages spoken by the two systems are completely different, with traditional systems using Signaling System 7 (SS7) and VoIP networks using Transmission Control Protocol/Internet Protocol or TCP/IP. This also explains why the Digium folks call VoIP disruptive. Everything about this system is different.

To finish this section, let's take a quick look at the skill sets required to run the two systems. Figure 1-3 shows a side-by-side comparison of the topologies and a short list of the basic skills required to work on each. At first glance, the topologies do not seem all that different, especially as they are drawn. But, the equipment used in each, while serving the same functions, performs these functions differently and in fact operates using a completely different set of protocols.

A Venn diagram comparing the skills for each topology would find very little intersection. Following this line of thought to the hiring or training activities in an organization, we have to conclude that there would be a different demand for someone knowledgeable in traditional telephony topics compared to someone possessing a data network background. When faced with the need to support a VoIP infrastructure, what would the two individuals have to learn? If we consider the typical deployment on the consumer side, the traditional telephony person may possess knowledge about dial plans, call routing, T-1s, and features but will not understand the operation of an IP-based wired/wireless network.

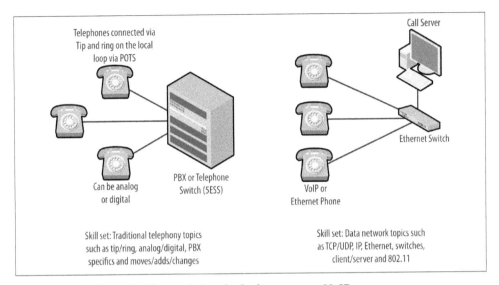

Figure 1-3. Skills needed for traditional telephony versus VoIP

A person possessing a data network background (Ethernet, 802.11, IP, TCP, UDP) would find that VoIP has migrated to the area of their expertise. They would be missing knowledge about the operation of a telephony system. However, many of the telephony skills would not be necessary. For example, moves or adds and changes are simply a matter of moving the phone and obtaining a new IP address. The debate over which individual would have an easier time transitioning has points on both sides, but there is no question that each side is missing something. This is somewhat mitigated by the proliferation of IP-based voice and location services, such as those offered by Google. It seems that we are all becoming a bit VoIP-ish whether we know it or not. Disruptive indeed.

Real-time Versus Nonreal-time Data

When you are downloading a file, delays are inconvenient and sometimes vexing, but they do not damage or prevent the transfer. Similarly, when visiting a website, if the page loads slowly, we are willing to give it a few seconds before navigating away. If some of the images from the page appear, we may be willing to wait even longer. These examples constitute transfers involving nonreal-time data. From a protocol standpoint, the transmission control protocol (TCP) is used to manage the connection, and all packets (or at least the bytes) are controlled via the associated sequence numbers. Lost or delayed data is retransmitted in order to ensure that the receiver has everything.

Figure 1-4 depicts a TCP packet with the sequence numbers circled. The two endpoints in the connection communicate not only the data sent (sequence numbers) but also, with the acknowledgment number, indicate the next chunk of data expected.

```
Ethernet II, Src: GiantEle_05:cb:11 (00:09:6e:05:cb:11), Dst: Avaya_e3:e3:d5 (00:04:0d:e3:e3:d5)
Internet Protocol Version 4, Src: 192.168.16.23 (192.168.16.23), Dst: 192.168.16.1 (192.168.16.1)
Transmission Control Protocol, Src Port: 4296 (4296), Dst Port: h323hostcall (1720), Seq: 1368, A(
  Source port: 4296 (4296)
  Destination port: h323hostcall (1720)
  [Stream index: 3]
  Sequence number: 1368     (relative sequence number)
  Acknowledgement number: 269     (relative ack number)
  Header length: 20 bytes
+ Flags: 0x10 (ACK)
  window size value: 7928
  [Calculated window size: 7928]
  [Window size scaling factor: 1]
+ Checksum: 0x3c8a [validation disabled]
+ [SEQ/ACK analysis]
```

Figure 1-4. TCP packet

Even though the bytes sent are closely monitored via the sequence numbers, the time it takes to receive them is not. So, packets may be delayed or even early. The important idea is that the user and the system are somewhat forgiving of delay, at least until the delay becomes so great the packet is considered lost. With TCP, the connection is strictly controlled and will not proceed without a complete set of packets. Most applications based on TCP are not real-time. From a user perspective, delays in applications are annoying but not prohibitive. We complain but we wait.

Real-time data is just the opposite. Real-time generally refers to something that is time sensitive. Delay that might have been acceptable for nonreal-time data can degrade performance and user experience to the point where the service or connection is unusable. Voice is a perfect example. Imagine a telephone conversation in which each participant must wait a second or two before receiving answers to statements or questions. We can see examples of this when watching a news broadcast in which the reporter is overseas. If, in the same conversation, the system were to lose a word here and there, the conversation becomes even more difficult. However, unlike the file transfer, we do not want the lost word returned. The connection would experience further delay waiting for the missing packet (packet loss), or it could be reinserted into the conversation in the wrong place. Lastly, if the packets arrived at a rate that varied (jitter), it might lead to unpredictable performance. Thus, the desire is to keep latency, packet loss, and jitter to much lower values on real-time data connections. From a protocol standpoint, the user datagram protocol (UDP) is usually deployed because we do not want retransmissions or the return of lost data. UDP does not keep track of sequence or acknowledgment values.

Figure 1-5 provides an example of a UDP packet. Besides the port numbers, the header does not include any information that might be significant for the connection. In fact, UDP is sometimes considered a fire-and-forget protocol because once the packet leaves the sender, we think nothing more about it. If the packet is lost, no response is required. Many real-time applications such as games and videos use UDP because the developers do not want to concern themselves with lost or delayed packets. Performance of the application might suffer if they did. The packet in Figure 1-5 also happens to encapsulate a Real-Time Transport Protocol (RTP) message. RTP is used by VoIP deployments to transfer voice and video data.

```
Ethernet II, Src: Avaya_ef:48:f8 (00:04:0d:ef:48:f8), Dst: GiantEle_05:cb:11 (00:09:6e:05:cb:11)
Internet Protocol Version 4, Src: 192.168.16.4 (192.168.16.4), Dst: 192.168.16.23 (192.168.16.23)
User Datagram Protocol, Src Port: clearvisn (2052), Dst Port: tsb2 (2742)
   Source port: clearvisn (2052)
   Destination port: tsb2 (2742)
   Length: 180
 ⊕ Checksum: 0xd11b [validation disabled]
Real-Time Transport Protocol
```

Figure 1-5. UDP packet

Why Change to VoIP?

With all of this disruption, why would we switch to Voice over IP? Probably the biggest reason for adopting a VoIP-based architecture is money. Instead of paying for a series of telephone lines or circuits, customers need only pay for a data connection. This is because the VoIP traffic travels in IP packets that can share the data connection. In addition, IP packets can flow to any destination connected to the Internet, and toll charges are much reduced. There are several business cases in which forklift (removing everything in favor of the new equipment) changes to telephony infrastructure are justified based on the savings in toll charges alone. VoIP architectures can pay for themselves in a relatively short period of time, giving the company a good Return on Investment, or ROI.

There are several other, less obvious, opportunities to save money with an IP-based VoIP solution. Networks deploying VoIP are often called converged networks because they share the data network. Once the data network is installed, all other devices are connected to it. This actually extends to other systems such as heating and cooling systems, security, and video cameras. The impact of this change is hard to overestimate:

- Single network to support
- Single set of devices
- Single set of maintenance requirements
- Single set of employee skills
- Many "off the shelf" components

- Single cable infrastructure
- Easier moves/adds/changes

All of these lead to a lower total cost of ownership, or TCO, for the network.

This is not to say that switching to VoIP eliminates specialized or expensive components. Indeed, some of the pricing structures or licensing fees for VoIP phones or PBXs are very similar to their traditional counterparts. VoIP desktop phones do not come cheap, with the more advanced models running hundreds of dollars. However, one advantage is the ability to deploy softphones instead of physical units. Softphones (phone software running on a laptop or handheld device) can be much less expensive and easier to manage.

The single set of employee skills is worth another look. VoIP systems run on the data network but are telephony systems that have been converted to IP-based protocols. The ideas and functions are the same. Companies consolidating infrastructure sometimes find themselves with a collection of employees that no longer possess the skills for the current infrastructure. As mentioned earlier, they may lack a background in the protocols and hardware associated with a data network. However, these employees are also the ones that understand the telephony side of things. On the other hand, data network administrators may have little or no knowledge of telephony. So a conversion to VoIP may require different types of training: vendor specific, basic network, and VoIP specific. Leveraging both groups of employees may provide the best possible outcome for the deployment.

The Business Case

And this brings us to the business case for VoIP. The justification for VoIP is often based on the Return on Investment. That is, how long will it take for the change to pay for itself? There are several situations in which VoIP has demonstrated a good ROI; these include upgrades to the current infrastructure, planned replacement of failed or out-of-date equipment, new installations, and many others.

However, there are some other, nonmonetary, benefits realized when converting to VoIP. For example, because VoIP equipment is very similar to the computers and network gear that is already deployed, the technical staff will be familiar with the issues associated with network connectivity. Thus, troubleshooting may be handled by the in-house staff. Additionally, this local expertise may reduce the mean time to repair (MTTR) and an increase in the mean time between failures (MTBF).

Employees using the VoIP endpoints may experience greater mobility if wireless phones are supported, but softphones and the ability to log into any phone may also increase mobility and productivity. Pundits often point to these advantages as well as integration with other applications as nonfinancial reasons to switch to VoIP.

Unified Communications (UC) also presents tremendous opportunities to realize improvements through integration of applications. UC systems are built upon a VoIP core, but, unlike VoIP, the case for UC is not always made through cost savings but productivity gains. The ability to collaborate, indicate presence, and use a single platform for email, messaging, and text can go a long way toward achieving these soft benefits.

However, not everyone agrees that switching to VoIP is the greatest idea. Companies that have a invested a great deal of time and money ensuring high quality of service levels, low downtime, and local expertise in their current telephony systems may not bite on VoIP for a few years yet, as the digital system provides the features and service they require.

VoIP and FCC Regulation

The telephony industry is highly regulated. What is on your bill, "do not call" lists, and 911 are all tightly controlled by the Federal Communications Commission. Pricing structure, number portability, and access are also controlled by these rules. But everything about the Internet and the services running on it are different, and so are the rules. For the last couple of years, there has been a continual debate regarding the regulation of the Internet. On one hand, there are those who believe that the Internet should be a free place where ideas and communications can flourish with no restrictions placed on anyone using it; for more information, look up *network neutrality*. On the other hand are people concerned about protection for consumers and young people. Issues with privacy and website willingness to share or sell your information seem to call for greater regulation and more stringent laws. Of course there are also those concerned with money. If everyone were to move to free telephony, what would happen to the cost model used by so many telephone companies? How would the government replace all of that tax revenue?

One look at a telephone bill reveals just how confusing this can be. In fact, one of the first documents offered on the FCC website clarifies what you might find on your bill. What it comes down to is that you pay for telephony service and the sales tax for that service. Almost everything else on the bill is also a tax or fee. At the time of this writing, the FCC does not regulate a lot of the VoIP market. In fact, as recently as June 2012, FCC Commissioner Robert M. McDowell stated:

> Governments should resist the temptation to regulate unnecessarily, get out of the way of the Internet and allow it to continue to spread prosperity and freedom across the globe. Internet connectivity, especially through mobile devices, is improving the human condition like no other innovation in world history.

A couple of the major exceptions include 911 service, discontinuance of service notification, number portability, support for the Law Enforcement Act of 1994, and contributions to the Universal Service Fund, or USF. The USF will show up on a voice service bill as a percentage (currently 9.85%) of the interstate and international call costs. The fund was established by the Telecom Act of 1996 and can provide assistance for locations such as schools, low income areas, the disabled, and health care facilities. Communications Assistance for Law Enforcement Act of 1994 (CALEA) requires that communication providers (including VoIP) enable law enforcement to perform lawful surveillance, including any modification to infrastructure that may be required. This may seem a bit heavy-handed, but the industry is largely responsible for setting standards and solutions. While all of this regulation or potential regulation is white noise to a network administrator, there are a couple of things that the professional has to worry about having available, and chief among them are 911 and power.

911

There is a significant difference between the operation of 911 service on traditional telephony systems and 911 on a system based on IP. The basic problem is that when a phone is identified by an IP address, geographic location is not part of the equation. By contrast, a traditional telephone is tied to a circuit that is terminated at a particular location. While it is true that an IP address is limited to an ISP and that a traditional telephone can be moved, VoIP phones are considered more mobile than telephony lines.

Adding to this are problems that are a regular part of data networks: outages, network address translation, movement or replacement of nodes, and so on. All of these elements can make it more difficult to locate an endpoint in the emergency call. Power outages can also create problems, as the VoIP service runs over powered Internet devices such as home gateways and cable or digital subscriber line modems.

Lastly, there is the very real question regarding the response to an incoming 911 call. Traditional systems have established public safety answering points (PSAP) to handle the call and connect it to the closest emergency response unit. While VoIP providers are required to establish the ability to locate an individual before offering service and must provide 911 on a nonopt-out basis, the challenges associated with locating an end node create a valid concern. Thus, finding the VoIP handset or softphone making the call becomes a very practical problem for the network administrator. This is made more difficult when we add wireless to the equation. Many vendors are beginning to offer location capabilities that made help address this challenge.

Another very practical problem is adding 911 to the dial-plan. This is not particularly new to VoIP but is worth mentioning, as it does have to be addressed. When a user dials 911, they expect a certain response. But what happens if a user remembers that they dial "9" to get off-site? In this case they may actually dial "9911" and expect the emergency response.

A Note on Power

Traditional telephony service provides power to customers from the central office. This means that the power source for telephones was completely different than the power supplied to outlets, lights, and your refrigerator. Thus, in a power outage, telephones might be the only thing still working—unless the customer uses cordless telephones, which get power from the outlet. In a VoIP solution, power outages also kill the VoIP service by shutting down the customer premises equipment (CPE). As an example, the local VoIP PBX would probably be installed in the closet with the rest of the networking gear. Desktop telephones typically get their power from the Ethernet switches via power over Ethernet (PoE), as would the wireless access points. Backup power supplies may provide power for a certain amount of time, but these are installed to provide enough time to manage a graceful shutdown of the equipment.

But with decreasing cellular costs and slow response from the traditional telcos, many customers adopted cellular phones. Charged cellular phones typically still have service in a power outage, thanks to backup power supplies for the cellular carrier equipment. Even if they have a VoIP solution, customers simply switch to cellular. Thus, the power-loss argument is not as strong. Of course, some folks never use a wireline telephone at all.

General VoIP Topologies

There are many topologies that can be used when constructing a VoIP solution. Each vendor has a collection of models that can be used to tailor a solution to the customer. But in a broader view, there are two general approaches: run the system yourself (on-site), or have someone else handle things, as in a hosted solution. Figure 1-6 provides an example of the first.

The left side of Figure 1-6 is the internal network, which houses the servers used to support the VoIP nodes and the VoIP phones themselves. The company is connected to the outside world via the Internet Service Provider, or ISP. Before VoIP, a company would also own a separate voice network, and these would be connected to the off-site local exchange carrier (LEC) in order to provide connectivity to the telephony endpoints. It is often the case that the ISP and LEC are one and the same. The VoIP endpoints also have to be connected to the telephony endpoints outside. Signaling traffic flows from the internal call server and gateway to the external gateway. Once again, it is possible that the ISP and VoIP gateway functions are provided by the same company. However, this is not always the case. For example, if Time Warner provides connectivity off-site via cable and gives you an IP address but your phones are managed by Vonage, the telephone signaling traffic flows through the ISP network to the VoIP carrier or trunk provider.

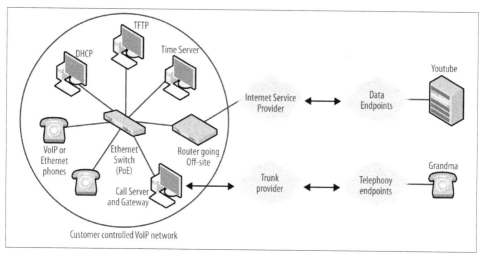

Figure 1-6. Running your own network

Companies that have a small staff or a small number of nodes or that simply do not want to run their own phone systems can opt for a hosted solution. In this scenario, very little customer premises equipment is necessary. It may be that only the desktop phones are installed within the company walls. All of the services necessary to run the phones are physically located at the provider. The provider may or may not be the ISP. This is shown in Figure 1-7.

If you decide to run your own IP PBX, there are several support components that must be part of the network. Deployment models depend on the size of the network, number of users, user requirements, and local skill level. There are also several small office home office (SOHO) solutions in which a small, low-maintenance gateway or PBX might be deployed on the customer premises. The customer may chose to administer the device or have a service contract. For even fewer headaches, the customer may opt for a full hosted solution like the one shown in Figure 1-7, and the only equipment on-site would be the phones.

Solutions scale up from there through small to medium business (SMB) models to enterprise deployments with massive integration, customer databases, and applications. Whatever the deployment model, several components must be present in order to handle several standard tasks. To start, all VoIP nodes must register with the call server. In this way, the call server understands what nodes require servicing. The call server may also be connected to several other call servers or to the outside world. Services such as directory listing or location may also be required. The following is a list of standard VoIP components; however, not all of them are required in every deployment.

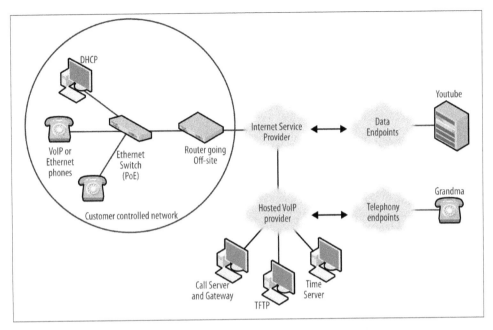

Figure 1-7. Hosted VoIP topology

Call server
> Phones register with the call server. The call server can handle security and admission control while connecting the phones. The voice data for the call, typically carried by the transport protocol, may or may not flow through the call server.

Gateway
> This device is typically used to connect an internal network to the rest of the world, or at least a different system. The system to which you are connecting may be a different technology or the same. For example, an internal network based on VoIP may connect directly to the PSTN. The PSTN is still largely controlled via SS7. The gateway will connect endpoints on either side, translate between the two systems, or provide features. On the other hand, a gateway may simply connect companies or providers together. In this case, the interconnected groups may be running the same signaling protocol.

VoIP protocols
> There are two types of VoIP protocols: signaling and transport. The signaling protocols handle all of the functions normally carried out by traditional protocols, such as the Integrated Services Digital Network (ISDN) Q.931. Standardized signaling protocols are described later in this chapter and given full attention elsewhere in this book. The transport protocol is used to encapsulate or carry the actual voice data, and the only protocol universally used for transport is the Real-Time

Transport Protocol (RTP), which is described in Chapter 4. The voice data packets are created with a codec and then encapsulated within RTP.

Codecs

This is short for a coder-decoder used for the purpose of converting the analog voice signal to a series of digital samples at the source and then back again at the receiver. Thus, the sending phone encodes the voice data with its codec, and the receiver decodes the voice packet with its codec. Codecs are present in both traditional and VoIP deployments. For a traditional system, the codec can be physically located in the phone or in the PBX, depending on the type and model deployed. VoIP phones always contain the codec. Codecs can also compress the voice data. While there are many different codecs, probably the most common audio codecs are from the ITU-T G series. The ITU-T H series contains the popular video codecs. Within the audio and video categories, codecs accomplish encoding and compression in different ways, though many are based on similar principles. Chapter 5 provides much greater detail on codecs, but a short list of these two collections would include:

- G.711—Pulse Code Modulation
- G.722 and G.723—Low bit-rate encoding
- G.726—Adaptive Differential Pulse Code Modulation
- G.729.1—Code Excited Linear Prediction variable bit-rate coder
- H.261—Early video codec for p x 64 Kbps
- H.263—Video coding for low bit-rate communication
- H.264—Advanced video coding for generic audiovisual services
- iSAC (Internet Speech Audio Codec)—a non-ITU-T audio codec developed by Global IP Solutions, used by Google Talk

Desktop phones and softphones

The phones (also known as endpoints) in a VoIP topology perform the same service that any other phone does, albeit in a different fashion. Early in the evolution of VoIP, there were attempts to get rid of the phone entirely in favor of phone applications installed on computers. However, people were used to the traditional telephone design and didn't like the change. The application also had to compete with whatever was running on the computer at the time. Today, we have a mix of desktop VoIP phones and telephony applications, or softphones.

Non-VoIP components

The VoIP system depends on a number of services that are not VoIP specific. Many of the services, such as the Dynamic Host Configuration Protocol (DHCP), are already part of the network architecture and can be expanded to include the VoIP components. Other services include Trivial File Transfer Protocol (TFTP), Domain Name Service (DNS), and Network Time Protocol, or NTP. It is common to see these components listed in the VoIP product requirements, as it may not run without them. A typical topology that includes these elements might look like the one shown in Figure 1-8.

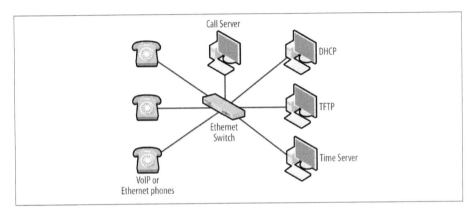

Figure 1-8. Typical VoIP topology

Power over Ethernet

There is another non-VoIP-specific piece to this infrastructure—power over Ethernet, or PoE. Devices such as access points and VoIP phones can be powered via injectors inserted between them and the network, but these require an outlet, as shown in Figure 1-9.

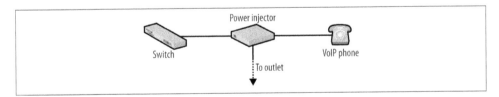

Figure 1-9. VoIP phone powered by injector

This does limit the deployment of the devices, since they must be near an outlet or have one installed. This is particularly true for access points, as they are often mounted on the ceiling. Rack-mounted PoE solutions can help if the environment and distances are favorable. Moving to a VoIP can introduce hundreds of phones that need to be powered. Even if the phones are in offices, this means a lot of outlets and power to manage. PoE-enabled switches get around this by providing power directly to the phone (or access point) without needing the injector. There are three PoE methods commonly deployed, two of which are IEEE standards.

IEEE 802.3af
> Carrier Sense Multiple Access with Collision Detection (CSMA/CD) and Physical Layer Specifications, Data Terminal Equipment (DTE) Power via the Media Dependent Interface (MDI) Enhancements

IEEE 802.3at
> Amendment to 802.3af

PoE Basic Operation

The standard defines two ends of the connection. Power is supplied via power-sourcing equipment (PSE) side and sent to the Powered Device or PD. There are a couple of configurations regarding the electrical connections which the PSE is supposed to support. Ethernet eight-wire connections have two data pairs (1 and 2, 3 and 6), and with PoE, direct current power can be supplied on pins 4, 5, 7, and 8. This positive pair runs on conductors 4 and 5 with conductors 7 and 8 being negative. The idea is that once a device requiring power is connected to the switch, it will be detected, and only then will power be applied. Discovery is via a PD detection signature at the time of connection. The PSE actually probes the connected device for the correct electrical characteristics, as defined in the standard. This is called the physical-layer classification. Devices may also support data-link-layer classification, which uses the local area network protocol. When this is active, data-link classification takes precedence.

PSEs, the link, and the PD are considered a system that is either Type I or Type II; each type has different electrical characteristics, such as direct current limitations, resistance, and cable type. Type II carries greater current and has greater cabling requirements. The power output by the devices is a function of the supply voltage and the current draw. The PSE has the requirements of locating PDs, providing power, monitoring the power provided, and removing the power when it is not needed. This also supposes that the PSE will not provide power to a non-PoE device. Type I PDs will advertise event-class signatures of 0, 1, 2, or 3 when queried. The default is class 0. Type II is more complicated but uses class 4 and a two part selection process. Some PDs can perform mutual identification, as they may require a Type II rather than a Type I PSE. The maximum power draw is a function of the class limitations and electrical characteristics (Table 1-1).

Table 1-1. PoE specifications

Class	Voltage	Current Min	Current Max	Min Power at output of the PSE	Average Power
0	14.5-20.5v	0	4mA	15.4W	13W
1	14.5-20.5v	9mA	12mA	4W	3.84W
2	14.5-20.5v	176mA	20mA	7W	6.49W
3	14.5-20.5v	26mA	30mA	15.4W	13W
4	14.5-20.5v	36mA	44mA	Defined by device	25.5W

The third PoE method is from Cisco. Cisco implemented PoE capability before the IEEE standards were ratified. The Cisco methodology differs from the IEEE standard in terms of negotiation, by utilizing the Cisco Discovery Protocol (CDP) and power level. Cisco also utilizes the fast link pulse to detect a connected PoE device. While Cisco devices may be IEEE compliant and support Cisco PoE, the two techniques are not compatible. Current Cisco devices support one or both of the IEEE standards.

The Cisco documentation notes an interesting problem that can crop up when a PoE device is connected and its type and class cannot be determined. The switch then allocates full power for the mystery device, though it may not be needed. The result is that power required by other devices connected to the switch cannot be supplied, thus resulting in an ersatz power-budget depletion.

 From a very practical side, knowledge of PoE operation is probably not necessary most of the time. An administrator might simply look up the power requirements of the connected devices in order to ensure that the switch provides the proper standard: 802.3af or 802.3at. This must also be part of purchasing decisions. Of course, troubleshooting is almost always aided by a little more domain expertise. In the example of power depletion, separating devices and understanding the signaling or potential problems can lead to quick problem resolution.

VoIP Protocols

As mentioned earlier, there are several VoIP-specific protocols but only two categories: signaling and transport. The signaling protocols handle the functions derived from the telephone system architecture, and the transport protocols carry the voice packets generated from the codec. Phones use the signaling protocol to register with the call server, set up, and tear down calls. Signaling protocols are also used for features such as directory services and screen displays. Once a call has been established, the voice data packets are typically sent directly between the phones using RTP encapsulation, though there are exceptions. The flow paths are shown in Figure 1-10.

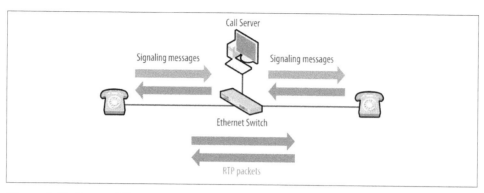

Figure 1-10. Protocol flow

RTP packets carrying the voice data may also flow from the phone to the call server and then to the other phone.

Signaling Protocols

Even though the VoIP architecture is completely different from that used by traditional telephony, we still have the basic requirement of signaling. Somehow, phones have to ring, numbers must be communicated, and routes have to be set up, and these functions are handled by the signaling protocol. The three most common types are H.323, Skinny, and the Session Initiation Protocol, or SIP.

Session Initiation Protocol

The Session Initiation Protocol (SIP) is a nonproprietary standard from the Internet Engineering Task Force, or IETF. The format of SIP messages is very close to that of Hypertext Transfer Protocol (HTTP) packets and so is very familiar to folks in the data networking world. SIP had a slow start but has largely taken over the world. Though the initial RFC was somewhat limiting, it is the signaling protocol used by most companies going forward, including Vonage and Skype. Even Cisco is transitioning from Skinny to SIP. In-depth coverage of SIP can be found in Chapter 3. A sample SIP packet can be seen in Figure 1-11.

From Figure 1-11, we can see that the packet is easy to read, it has an obvious purpose, and the parties involved are clearly defined. These characteristics and the integration with many forms of addressing are some of the reasons for the popularity of the protocol.

```
Internet Protocol Version 4, Src: 10.210.200.111 (10.210.200.111), Dst: 10.210.200.112
Transmission Control Protocol, Src Port: sip (5060), Dst Port: sip (5060), Seq: 1, Ack:
Session Initiation Protocol
⊟ Status-Line: SIP/2.0 180 Ringing
    Status-Code: 180
    [Resent Packet: False]
⊟ Message Header
  ⊞ v: SIP/2.0/TCP 10.210.200.112:5060;branch=z9hG4bK2965924072-14
  ⊞ f: <sip:10.210.200.112>;epid=10021002000112;tag=plcm_2965924072-15
  ⊞ t: <sip:10.210.200.111>;tag=plcm_1663913224-7
    i: 2965924072-13
  ⊞ CSeq: 1 INVITE
    k: timer
  ⊞ m: <sip:10.210.200.111:5060;transport=tcp>
    User-Agent: Polycom ViaVideo Release 8.0
    l: 0
```

Figure 1-11. SIP packet

H.323

This is actually an ITU-T suite of standards that focuses on video conferencing. It was developed earlier than its competitors and thus was the de facto standard used in many deployments. It uses many of the signaling ideas from traditional telephony, and some might say that it suffers as a result of the corresponding baggage. There are several subprotocols in an H.323 session, including Q.931, H.225, and H.245. More detail about H.323 can be found in Chapter 6. A sample H.225 packet can be seen in Figure 1-12.

```
⊞ Internet Protocol Version 4, Src: 192.168.16.23 (192.168.16.23), Dst: 192.168.16.1
⊞ Transmission Control Protocol, Src Port: 4296 (4296), Dst Port: h323hostcall (1720)
⊞ TPKT, Version: 3, Length: 1367
⊞ Q.931
⊟ H.225.0 CS
  ⊟ H323-UserInformation
    ⊟ h323-uu-pdu
      ⊟ h323-message-body: setup (0)
        ⊟ setup
            protocolIdentifier: 0.0.8.2250.0.5 (Version 5)
          ⊟ sourceInfo
              terminal
              .0.. .... mc: False
              ..0. .... undefinedNode: False
              ...0 .... activeMC: False
              conferenceID: 00000000-0000-1000-0000-0000c0a81017
          ⊞ conferenceGoal: callIndependentSupplementaryService (4)
          ⊞ callType: pointToPoint (0)
          ⊞ callIdentifier
          ⊞ fastStart: 36 items
              1... .... mediaWaitForConnect: True
              1... .... canOverlapSend: True
          0... .... h245Tunnelling: False
```

Figure 1-12. H.323 packet

Examining the packet in Figure 1-12, we do not have to go very far to see the number of sublayers and fields involved. Within the TCP packet there are three sublayers (TPKT, Q.931, and H.225) before we come to the actual message information. A little further on is the "fastStart" section, which has 36 items. This complexity might be one of the reasons for its declining popularity. However, some VoIP experts point out that SIP complexity can increase depending on the endpoints and their capabilities.

Skinny Client Control Protocol

The Skinny Client Control Protocol (SCCP), or Skinny, is a Cisco product. It is highly proprietary, and much of its operation differs significantly from what might be considered a normal VoIP deployment. However, Cisco has had great success with its VoIP products, and there are a significant number of Cisco networks running Skinny. Chapter 7 provides an examination of Skinny. A sample Skinny packet can be seen in Figure 1-13.

```
Internet Protocol Version 4, Src: 192.168.1.254 (192.168.1.254), Dst: 192.168.1.1 (192.168.1.1)
Transmission Control Protocol, Src Port: cisco-sccp (2000), Dst Port: 50202 (50202), Seq: 1205,
Skinny Client Control Protocol
  Data length: 88
  Header version: Basic (0x00000000)
  Message ID: StartMediaTransmission (0x0000008a)
  Conference ID: 2
  Pass-thru party ID: 0
  Remote IP address: 192.168.1.3 (192.168.1.3)
  Remote port: 27368
  MS/packet: 20
  Payload capability: G.711 u-law 64k (4)
  Precedence: 0
  Silence suppression: Media_SilenceSuppression_Off (0x00000000)
  Max frames per packet: 0
  G723 bitrate: Media_G723BRate_6_4 (2)
```

Figure 1-13. SCCP packet

One of the nice things about the Skinny messages is that, like SIP, they are very easy to read, at least if you have an older version or recent dissectors. Most Skinny messages are short and to the point. However, Skinny is proprietary and does have some behaviors that are not seen elsewhere, such as a limited or nonexistent use of Real-Time Control Protocol (RTCP), the companion protocol to RTP.

Transport Protocol

The Real-Time Transport Protocol (RTP) is the hands-down favorite for transporting voice packets containing the voice data. While there have been other mechanisms deployed, RTP is widely accepted. RTP, defined in RFC 3550, is a simple protocol that uses source IDs to collect packets from the same source, and it has a field that identifies the payload so that the receiver can determine which codec was used to create the voice packet. An RTP packet is shown in Figure 1-14.

```
Internet Protocol Version 4, Src: 192.168.16.23 (192.168.16.23), Dst: 192.168.16.24
User Datagram Protocol, Src Port: tsb2 (2742), Dst Port: acc-raid (2800)
Real-Time Transport Protocol
⊞ [Stream setup by H245 (frame 597)]
  10.. .... = Version: RFC 1889 Version (2)
  ..0. .... = Padding: False
  ...0 .... = Extension: False
  .... 0000 = Contributing source identifiers count: 0
  0... .... = Marker: False
  Payload type: ITU-T G.711 PCMU (0)
  Sequence number: 11639
  [Extended sequence number: 77175]
  Timestamp: 998248329
  Synchronization Source identifier: 0x196d27c5 (426584005)
  Payload: cec4e14b60cb61f8684a70febfcd5f51494d70c1cdde3f4a...
```

Figure 1-14. RTP packet

RFC 3550 also includes the Real-Time Control Protocol (RTCP), which provides in-formation about the flow of RTP packets. Its primary use is to provide feedback on the quality of the voice stream. An RTCP packet is shown in Figure 1-15.

```
User Datagram Protocol, Src Port: lot105-ds-upd (2053), Dst Port: upgrade (2537)
Real-time Transport Control Protocol (Sender Report)
⊞ [Stream setup by H245 (frame 22700)]
  10.. .... = Version: RFC 1889 Version (2)
  ..0. .... = Padding: False
  ...0 0000 = Reception report count: 0
  Packet type: Sender Report (200)
  Length: 6 (28 bytes)
  Sender SSRC: 0x07fff4aa (134214826)
  Timestamp, MSW: 18560 (0x00004880)
  Timestamp, LSW: 1941307392 (0x73b60000)
  [MSW and LSW as NTP timestamp: Not representable]
  RTP timestamp: 148483616
  Sender's packet count: 2
  Sender's octet count: 320
Real-time Transport Control Protocol (Source description)
[RTCP frame length check: OK - 80 bytes]
```

Figure 1-15. RTCP packet

Comparing these packets, we can see that the RTP packet provides an indication of the codec used to create the voice packet, the source identifier, and the data itself. The RTCP packet contains none of this. Instead, RTCP keeps track of the timing and bytes sent between the endpoints. In this way, an idea of the link performance can be obtained. Chapter 4 provides greater detail regarding both RTP and RTCP.

VoIP Basic Operation

This book contains a chapter for each of the signaling protocols, and the topologies used for the explanation were built using different vendors, including Cisco, Avaya, and As-terisk. As we work through each, we will see that most VoIP deployments follow a similar template for operation and have nearly the same set of components. This section will provide the template for operation, and the chapters will provide the details specific to the topology and protocol used. For right now, the topology shown in Figure 1-16 will form the basis of our discussion.

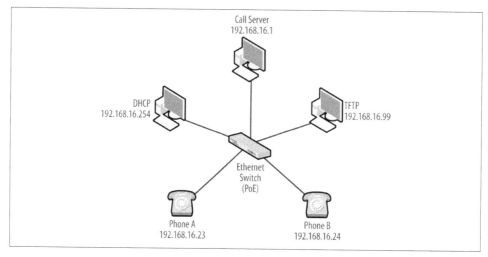

Figure 1-16. Topology for basic operation

The packet list shown in Figure 1-17 depicts the packets generated as a phone starts up and then makes a call. For space, this list has been edited so that examples are shown rather than the entire conversation series. This list is from a nonproprietary H.323 connection. As can be seen, there are several parts beginning with Dynamic Host Configuration Protocol, or DHCP. After DHCP, the phone contacts a Trivial File Transfer Protocol (TFTP) server to obtain any recent updates and then moves into the VoIP-specific messaging.

Just for fun, I've included another list from the proprietary Cisco architecture so that we can see both formats following a similar set of procedures. The packets shown in Figure 1-18 also progress from DHCP to TFTP and then to the VoIP-specific protocols.

Dynamic Host Configuration Protocol (DHCP)

As we saw in the proprietary and nonproprietary packet lists, almost all VoIP deployments begin with DHCP. In addition to standard items such as an IP address and default gateway, VoIP phones require the addresses of the TFTP and call-server address. Of the two addresses, TFTP is the next step for the phones simply because there are different mechanisms used to obtain the call-server address. For example, a configuration file can be installed on the TFTP server. This file will provide values such as the call server, language, and button arrangement. Some sample Cisco

Source	Destination	Protocol	Info
0.0.0.0	255.255.255.255	DHCP	DHCP Discover - Transaction ID 0xc6e03148
192.168.16.254	255.255.255.255	DHCP	DHCP Offer - Transaction ID 0xc6e03148
0.0.0.0	255.255.255.255	DHCP	DHCP Request - Transaction ID 0xc6e03148
192.168.16.254	255.255.255.255	DHCP	DHCP ACK - Transaction ID 0xc6e03148
192.168.16.23	192.168.16.99	TFTP	Read Request, File: 46xxupgrade.scr, Trans
192.168.16.99	192.168.16.23	TFTP	Data Packet, Block: 1
192.168.16.23	192.168.16.99	TFTP	Acknowledgement, Block: 1
192.168.16.99	192.168.16.23	TFTP	Data Packet, Block: 2
192.168.16.23	192.168.16.99	TFTP	Acknowledgement, Block: 2
192.168.16.23	192.168.16.1	H.225.0	RAS: gatekeeperRequest
192.168.16.1	192.168.16.23	H.225.0	RAS: gatekeeperConfirm
192.168.16.23	192.168.16.1	H.225.0	RAS: registrationRequest
192.168.16.1	192.168.16.23	H.225.0	RAS: registrationConfirm
192.168.16.23	192.168.16.1	H.225.0	CS: setup OpenLogicalChannel
192.168.16.1	192.168.16.23	H.225.0	CS: callProceeding
192.168.16.1	192.168.16.23	H.225.0	CS: connect OpenLogicalChannel
192.168.16.1	192.168.16.23	H.225.0	CS: empty
192.168.16.1	192.168.16.23	H.225.0	CS: facility OpenLogicalChannel
192.168.16.23	192.168.16.24	RTP	PT=ITU-T G.711 PCMU, SSRC=0x196D27C5, Seq=
192.168.16.24	192.168.16.23	RTP	PT=ITU-T G.711 PCMU, SSRC=0x49FF2367, Seq=
192.168.16.23	192.168.16.24	RTP	PT=ITU-T G.711 PCMU, SSRC=0x196D27C5, Seq=
192.168.16.24	192.168.16.23	RTCP	Sender Report Source description Seq=
192.168.16.23	192.168.16.24	RTP	PT=ITU-T G.711 PCMU, SSRC=0x196D27C5, Seq=
192.168.16.24	192.168.16.23	RTP	PT=ITU-T G.711 PCMU, SSRC=0x49FF2367, Seq=
192.168.16.1	192.168.16.23	H.225.0	CS: empty
192.168.16.1	192.168.16.23	H.225.0	CS: facility OpenLogicalChannel
192.168.16.1	192.168.16.23	H.225.0	CS: facility OpenLogicalChannel

Figure 1-17. H.323 packet list from startup

0.0.0.0	255.255.255.255	DHCP	DHCP Discover - Transaction ID 0
192.168.1.254	255.255.255.255	DHCP	DHCP Offer - Transaction ID 0
0.0.0.0	255.255.255.255	DHCP	DHCP Request - Transaction ID 0
192.168.1.254	255.255.255.255	DHCP	DHCP ACK - Transaction ID 0
192.168.1.1	192.168.1.254	TFTP	Read Request, File: SEP0013C4615
192.168.1.254	192.168.1.1	TFTP	Data Packet, Block: 1
192.168.1.1	192.168.1.254	TFTP	Acknowledgement, Block: 1
192.168.1.254	192.168.1.1	TFTP	Data Packet, Block: 2 (last)
192.168.1.1	192.168.1.254	TFTP	Acknowledgement, Block: 2
192.168.1.1	192.168.1.254	SKINNY	RegisterMessage
192.168.1.254	192.168.1.1	SKINNY	RegisterAckMessage
192.168.1.254	192.168.1.1	SKINNY	CapabilitiesReqMessage
192.168.1.1	192.168.1.254	SKINNY	HeadsetStatusMessage
192.168.1.1	192.168.1.254	SKINNY	CapabilitiesResMessage
192.168.1.1	192.168.1.254	SKINNY	ConnectionStatisticsRes
192.168.1.1	192.168.1.254	SKINNY	OpenReceiveChannelAck
192.168.1.254	192.168.1.1	SKINNY	StopToneMessage
192.168.1.254	192.168.1.1	SKINNY	StartMediaTransmission
192.168.1.1	192.168.1.3	RTP	PT=ITU-T G.711 PCMU, SSRC=0x165F
192.168.1.1	192.168.1.3	RTP	PT=ITU-T G.711 PCMU, SSRC=0x165F
192.168.1.1	192.168.1.3	RTP	PT=ITU-T G.711 PCMU, SSRC=0x165F
192.168.1.1	192.168.1.3	RTP	PT=ITU-T G.711 PCMU, SSRC=0x165F
192.168.1.1	192.168.1.3	RTP	PT=ITU-T G.711 PCMU, SSRC=0x165F
192.168.1.254	192.168.1.1	SKINNY	ConnectionStatisticsReq
192.168.1.254	192.168.1.1	SKINNY	CloseReceiveChannel
192.168.1.254	192.168.1.1	SKINNY	StopMediaTransmission
192.168.1.254	192.168.1.1	SKINNY	ConnectionStatisticsReq

Figure 1-18. SCCP packet list from startup

DHCP configuration lines follow, and the last four lines indicate various methods for providing the address of the TFTP or call server.

```
ip dhcp pool voip
network 192.168.16.0 255.255.255.0
default-router 192.168.16.254
next-server 192.168.16.99
option 66 ip 192.168.16.99
option 150 ip 192.168.16.99
option 176 ascii "TFTPSRVR=192.168.16.99,
MCIPADD=192.168.16.1"
```

Trivial File Transfer Protocol (TFTP)

As the name suggests, TFTP transfers are bare bones; there are no usernames, passwords, or fancy transfer types. A TFTP server is used to update the firmware used by the phone and perhaps provide a settings file that might contain operational parameters for the VoIP network. A sample from a settings file might look like this:

SET MCIPADD 192.168.16.1

But TFTP servers are also used to provide files that describe codes or tones used in a particular region. For example, a wide variety of downloadable files might be used when configuring Cisco's localization support. The capture shown in Figure 1-17 is from the perspective of Phone A, which receives an IP address of 192.168.16.23. Following the conversation up to this point, we can modify the topology as shown in Figure 1-19.

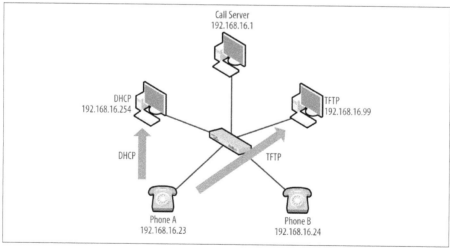

Figure 1-19. Topology with DHCP and TFTP conversations

Phone registration

Before a VoIP endpoint can make a call, it must first register with the call server, or gatekeeper. This process makes the call server aware of the phone and provides information for the interface on the phone. With a new installation or registration, a user will log into a phone using the phone number assigned to him or her. At this point, the IP and MAC address of the phone are now tied to that particular phone or dial number.

Registration occurs via the signaling protocol, and each signaling protocol uses a slightly different set of messages to accomplish the task. From the two conversation diagrams, we can see that H.323 uses RAS, or Registration, Admission, and Status messages, while Skinny use a registration message. In either case, it is pretty clear what is happening and that the phones perform this task before any other. Figure 1-20 depicts some variations in the register messaging.

```
H.225.0 RAS                                    Skinny Client Control Protocol
⊟ RasMessage: gatekeeperRequest (0)               Data length: 56
  ⊟ gatekeeperRequest                             Header version: Basic (0x00000000)
      requestSeqNum: 2                            Message ID: RegisterMessage (0x00000001)
      protocolIdentifier: 0.0.8.2250.0.5 (version 5)  Device name: SEP0013C4615F16
    ⊞ nonStandardData                             Station user ID: 0
    ⊞ rasAddress: ipAddress (0)                   Station instance: 1
    ⊞ endpointType                                IP address: 192.168.1.1 (192.168.1.1)
    ⊞ endpointAlias: 1 item                       Device type: TelecasterMgr (7)
    ⊞ tokens: 1 item                              Max streams: 0
    ⊞ authenticationCapability: 2 items
    ⊞ algorithmOIDs: 2 items
    ⊞ featureSet
```

Figure 1-20. Registration messages

Phone setup

Depending on the phone model, topology configuration, and signaling protocol, there may be several H.323, Skinny, or SIP messages passed between the call server and the phone. These may be used to inform the phone of events, provide feature support, or populate the interface. Each of the signaling chapters will provide greater detail, but some of these messages can be seen in Figure 1-21 and Figure 1-22.

These messages are exchanging permitted methods (Figure 1-21) and receiving directions regarding the screen (Figure 1-22).

```
Session Initiation Protocol
⊕ Request-Line: OPTIONS sip:4752222@172.30.1.19:5060 SIP/2.0
⊟ Message Header
  ⊕ Via: SIP/2.0/UDP 172.30.1.20:5060;branch=z9hG4bK0d4cc467
    Max-Forwards: 70
  ⊕ From: "Unknown" <sip:Unknown@172.30.1.20>;tag=as0b153664
  ⊕ To: <sip:4752222@172.30.1.19:5060>
  ⊕ Contact: <sip:Unknown@172.30.1.20:5060>
    Call-ID: 4bbe8bc25b1313d40a3f2e931d9718b1@172.30.1.20:5060
  ⊕ CSeq: 102 OPTIONS
    User-Agent: FPBX-2.10.0rc1(1.8.11)
    Date: Thu, 09 Aug 2012 20:08:59 GMT
    Allow: INVITE, ACK, CANCEL, OPTIONS, BYE, REFER, SUBSCRIBE, NOTIFY, INFO, PUBLISH
    Supported: replaces, timer
    Content-Length: 0
```

Figure 1-21. SIP options packet

```
Skinny Client Control Protocol
  Data length: 48
  Header version: Basic (0x00000000)
  Message ID: DisplayPromptStatusMessage (0x00000112)
  Message time-out: 0
  Display message: \200
  Line instance: 1
  Call identifier: 13
```

Figure 1-22. SCCP message

Both were received after the registration phase.

Call setup and connection

In a traditional network, lifting the receiver closes a circuit in preparation for the voice signal. Users dial numbers, creating tones that are sent to the telephone switch. The switch converts the tones to digital information via the codec. The switches must establish an end-to-end circuit to the destination. None of this is packetized, meaning it is not IP-based on protocols. For VoIP, this process must now be changed from Signaling System 7 messages and telephone frequencies (such as those coming from a dual-tone multifrequency, or DTMF, endpoint) to messages encapsulated in protocols such as those outlined in this section.

The VoIP signaling protocol (H.323, Skinny, SIP) sends messages to the call server, indicating the number dialed, and the call server must contact the destination. While the protocols have different methodologies, and in fact vendors may create additional differences, these messages typically appear just before the start of the RTP stream. Figure 1-23 shows some variations on the messages starting the connection.

```
Q.931                                           Skinny Client Control Protocol
  Protocol discriminator: Q.931                   Data length: 36
  Call reference value length: 2                  Header version: Basic (0x00000000)
  Call reference flag: Message sent to originating side   Message ID: DialedNumberMessage (0x0000011d)
  Call reference value: 0001                      Called party number: 4755002
  Message type: CONNECT (0x07)                    Line instance: 1
 ⊞ User-user                                      Call identifier: 13
H.225.0 CS
 ⊟ H323-UserInformation
  ⊟ h323-uu-pdu
   ⊟ h323-message-body: connect (2)
    ⊟ connect
        protocolIdentifier: 0.0.8.2250.0.5 (version 5)
       ⊞ destinationInfo
        conferenceID: 00000000-0000-1000-0000-0000c0a81017
       ⊞ callIdentifier
       ⊞ fastStart: 2 items
        1... .... multipleCalls: True
        1... .... maintainConnection: True
        0... .... h245Tunnelling: False
```

Figure 1-23. Connection messages

As we can see from the capture trace in Figure 1-18, the registration, setup, and connect messages all flow to the call server at 192.168.16.1. Updating our topology diagram, we get the result shown in Figure 1-24.

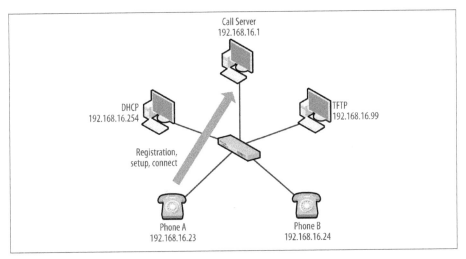

Figure 1-24. Topology with registration and connection transactions

RTP conversation

RTP is used to convey voice data. Once the RTP packets are flowing, the call has been established. However, RTP can also be used to convey samples created for other sounds. For example, a dial tone can be placed in RTP packets sent from the call server, and these packets will occur before the voice data for the call—so keep an eye on the IP addresses. The RTP packet contains a payload ID indicating the codec used. When the end user speaks into the handset, the codec takes the analog voice and creates the voice packets sent in the RTP stream. Taking a snippet from the H.323 conversation in Figure 1-17, we can see that the RTP packets are flowing between the phones. The diagram in Figure 1-16 indicates that the phones have the IP addresses of 192.168.16.23 and 192.168.16.24.

At the receiving end, the voice packets are decoded and played into the earpiece. Note that the Synchronizing Source (SSRC) values are consistent in these packets, allowing the stream to be reconstructed at either end. From the two conversations in Figure 1-17 and Figure 1-18, it can be seen that both architectures are using RTP. SIP deployments also use RTP. Another look at the RTP conversation in Figure 1-25 reveals that an RTCP packet stole in.

```
192.168.16.23    192.168.16.24    RTP     PT=ITU-T G.711 PCMU, SSRC=0x196D27C5, Seq=
192.168.16.24    192.168.16.23    RTP     PT=ITU-T G.711 PCMU, SSRC=0x49FF2367, Seq=
192.168.16.23    192.168.16.24    RTP     PT=ITU-T G.711 PCMU, SSRC=0x196D27C5, Seq=
192.168.16.24    192.168.16.23    RTCP    Sender Report   Source description    Seq=
192.168.16.23    192.168.16.24    RTP     PT=ITU-T G.711 PCMU, SSRC=0x196D27C5, Seq=
192.168.16.24    192.168.16.23    RTP     PT=ITU-T G.711 PCMU, SSRC=0x49FF2367, Seq=
```

Figure 1-25. RTP conversation

RTCP

As mentioned previously and as seen in Figure 1-15, RTCP packets carry information about the RTP stream that is used to provide details about quality or performance. RFC 3550 states that RTCP will be deployed whenever RTP is used. The list of packets bears this out. However, not every deployment will obey the rules. While the lists of packets are edited, they are not edited in such as way that should mislead the reader. So, if in examining the Cisco topology, you noticed that there were no RTCP packets, your eyes are not deceiving you. Cisco uses another SCCP mechanism to accomplish the goal of RTCP, and this is shown in Figure 1-26.

```
Skinny Client Control Protocol
  Data length: 64
  Header version: Basic (0x00000000)
  Message ID: ConnectionStatisticsRes (0x00000023)
  Directory number: 4755001
  Call identifier: 13
  Stats processing type: doNotClearStats (1)
  Packets sent: 389
  Octets sent: 66908
  Packets Received: 380
  Octets received: 65360
  Packets lost: 0
  Jitter: 0
  Latency(ms): 0
```

Figure 1-26. Cisco SCCP Connection Statistics Message

If we take another look at our topology, we see that the endpoint IP addresses are communicating directly via the RTP stream, as shown in Figure 1-27. Note that all of the other devices are out of the conversation at this point.

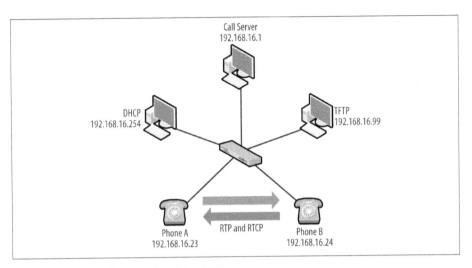

Figure 1-27. Topology updated for RTP

Call termination

In most VoIP deployments, every attempt to facilitate a graceful disconnect is made. This ensures that the channel or session is shutdown, resources are recovered, billing is determined, and no other connection data is accepted for that Call-ID. This is as opposed to simply severing the connection from one endpoint. Reviewing Figure 1-17, the signaling protocol comes back into the connection at this point and provides messages to the involved parties in order to tear down the logical circuit and recover resources. The phones are back to communicating with the call server IP address at 192.168.16.1.

Performance

With protocols such as RTCP or Skinny messages, like those shown in Figure 1-15 and Figure 1-24, paying so much attention to quality metrics for the RTP stream, one might be led to believe that VoIP performance is a big deal. Well, it is. With so many systems converting to IP, it is easy to be lulled into thinking that these are just additional applications running on the network and that the network can continue to support the additions. While some applications may survive in an increasingly busy network, voice is a very important and sensitive application. Other types of traffic (FTP, HTTP, mail, etc.) can usually weather an outage or service problem. But without voice communication, problems can get very serious for a business. If you are a network administrator, you may get some unwanted attention if voice communications fail. Thus, it is not uncommon for VoIP systems to receive additional budget consideration and personnel. We often allocate resources to ensuring that not only does the system keep running but that it has a high level of quality.

As mentioned earlier in this chapter, the three enemies to VoIP performance are latency (delay), jitter, and packet loss. Almost every object or process in the path adds latency —from the codec used, routing and switch tables in hops along the way, and the inherent behavior of the network. Jitter, or the variation in packet-arrival times, leads to unpredictable performance. Normally, jitter problems are managed with buffering. But with real-time data, the ability to provide buffering is extremely limited. Packet loss is another significant problem for any application, as retransmissions can really eat into the quality of the call. Table 1-2 provides some indication of a quality metric for calls.

Table 1-2. VoIP Quality Metrics

	Cisco	Avaya	ITU-T
Maximum Latency (end to end)	150msec	80-180msec	150msec
Maximum Packet Loss	Less than 1%	Target of 1%; 3% is acceptable	Less than 1%
Maximum Jitter	Less than 30msec	Less than 20msec	Varies based on deployment

Though some of the values might vary a small amount, we can see that most vendors and standards are pretty close.

Unified Communications

While this book is intended to help with the networking side of VoIP, we should at least touch on the subject of unified communications, or UC for short. UC describes what many people think of as the next step after VoIP. Many UC solutions have a VoIP core but go well beyond using the data network for audio and video. UC is perhaps best described by the problems it tries to address, namely:

- Many different kinds of devices
- Many different platforms
- Many methods used to communicate
- Many usernames, IDs, and addresses to coordinate

Unified Communications are broad attempts to collect these into a single interface or service. As a colleague of mine likes to say, "I decide what I want to send to you and how. You decide how to pick it up and in what format." This means that a vendor offering UC services might include voice, video, email, messaging, collaborative workspace, conference, presence, and the list goes on.

It is a challenge that vendors have different definitions of UC, and they all read like a collection of buzzwords. Examples include "enhancing the quality of the interactive experience across the entire enterprise" and "the convergence of real-time and nonreal-time business communication applications." While these definitions don't really tell us very much, by digging a little deeper, we find that most solutions agree on a couple of key areas:

- Integration with voice capabilities
- Presence, both online and off-hook
- Single A single user interface
- Collaboration

Another piece that most agree on is that, unlike VoIP, unified communications are not sold on savings or cost improvements but on improving business processes and human productivity. Sometimes unified communications can do both, as is the case with using high-definition video conferencing instead of travel.

Summary

Voice over IP (VoIP) is quickly becoming a central component to networks, regardless of the size or type of business. System and network administrators are often asked to deploy VoIP natively or migrate traditional telephony systems to a VoIP solution. Understanding the operation of VoIP protocols and the services necessary is critical to create a successful solution. This chapter discussed a standard VoIP topology, including non-VoIP-specific components such as the Dynamic Host Configuration Protocol and the Trivial File Transfer Protocol. Signaling protocols including H.323, SIP, and SCCP were reviewed, as well as RTP, which servers use to transport voice data. Further details can be found in the chapters dedicated to these protocols. This chapter is also supported by capture files on the book's website.

Standards and Reading

While each chapter in this book has a reading list specific to the chapter topic, this section will provide a "getting started" list. The Federal Communications Commission website (*http://www.fcc.gov*) has a tremendous amount of good information regarding the state of legislation and requirements for telephony service over the Internet. A good place to start is this website (*http://fcc.us/XMCyBH*).

This book does not cover the justification for VoIP and Unified Communications, as that appears to have already been made. But if you would like a little more information on the business case, you can start with the Techtarget folks—and no, I didn't get paid to say that. The work done by Digium is a great resource as well:

- United Communications (*http://bit.ly/11TIfWY*)
- Asterisk—one of the documents that helped start it all: "The Future of Telephony" (*http://www.asteriskdocs.org/*)
- RFC 3261—SIP: Session Initiation Protocol
- RFC 3550—RTP: A Transport Protocol for Real-Time Applications
- International Telecommunications Union–Telecom Recommendations, G and H series (*http://bit.ly/XMCTV8*)

Review Questions

1. What are the major signaling protocols? Which of these are proprietary?
2. What are the two protocols defined by RFC 3550 and their purposes?
3. Name three non-VoIP components used by VoIP architectures.
4. Describe the general order of operations for a disconnected phone that is first plugged into the network and then makes a call.
5. True or false: all codecs in a VoIP system reside on the call server.
6. Name a couple of methods by which a VoIP phone may learn about the call server.
7. What are the three main impairments to good voice quality on a VoIP system?
8. What are the target values for these impairments in order to maintain good voice quality?
9. True or false: the business case for VoIP and UC are made in the same way.
10. What are the two IEEE PoE standards?

Review Question Answers

1. Skinny (proprietary), SIP, and H.323.
2. RTP—transport of voice data, RTCP—quality and performance feedback for the RTP stream.
3. DHCP, TFTP, NTP.
4. DHCP, TFTP, registration via signaling protocol, phone configuration and call setup/connecting via signaling protocol, voice transfer via RTP, RTCP feedback, call termination and teardown via signaling protocol.
5. False; codecs reside in the VoIP endpoint.
6. DHCP, TFTP-based settings file, signaling protocol message.

7. Packet loss, latency, jitter.

8. Less than 1 percent; less than 150ms one-way; less than 30ms.

9. False; VoIP is sold on cost savings, while UC is sold on productivity or efficiency improvements.

10. 802.3af, 802.3at.

Lab Activities

This chapter is supported by the book website. So, if the activity lists equipment or software that you do not have, go to the book website for additional content.

Activity 1—Review of the Standards

Take a look at the reading list for this chapter. Review the standards and recommendations that were part of the discussions. Pay special attention to SIP, H.323, and RTP.

Materials: computer with web access

1. Explain the structure of these documents, what they contain, and where they can be found.

2. Discuss the basic operation of each protocol.

Activity 2—Download Wireshark and the Capture Files for This Chapter

This activity develops reader familiarity with the VoIP protocols and topics covered in this book.

Materials: computer with web access, Wireshark

1. Open the capture files and examine the packets for protocol families.

2. Explain the basic flow of packets as they move through each of the stages.

3. Open packets that are specific to each of the protocols. Examine the fields contained. How much can you identify?

Activity 3—Examine VoIP Offerings in Your Area

In addition to services such as Skype and Vonage, what are your local service offerings for VoIP?

Materials: N/A

1. Take a look at the Vonage and Skype sites. How is their service described? How do they handle 911 service? What are the reviews for their service? How does the cost compare with traditional landline? Cellular service?

2. Discover the signaling protocol that is used by your local provider or company. What are the benefits? Problems?

3. If you own a handheld device, does it have a voice or video app? What protocols does it use? What are the pros and cons of its performance? What can affect the performance and why?

Activity 4—Take a Look at the FCC Website

Materials: Computer with web access.

1. Search the FCC website for information on the current state of regulation for VoIP.

2. What is the FCC position on regulating VoIP?

3. What is net neutrality, and how is this affected by the FCC?

Activity 5—Latency, Packet Loss, and Jitter

The goal of this activity is to familiarize the reader with some of the tools in Wireshark and some of the performance values that are important to VoIP.

Materials: Computer with web access, Wireshark.

1. Open the capture files from the book website.

2. Using the "Telephony" menu, select RTP and "Show all streams". At the time of this writing, Wireshark 1.8.2 was used.

3. Select one of the identified streams to analyze.

4. Can you find the packet loss, jitter, and latency values for these streams?

5. Do the numbers meet or improve upon the values listed in this chapter?

6. Do a little experimentation with the available tools—what else can you learn?

CHAPTER 2

Traditional Telephony

> *Telecommunication: Any transmission and/or emission and reception of signals representing signs, writing, images and sounds or intelligence of any nature by wire, radio, optical or other electromagnetic systems.*
>
> —ITU-T G.701 Vocabulary of digital transmission and multiplexing and pulse code modulation terms (PCM)

Introduction

Whether you are converting to Voice over IP or already have, network administrators will be required to handle a collection of issues of a more traditional nature and connect to the outside world. So even though we may have embraced the future, it is difficult to divorce ourselves entirely from the past. For the foreseeable future, an understanding of analog and digital circuit-switched technology, telephony wiring, and the tried-and-true methods for connecting to ISPs is necessary. For example, one of the most popular circuits sold is still a T-1. In addition, data from the International Telecommunication Union indicates that while the growth in Internet use and devices accessing the Internet is significant, it does not signal the death knell of more traditional fixed services. This data is shown in Figure 2-1.

It is quite common for graduates entering the workforce armed with network degrees and certifications to be told upon being hired that their responsibilities include the care and feeding of a legacy PBX or a bundle of blue-and-white wires.

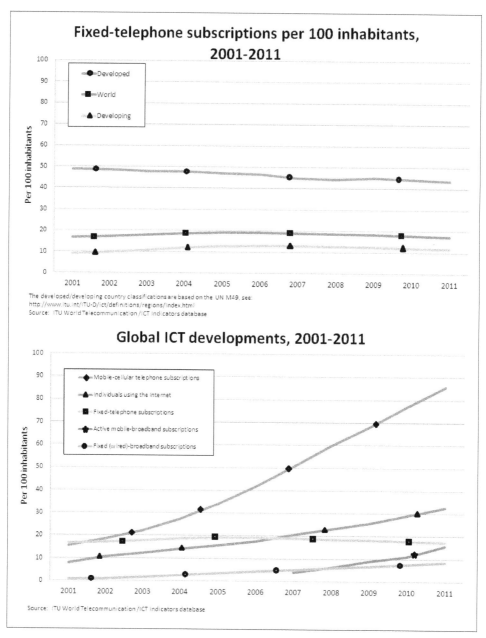

Figure 2-1. Data from the ITU

Since the Public Switched Telephone Network (PSTN) is huge and quite complex, this chapter will examine the parts likely to be useful to a VoIP administrator. It covers the components of a small, traditional deployment featuring the PBX and the telephones. Included in the discussion are the wiring and interconnections used. The chapter will also cover the connections used to interconnect sites and switches, such as T-1s.

Overview

One simplified way to think of things, at least to get started, is that the Internet and the telephone networks used to be two completely separate entities, running different standards and rules, as shown in Figure 2-2.

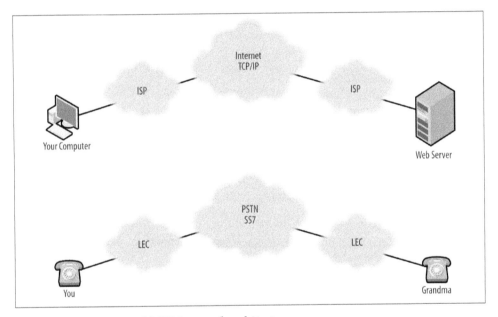

Figure 2-2. Internet and PSTN general architectures

The Internet runs on the suite of protocols from the Transmission Control Protocol/ Internet Protocol model, or TCP/IP. The PSTN runs on something called Signaling System 7, or SS7. It is interesting to consider that in the days of dial-up access, you connected to your Internet Service Provider (ISP) through the PSTN. In addition, most of the companies providing service on the PSTN are also the companies acting as ISPs. This is especially true if we look at the evolution of these connections since 1996. So from the viewpoint of the computer with a modem, the actual topology might have looked more like the one shown in Figure 2-3.

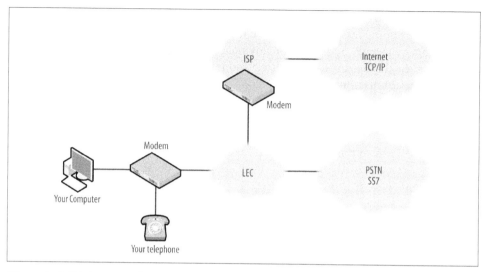

Figure 2-3. Dial-up topology

In this case, the local exchange provider connects your modem (modulator-demodulator) with the modem pool at the ISP when you dial the telephone number of the ISP. Once established, the connection essentially acts as a direct wire between the two devices. All modems modulate a carrier wave in order to indicate the binary values that need to be transmitted. Whether it is voice information or a modulated carrier wave, the behavior of the local exchange provider's equipment is the same.

 The frequency of the carrier wave must fall within the 300–3400Hz range allowed for the local loop.

With a high-speed cable Internet connection, the local exchange carrier is not needed at all. Digital subscriber lines (DSL) still use the local loop wiring, but the office will be provisioned to handle the additional signal components and bandwidth required for DSL. The local loop is covered in more detail later in this chapter.

Organizations

There are several institutions that will be referred to throughout this (and other) chapters. These bodies are responsible for either the standards or regulation upon which we based our communication systems.

International Telecommunications Union-Telecom (ITU-T)

Founded in 1865, the ITU-T has the primary goal of creating universally accepted infocommunications standards. In 1947 it became an agency of the United Nations. The ITU-T is also concerned with telecom development around the world but especially in third-world countries. In the United States, this means telephone and data. The ITU-T comes out with what are called recommendations, but they are really intended as standards. Most of the rules for the PSTN network shown in Figure 2-3 (codecs, wiring, signaling, etc.) come from the ITU-T. The telephone number is described in ITU-T Recommendation E.164 and is called the international public telecommunications numbering plan. In North America, we use the North American Numbering Plan (NANP), which complies with E.164. The format is shown in Table 2-1. In this table, N is a digit from 2 to 9, and x is a digit from 0 to 9. The area code is a geographic assignment, the office code is the Class 5, or local exchange switch assignment, and the station code is the port or circuit assignment. More than one office code may be assigned to a particular local exchange switch.

Table 2-1. E.164 number format

Area Code	Office code	Station Code
1-N X X	N X X	X X X X

Federal Communications Commission (FCC)

The FCC is a US regulatory body that was formed by the Communications Act of 1934 and answers to Congress. To quote from the FCC site, the agency:

> regulates interstate and international communications by radio, television, wire, satellite and cable in all 50 states, the District of Columbia and U.S. Territories.

The FCC sets prices for interstate telephone, data, and video, handles the allocation of the wireless spectrum, determines what vendors are allowed into the various markets, and is involved in the development of electrical and physical standards. The FCC is also an investigative organization, handling complaints and consumer protection.

Public Utilities Commission (PUC) and Public Services Commission (PSC)

As the name suggests, these two bodies (usually one and the same, as states use the terms interchangeably) are concerned with all of the services within the state boundaries, such as electricity, gas, steam, water, and telecommunications. These are state-run organizations that can also impose restrictions and provide oversight within their jurisdictions.

Connecting to the Traditional World

The Public Switched Telephone Network (PSTN) is the worldwide topology that inter-connects all of the telephones to each other. So, when your home telephone was connected via your telephone company, your telephone line and all of the other telephone lines, including those that interconnect the telephone companies, are part of the PSTN. The local loop and the connected telephones are some of the last analog holdouts. Some companies also have internal analog lines, but for the most part, the entire PSTN is digital. The PSTN is described as a circuit-switched network in which connections are set up and torn down as needed. Circuit switching connects the two ends across the entire network by dedicating resources to the lines in use, as opposed to simply sending packets into the network (packet switching) for best effort delivery. For this reason, the PSTN has enjoyed the reputation of having a high quality of service for customers.

The PSTN is composed of two networks—the traffic-bearing network and the signaling network. We speak and send information over the traffic-bearing network. These connections are controlled by the signaling network. The signaling network employs its own architecture and protocol. The signaling network can also carry data traffic. We will talk about this when we cover Integrated Services Digital Network (ISDN). The language of the PSTN signaling network is Signaling System 7 (SS7), as opposed to the TCP/IP-based language of the Internet. Even though the PSTN and the Internet speak different languages, they have many of the same concerns: interconnecting endpoints and routing calls, keeping track of usage, addressing, and implementing resource control to name a few. In the United States, the PSTN was often referred to as the AT&T network or the Bell System.

As for structure, the PSTN is made up of areas codes, local exchange and transport areas, local exchange carriers (incumbent and competitive), and the inter-exchange carriers. It is organized in a highly geographic fashion and regulated for cost, service, and competition. Updating our diagram using the upcoming definitions, we would have the topology pictured in Figure 2-4.

Some other helpful definitions as we wade through this topic include:

Local Access and Transport Area (LATA)
> The country is divided into 196 local access and transport areas, or LATAs. A LATA defines a geographical area in which a local exchange carrier (LEC) can offer services. The local exchange carrier is also known as your local telephone company. LATAs and area codes are loosely associated, as population densities can affect the number of areas codes required by a particular region. LATA numbering is a three-digit value, beginning with a region code. In our example, all of the LATAs within the south-central region begin with a "5." A comparison between LATAs and area codes can be seen in Figure 2-5.

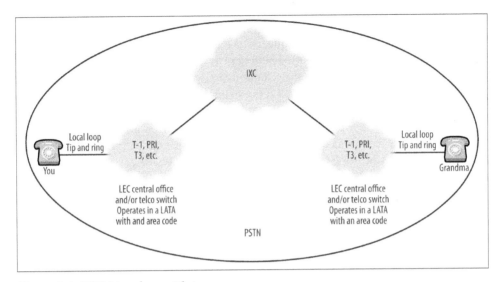

Figure 2-4. PSTN topology with terms

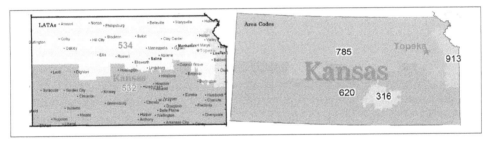

Figure 2-5. LATA and area code comparison

Kansas was chosen because the population density is not all that great, and thus the state makes for a more straightforward comparison. As can be seen from these maps, Kansas has a pair of LATAs and four area codes. This means that telephone numbers such as 785-111-2222 and 913-333-4444 would be in different area codes and therefore likely a long distance call. However, since they are in the same LATA, it is possible that they might not be, depending on the coverage of the LEC.

Inter-exchange carriers (IXCs)

The inter-exchange carriers are the long-distance, or inter-LATA, carriers. These were companies like AT&T, Sprint (hailing from the Southern Pacific Railroad—SPRint), and the old MCI. Some IXCs can now operate as competitive LECs or CLECs.

Telecommunication Companies

Almost every book about telecommunications has a section for the Modified Financial Judgment against AT&T. It is included here to provide a little insight into a very murky collection of companies. To start, the telephone network has been around for decades and recalls a time when the operator sat at the switchboard, manually connecting callers. The Internet is much younger, with most agreeing that the grand opening goes back to the early 1990s, although purists will certainly point to earlier activity. These are two different networks that speak two different languages. What adds to an already complex picture is that many of the same companies run the two networks.

To provide more background, we have to go prior to 1982, when the American Telephone and Telegraph Company (AT&T) had a monopoly on the entire telephone system. It could set prices and control access. In 1982, the Department of Justice decreed that as of December 30, 1983, AT&T would be broken into seven Regional Bell Operating Companies, or RBOCs. This was a reorganization of the 22 Bell Telephone companies existing at that time. The RBOCs were to provide local exchange service, and AT&T would provide long distance. This makes the RBOCs local exchange carriers (LECs) and AT&T an inter-exchange carrier (IXC). The RBOCs were not allowed to provide long-distance service, and AT&T was not to offer local service. However, the always clever AT&T secured the right to offer data services.

The Telecommunications Act of 1996 changed the rules to allow greater competition in the marketplace. New telephone companies emerged, and the restrictions on providing service were loosened. As of the date the act went into effect, the RBOCs were referred to as the incumbent local exchange carriers (ILECs), and the competitive local exchange carriers (CLECs) entered the telecom fray. To quote from this act, part of its intention is the following:

> To promote competition and reduce regulation in order to secure lower prices and higher quality of service for American telecom consumers and encourage rapid deployment of new telecom technologies.

Today, telephone companies are indistinguishable from Internet or data-service companies. When we combine this with the conversion of voice samples to voice data packets, one can envision a time in which circuit-switched connections are no longer part of the network. Providers are busy converting their infrastructure and application models to anticipate the demand for IP-based services.

One other interesting detail is just how powerful these companies can be. In the early days of the Internet, its structure was based on network access points, or NAPs. Originally there were four of them located in California, New Jersey, Michigan and Washington D.C. The idea was that all those wishing to connect to the global data network would interconnect via the NAPs. It didn't take the large companies very long to realize that if they withheld their routing tables, small companies could not provide their customers full connectivity without a little help. After all, what are the sharing benefits to a global ISP? Large ISPs developed peering agreements and private peering points (PPP) in order to exchange data traffic. The fate of a small ISP was usually to be bought out, obtain service through the larger ISPs, or go out of business; it was difficult to continue to make a living selling dial-up service.

Central office (CO)

The CO houses the local exchange switch. Traditionally, a telephone number prefix (the exchange) identifies a particular central office local exchange switch. A central office local exchange switch may be programmed with more than one local exchange.

Private Branch Exchange (PBX)

This device handles almost all of the features and functions of the central office or telephone switch. Internal telephones connect to the PBX, which in turn is connected to the outside provider network. A PBX can provide service to all types of telephones, including VoIP. An Avaya PBX is shown in Figure 2-6. The arrows indicate installed cards to support analog and digital phones. The left most arrow points to the Ethernet ports on the bottom of the chassis. Thus, the PBX can be connected to the data network to support VoIP phones.

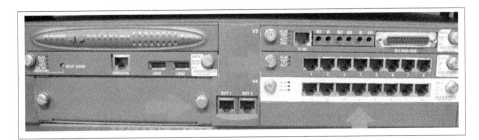

Figure 2-6. Avaya PBX chassis

The analog and digital telephones are connected to the PBX via patch cables or punchdown blocks. Examples of punchdown blocks can be seen in Figure 2-7.

These happen to be examples of BIX (building industry cross-connect) and 66 blocks. Both have the capability to terminate 25-pair cables like the one shown in Figure 2-8.

PSTN distribution frames

These are high-density cross-connection points sprinkled around the CO for the purpose of providing connectivity and service to the surrounding areas via the local loops. Cables at this point may have densities from 50 to 800 pairs or households.

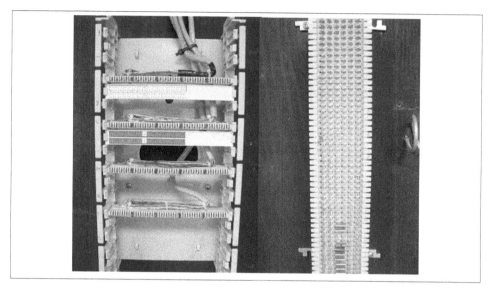

Figure 2-7. Punchdown blocks

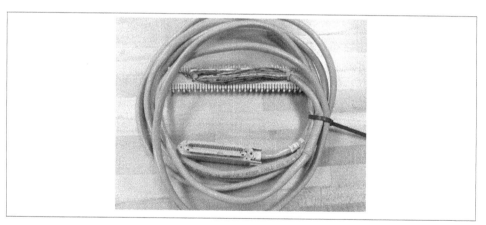

Figure 2-8. 25-pair cable

Lower density connections running to the distribution frame will have 2 – 25 connections or pairs.

Main distribution frames

These areas are often powered and have switching or encoding equipment. They can combine or aggregate users into much more dense feeds, such as fiber, for connecting to the CO. An arrangement of distribution frames can be seen in Figure 2-9.

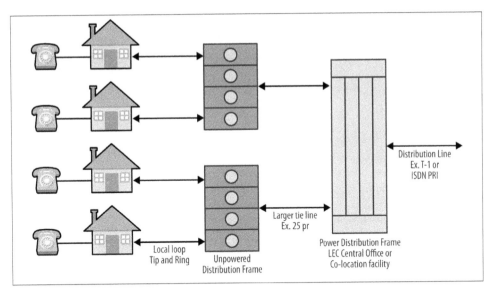

Figure 2-9. Distribution frames

Local loop

This is a term used to define what is located outside the central office. It is composed of a myriad of outside plant (OSP) equipment and wiring that provides access and connectivity to the service provider of that local area. POTS lines are run from homes or small offices using this equipment and connected to the telephone switch that serves that local loop. These lines are run within larger cables that are often buried. Each telephone line is made up of a pair of wires called tip and ring. At the customer premises, the ring wire is red and the tip wire is green. Should a second line be present, the second pair of wires can use black and yellow for tip and ring, respectively.

Telephones

It seems kind of silly to provide a definition for a telephone, but it is worth noting that telephones come in many styles, shapes, and configurations. The three basic types are shown in Figure 2-10.

Analog—A simple analog telephone (or cordless telephone) is connected via a four-wire patch cable that contains both the red and green pair along with the yellow and black pair. This is a direct connection to the local loop, and the telephone derives its power from the telephone company switch. The signal sent down the line is an electrical version of your voice. From the sender, signals must be converted to digital values for use on the PSTN. The conversion occurs on the subscriber line card.

Figure 2-10. Telephone types

Digital—Digital telephones use the same wiring as the analog line. The difference is that the outgoing digital signal starts at the telephone. Incoming digital signals can be sent right to the telephone. The nice thing about the digital line is that it can be used to multiplex transmissions so that a telephone can have multiple lines without extra wiring. In addition, the number of possible values on a digital signal exceeds the analog line, and so the number of possible features also increases.

Voice over IP (VoIP)—The words VoIP and digital are sometimes used interchangeably. This is misleading, as a VoIP phone uses data networking protocols and a completely different infrastructure in order to function. Digital and analog telephones live in the SS7 world. An analog telephone can be still connected to a VoIP provider such as Vonage through the Internet if it is first connected to an analog telephone adapter, or ATA device. Some home gateways have built-in adapter ports. Once connected in this fashion, your transmission that started as analog ends up as VoIP. But, to be clear, when you think of different phone types, think analog, digital, and VoIP.

The way we define distribution frames, central offices, local exchange and long distance carriers, and even LATAs from the previous section should be taken with a grain of salt. Since the break up of AT&T, deregulation, and the advent of VoIP, what companies do and how they accomplish service provision varies greatly. You never know what a company is doing or how they are leveraging their infrastructure. In addition, every neighborhood has different telephone wiring based on their needs. Company wiring closets and distribution frames vary quite a bit, as they may handle their own telephony systems or use hosted services. The devices and connections change almost daily. But upgrades are expensive, so companies vary in their rate of change. However, as long as analog or digital telephony is around, one thing will never change—tip and ring. Opening and closing the connection between tip and ring wires allows the circuit to be connected and disconnected as needed. When you pick up the receiver of a POTS phone, you close the connection between tip and ring, allowing data transfer.

Telephone Wiring

Patch cords are typically terminated with a four-wire RJ11 jack. The four wires are the two tip and ring pairs (red and green, yellow and black). A telephone patch cable can either be straight-through or a roll-over. Straight-through cables have the same pin alignment on both ends. So, pin 1 goes to pin 1 and so on. A rollover cable does the exact opposite; pin 1 goes to pin 8, pin 2 goes to pin 7, etc. It turns out that an RJ11 fits nicely into an RJ45 jack, as the blue telephony pair is in the center of the RJ-45. Data networks use RJ45 jacks almost exclusively for infrastructure. Ethernet patch cables, wall jacks, computer network cards, VoIP phones, and data closets all use RJ45s for terminating connections. Because the RJ11 fits in the RJ-45, it is common to see data wiring supporting both traditional and VoIP voice connections. RJ45 and RJ11 male jacks are shown in Figure 2-11.

Figure 2-11. RJ11 (left) and RJ45 (right) jacks

So, a telephone patch cord containing tip and ring goes to the wall outlet. From there, the telephone wiring goes from the property's connection with the local exchange carrier to the central office via the OSP. On the way, it might be bundled with many connections from the neighborhood or other buildings, but it is still the same two-wire signal that started at the house or business. These two wires carry speech in both directions.

Data Cabling, EIA568 A and B

VoIP networks are sometimes called converged networks because the voice circuit and the data connections run over the same physical infrastructure. It is one thing to follow tip and ring from the telephone to the circuit on the telco switch, but as soon as a telephone infrastructure merges with data, it can be a little more confusing. The Ethernet cable plant is constructed using Category 5/5e/6 wiring having eight conductors, of which Ethernet uses four. Pins 1, 2 (transmit) 3, and 6 (receive) are used for an Ethernet node. These are the orange and green pairs. Many of the guide lines for the wiring come from Electronic Industries Association (EIA) 568B. The color codes used by networks are shown in Table 2-2. Network nodes all use the same pairs, and so in order to connect nodes, the transmit and receive pairs must be crossed. This is accomplished by either a crossover cable or through the network equipment, such as a switch.

Table 2-2. 568 pins and colors

568A Pin	568A Color	568B Pin	568B Color	Punchdown Block Pin	Punchdown Block Color	Matching RJ-45 Pin
1	White/Green	1	White/Orange	1	White/Blue	5
2	Green	2	Orange	2	Blue	4
3	White/Orange	3	White/Green	3	White/Orange	1
4	Blue	4	Blue	4	Orange	2
5	White/Blue	5	White/Blue	5	White/Green	3
6	Orange	6	Green	6	Green	6
7	White/Brown	7	White/Brown	7	White/Brown	7
8	Brown	8	Brown	8	Brown	8

Punchdown blocks have a different construction, so the pins and their associated signals are moved a bit. However, with two punchdown blocks in the topology (telephone to PBX), the result would be that the overall connection is straight through.

 When using an Ethernet crossover cable, one end is terminated using 568B and the other with 568A; both ends will use RJ45 jacks. Note that in the case of the crossover (not rollover), the only pins affected are the orange and green pairs. The wires for the blue pair (telephone) always wind up in the same place.

When integrating the voice with the data network, it is often the case that traditional analog and digital telephones continue to be used. It may even be the case that integration of the two networks is not planned even though the cable plant has been upgraded. In either case, the same internal wired infrastructure can be used. As mentioned earlier, traditional analog telephones can be directly connected to a data network cable plant, as shown in Figure 2-12. On the left is an RJ45 male and on the right is an RJ11 male. Both are plugged into RJ45 terminated infrastructure.

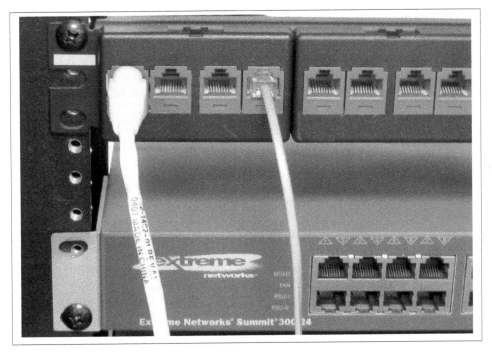

Figure 2-12. RJ45 and RJ11 jacks in the same infrastructure

Recall that the connections shown in Figure 2-12 both work because the tip and ring wires terminated with an RJ11 use pins 4 and 5 in the RJ45 connector. This means that the wires used are right in the middle of both jack types. Figure 2-13 depicts an analog telephone and its connections through the data network to the PBX.

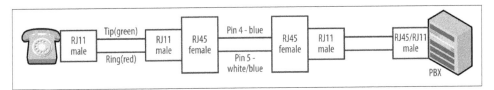

Figure 2-13. Telephone to PBX wiring

When the telephones are transitioned to VoIP phones, these wiring issues fall away, as the phones are actually Ethernet nodes obeying the same rules as computers. This means that the phones use the same orange and green wires (1, 2, 3, and 6) that the computers do. The only remaining problem to be solved is supplying power to the phone. This can occur on the now unused blue pair or the brown pair located on pins 7 and 8, although some devices may even use the conductors dedicated to data.

POTS and the Local Loop

For households and small businesses, local loop connections are still typically analog, while the connections between switches or offices are digital. Because it is low bandwidth and analog, the POTS connection to a house is somewhat limited. This is because features must be implemented within this same small bandwidth. The service offered to local loop users is called Plain Old Telephone Service, or POTS. Electrically, it is a two-wire (one pair), simple electrical loop with low information-carrying capacity. Each analog connection is allocated about 4000Hz of bandwidth because most of the sounds we make when talking fall within this frequency range.

To be a little more precise, the electrical structure of the local loop connection is detailed in ITU –T Rec G.107, which describes narrowband E-model. The E-model specifies a 3.1kHz channel for subscriber lines from 300 to 3400 Hz. This was later amended to the wide band E-model that spans 50–7000Hz. This also means that all of the signaling (numbers, dial tone, etc.) must fall within this 3.1kHz range. These signals use not only the same frequency range but the same physical pathway as the voice. This is called in-band signaling. The tones themselves are specified in ITU-T Rec E.180 (Q.35). For example, dial tone should be 400–450Hz if a single tone is to be used. The busy tone is also recommended for this range, but it is used at a different time and has an associated interval. The tones or frequencies used when dialing a telephone also fall into this 3.1kHz range. See the dual-tone multifrequency (DTMF) section later in this chapter.

Tip and ring are the wires of the circuit assigned to that location from the telephone company local exchange carrier, or LEC. So, these wires can be traced all the way back to a particular port on a telephone switch or PBX. The card with connections from an Asterisk PBX is shown in Figure 2-14. Asterisk is an open-source project that can provide connections for both traditional and VoIP endpoints. In this case, the Asterisk box has an analog card and an Ethernet interface to connect to the network.

Each one of these ports is a circuit that goes to an analog telephone via the tip-and-ring pair. Note that the color of the wires does not affect the operation of the analog phone. Here we show pairs based on the color yellow. Asterisk differentiates ports as either FXO or FXS. FXS and FXO ports name the two interfaces used to interconnect customers and the network. FXS stands for foreign exchange station and FXO is for foreign exchange office.

Figure 2-14. Asterisk PBX connections

Recall from Table 2-1 (E.164) that a telephone number has a station or circuit code for the last four digits. These lines flow out from the house or office to the telephone pole and then to either a distribution frame (sometimes seen in your neighbor's yard) or telco OSP space. This is referred to as an aggregation point. The lines eventually terminate into a telephone switch. One of the most common telephone switches is called a Class 5 or 5ESS switch. It contains the subscriber line cards that serve as the physical termination point for the telephone lines. Thus, an entire neighborhood will reach the local distribution facility in similar fashion.

All of these lines are bundled together at the aggregation point into a larger wire or cable. One common cable used in building wiring systems is a 25-pair cable, shown in Figure 2-8. This cable is a little tougher than a single pair and is often sheathed in a gray insulating cover.

At the center of the image, the individual pairs terminate onto a removable block. The opposite end has terminates with an AMP Champ connector, which allows simple connections to most telco gear.

In order to keep all of the circuits separate from each other, the 25-pair line has a strict color code. In this way, the neighborhood lines are connected to the telco outlet and then split up again to connect to their individual circuits, as shown in Figure 2-15.

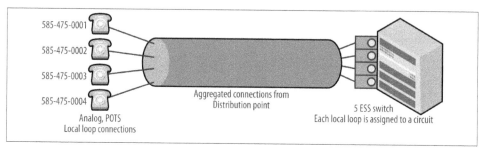

Figure 2-15. Local loop aggregation to the telco switch

When telephone calls are made or received, signals are sent either to or from the telephone. The eventual connection between two telephones is governed by the SS7 network. Dialing a telephone number provides the serving switch with the destination circuit you would like at the other end. When someone calls you, signals must be sent to notify you of an incoming call (ringing) and then notify the switch when the person hangs up (disconnects) the telephone on the other end.

At this point, we come to a basic problem: analog to digital conversion. The core of the PSTN is digital. That is, the signals and messages sent between nodes on the network are binary ones and zeros. The local loop represents one of the last wired network sections that are still analog. When you dial a telephone number, the signals you send are actually low-frequency analog tones or waves. In fact, the analog telephones that populated many American homes are called a dual-tone multifrequency, or DTMF, telephone. These actually send a pair of frequencies with each key pressed. These tones must be converted to digital signals once they get to the serving telco switch. This is commonly done in the subscriber line card and accomplished through the use of a coder/decoder, or codec. Chapter 5 describes codecs in detail, but a brief description follows.

The most common method used by the PSTN to handle this conversion is called pulse code modulation, or PCM. PCM is described in the International Telecommunications Union–Telecom (ITU-T) Recommendation G.711. G.711 is also commonly deployed with VoIP. G.711 works by sampling (taking a snapshot of) the waveform as it comes in and creating a digital value for that sample. The goal is to sample at a rate greater than or equal to twice the bandwidth of the original signal. The work leading to this sampling rate was begun by Harry Nyquist in the 1930s. Telephone conversations are sampled at a rate of 8000 times per second, and each sample is allocated 8 bits for the value. Remember that the bandwidth allocated to a local loop connection is about 4000Hz. Each sample must be given a value. For G.711, 8 bits are allocated for each sample. Thus the standard telephone circuit has a bandwidth requirement of 64Kbps.

```
64,000 = 8 bits/sample x 8000 samples/sec
```

This is also referred to as a digital signal, level 0, or DS-0. It is usually written DS-0.

T-1

So, telephone calls on local loops are converted to DS-0s when they reach the central office. If the calls continue into the PSTN, they must be sent to the next central office or switch down the line. Circuits that terminate on a telephone switch connect to the next switch and so on through a series of digital trunk lines. Commonly, this is via a T carrier such as a T-1. T-1s are DS-1s in terms of their data formatting. T-1s have the ability to multiplex 24 separate telephone circuits, or channels. Each channel is sized to accommodate a 64Kbps voice conversation based on G.711 encoding. The structure of the T-1 can be found in ITU-T Rec G.704 but was originally published as Bell/AT&T publication 62411. Since the utilization on a telephone system is often less than 10 percent, a single T-1 line may be able to service many more than 24 users. It is not uncommon to see an office building housing several hundred workers connected via a handful of T-1 lines. Connections within the telephone network will use much higher-capacity lines, such as T-3 (44.736 Mbps) or OC-3 (155.52Mbps). SONET (Synchronous Optical Network) uses OC, or Optical Carriers.

The T-1 transmission rate is 1.544Mbps and carries 24 channels in both directions. The derivation of the rate is a little confusing because of the way a T-1 frame is constructed. As the active circuits are multiplexed together, a sample from each is placed in one of the time slots for the T-1 frame. Each sample has 8 bits, giving us twenty-four 8-bit samples, for a total of 192 bits. The T-1 is constructed of time division multiplexed (TDM) connections. So, as each sample is generated on a channel, it is placed in one of the time slots. Twenty-four samples will fill the available slots. The T-1 frame is shown in Figure 2-16.

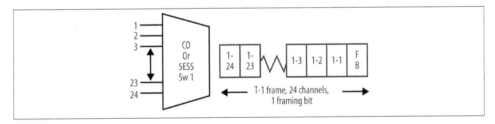

Figure 2-16. T-1 frame and multiplexer

Recall that the 64Kbps rate for each channel is reached because there are 8000 samples per second. Following the same pattern, T-1 frames are created at the same rate. First, the T-1 frame is built.

```
24 x 8 = 192
```

Each frame is given a framing bit, which is used for alignment, performance monitoring, or some other data. The alignment bit pattern of 001011 repeating provides an indication of the frame position in a group.

```
192 + 1 = 193
```

The process repeats as more samples are collected, for a total of 8000 frames per second, which results in the T-1 data rate.

```
193 x 8000 = 1,544,000 bps
```

If we think about this another way, the single framing bit is actually an 8Kbps communication channel. Bits are sometimes stolen from DS-0s to provide a means for DS-0 signaling. That is, stolen bits represent a signaling channel used for call information. Transmission rates that are often part of the same conversation are the E-1 and T-3. An E-1 is a larger European frame, housing up to 30 voice channels and a data rate of 2.048Mbps. Signaling (CCS and CAS) are similar. T-3s (E-3s) correspond to the next step up in terms of deployment. The T-3 data rate is 44.736Mbps and is a collection of 672 DS-0 channels. This matches the capacity of 28 T-1s.

T-1 signaling

Telephone calls are not only assigned to a channel; the telephone number must be provided and a route across the network configured. There are a couple of methods for handling this signaling for the T-1. First, configuration options for T-1s are based on the type of framing and the signaling method used. In North America, we see either the superframe (AT&T pub 62411), which is a group of 12 frames or the extended superframe (ESF) format of 24 channels. Each frame is the T-1 frame discussed earlier. Second, the structure of the channels can be modified. For example, in ISDN, all of the signaling may be sent via one of the 24 frames. This would give a 64Kbps circuit for the information regarding the other 23 channels. This is called common channel signaling, or CCS. Channel associated signaling (CAS) steals bits from a collection of channels to provide this information. For example, a voice channel may steal the eighth bit of every sixth frame for signaling information. ITU-T Rec G.704 provides a table for the identification of these bits.

When using ESF, some of the T-1 bandwidth is allocated to 4Kbps maintenance (a.k.a. facilities data link), cyclical redundancy check (CRC-6) checksum (2Kbps), and framing and synchronization (2Kbps). This capability comes from using the 8Kbps framing bit. G.704 provides a table that describes what bits within the 24 channel T-1 frame will be used for these purposes. Lastly, T-1 channels do not have to be 64Kbps in size, and a company does not have to purchase a full T-1. For example, a channel may have a bit stolen (robbed bit) for signaling, which results in a 56Kbps data channel. When fewer than 24 channels of the T-1 are needed, companies purchase fractional T-1s.

T-1 physical layer and wiring

The modulation technique used on T-1 lines is commonly either alternate mark inversion (AMI) or binary eight zero substitution (B8ZS); the later prevents a long string of zeros from causing a loss of synchronization. B8ZS is more common. Binary 1's are inserted into the stream to help maintain synchronization. More detail on these techniques can be found in ITU-T Rec G.703.

T-1 wiring consists of two-pair copper, using pins 1 and 2 (Rx from the network) and pins 4 and 5 (Tx to the network). T-1 crossovers swap the connections in order to connect like interfaces. T-1 pinouts are shown in Figure 2-17.

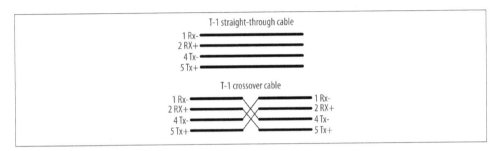

Figure 2-17. T-1 pinouts

T-1 and E-1 circuits are often terminated with RJ45s, but the RJ48 is another connector used.

Integrated Services Digital Network (ISDN) primary rate interface (PRI) has the same data rate as the T-1, but the channels are organized differently. Twenty-three of the channels are used for data or voice. These are called bearer (B) channels (64Kbps), while the 24th is a data (D) channel used for common channel signaling, or CCS. This means that the one channel is used to provide information about the others, and bits are not robbed from the user channels in every sixth frame.

Integrated Services Digital Network

A VoIP administrator may also have to work with ISDN, which is described in the ITU-T I series recommendations. ISDN connections are designed to support both voice and nonvoice applications but with a limited set of connection types. The two common interfaces are called PRI and BRI, or the primary and basic rate interfaces. The ISDN connections are also designed to be compatible with the 64Kbps circuits seen in T-1s. ISDN signaling is described in ITU-T Recommendation Q.931, which forms the basis for an H.323 VoIP deployment.

ITU-T Recommendations I.412 and I.430 define the basic rate interface as two bearer channels of 64Kbps each and one data channel of 16Kbps, or 2B+D. Like the standard PSTN circuit, a B-channel encodes voice per G.711. The channels are designed to support data streams at less than or equal to 64Kbps. The D-channel is used to carry the circuit-switched signaling information for the B-channels. The bearer channels can work independently of each other. ISDN also defines an H channel at 384Kbps.

The primary rate interface corresponds to the ANSI 1.544 and CCITT 2.048Mbps data rates. The channel configuration for the two data rates are 23B+D and 30B+D, respectively, similar to the T-1 and E-1 rates mentioned previously. For the PRI, both the bearer and the data channels are 64Kbps. The PRI framing is essentially the same as that defined for T-1s except for the standard use of the D channel. The basic PRI framing is shown in Figure 2-18.

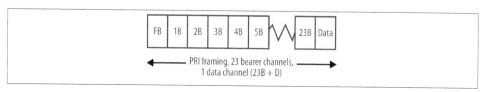

Figure 2-18. ISDN PRI framing

Basic Telephone-Call Operation

As discussed previously, the network control language of the PSTN is Signaling System 7. While complex, it has been an extremely effective architecture for handling traffic on the telephone network as well as some of the demands of IP-based data traffic. Like the Internet with its routers and switches, the PSTN has elements that perform the same tasks. For those used to thinking in terms of layers and models, the SS7 architecture is constructed in the same way as the Open Systems Interconnect (OSI) and Transmission Control Protocol/Internet Protocol (TCP/IP) models. The lower layers are concerned with electrical and physical characteristics of the link, while the upper layers are concerned with messaging and applications. A good resource to start off with is ITU-T Rec Q.700, which provides an overview of SS7. Q.700 actually describes the evolution of the SS7 architecture as being based on the OSI model since 1984.

Information of all types (not just telephone calls) flows constantly through the network as databases are updated, information about links is transmitted, and accounting data transactions are occurring. Per Q.700, the network is a collection of nodes interconnected via links using common channel signaling, and these nodes implement some part of SS7 and become signaling points. Signaling point examples include exchanges, service control points, signal transfer points, and nodes handling administration, operation, and maintenance. The link type between the signaling nodes is dependent upon their relationship. For example, exchanges forwarding user call data will have a different relationship with each other than with a node accessed for database lookups.

Service Switching Point (SSP)
> The originating and destination signaling points are switches that originate or terminate calls. Typically, SSPs understand a wide variety of signaling types and interfaces. These are local exchange switches that are SS7 capable and can talk to the STPs and other SSPs of the SS7 network.

Signal Transfer Point (STP)

These nodes route all signaling messages in the SS7 network and transfer the connection from one link to another. In other words, these are not the source and destination nodes, but they form the backbone of the SS7 network.

Service Control Point (SCP)

These nodes provide database access for additional routing and application delivery.

Lastly, signaling nodes have a hierarchy in terms of functionality, with some nodes acting as gateways or with the ability for regional, national, or international reach. ITU-T Rec. Q.724 provides a detailed description of the myriad procedures involved when a call is placed, but we'll try to boil things down a bit in the next couple of paragraphs.

Recall from our earlier discussion that an analog telephone operating on a local loop provisioned for POTS receives signals from and sends signals to the local telephone network or switch. So, when you pick up the receiver, you get a dial tone from the same switch. When you dial the telephone, you are sending analog signals to the telco switch. The signals are also called tones, as they are audible. For the telephone number or address, signaling telephones actually send a pair of tones, one for the number column and one for the number row. This is called dual-tone multifrequency. We also used these signals to interact with systems we call, such as menus. The frequency distribution is shown in Table 2-3.

Table 2-3. DTMF frequencies

	1290 Hz	1336 Hz	1477 Hz
697 Hz	1	2	3
770 Hz	4	5	6
852 Hz	7	8	9
941 Hz	*	0	#

Signals from the telephone network are structured in similar fashion. For example, the busy signal is a combination of 480 and 620Hz.

The subscriber line card converts the numbers dialed in the CO or telephone switch to provide the address of the destination. This signaling or service switching point takes the dialed numbers and begins the connection, sending messages to the other signaling nodes. Based on the location of the destination, intervening switches communicate to allocate resources for the call. One such negotiation is the channel in the T-1 that will be used for that call. The signaling points use their routing tables to determine the outgoing trunk group and circuit needed. The originating signaling service point (SSP) sends the setup message to the destination SSP via the STPs requesting a connection on the specified circuit. Upon acknowledgment, the circuit is allocated.

Along the way, there may be many other messages, such as clearing, answer, and congestion. An example of the circuit configuration can be seen in Figure 2-19. The section shown depicts a central switch with several multiplexed lines coming in and one going out. On the left, users are time division multiplexed (TDM) into their channel, but upon reaching the next switch, the channels may have to be changed due to destination or resource availability.

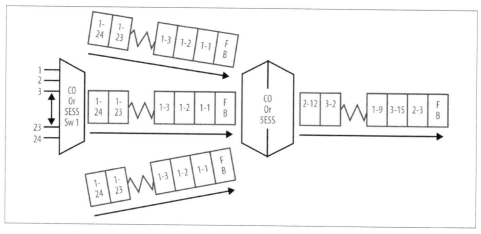

Figure 2-19. Call virtual circuits

Once the circuit is set up, the destination is sent ringing voltage from the local exchange carrier. This is a 75–90vac signal that causes the telephone to ring. As the destination picks up and the customers begin conversing, the codecs in the switches at either end perform the pulse code modulation conversions as outlined earlier in this chapter and detailed in Chapter 5. At the source, the voice is converted to digital samples, and at the destination, the reverse process occurs. Thus, when you are hearing the voice from the other end, it is actually a reasonable facsimile of the actual sounds made by the person at the other end.

As we transition from one type of telephone system to another, and even as we move to VoIP, the basic ideas described here hold true. However, even though the same processes and functions continue to happen, how they happen and where they happen changes completely. For example, dial tone might be locally generated, and a codec can exist in the phone itself.

Summary

Companies and organizations are adopting Voice over IP and Unified Communications at ever increasing rates. Some have already deployed these systems or are migrating. Regardless of the state of the current deployment, VoIP administrators cannot afford to ignore traditional telephony connections and ideas. Even if the system currently runs VoIP natively, it must eventually connect to the PSTN and the SS7 architecture.

Central ideas include telco wiring from the telephone to the PBX and the connections to the provider. Among these connections, running off-site T carriers and ISDN are still popular. This chapter provides coverage of these areas and an explanation of call processing along with the components, the architecture, and the organizations involved.

Standards and Reading

- ITU-T Rec E.164: The international public telecommunications numbering plan
- ITU-T Rec E.180: Technical characteristics of tones for the telephone service
- ITU-T Rec G.107: The E-model: A computational model for use in transmission planning (3.1kHz)
- ITU-T Rec G.107.1: Wideband E-model for use in transmission planning (50-7000Hz)
- ITU-T Rec G.703: Physical/electrical characteristics of hierarchical digital interfaces
- ITU-T Rec G.704: Synchronous frame structures
- ITU-T Rec G.711: Pulse code modulation of voice frequencies
- ITU-T Rec. Q.700: Introduction to CCITT Signalling System No. 7
- ITU-T Rec. Q.931: ISDN user-network interface layer 3 specification for basic call control

Review Questions

1. True or false: digital and VoIP phones are the same thing.
2. How much bandwidth is allocated to a single POTS local loop?
3. What is meant by the phrase "dual-tone multifrequency"?
4. How many channels are contained in a T-1?
5. Derive the T-1 data rate.
6. After 1996, a regional Bell operating company offering service in the local exchange is called what?
7. What pins are used by a T-1 cable?
8. Which ITU-T recommendation contains the electrical characteristics for the connections discussed in this chapter?

9. In what year was the breakup of AT&T to take affect?

10. True or false: an RJ45 jack fits into an RJ11.

Review Question Answers

1. False.

2. 4000 Hz in general, 3100 Hz by the standard.

3. Each number or symbol on the telephone keypad generates a pair of frequencies or tones when pressed.

4. 24.

5. $((24 \times 8) + 1) \times 8000 = 193 \times 8000 = 1{,}544{,}000$ bits per second.

6. An incumbent local exchange carrier (ILEC).

7. Pins 1 and 2 are the receive pair, while pins 4 and 5 are the transmit pair.

8. G.703.

9. 1983.

10. False—an RJ11 fits into an RJ45.

Lab Activities

This chapter is supported by the book website. So, if the activity lists equipment or software that you do not have, go to the book website for additional content.

Activity 1—Review Your Local Telephone Connections

Materials: flashlight

1. Examine the telephony equipment in your office, lab, or home.

2. What type is it? Where do the wires go?

3. What kind of patch cable are you using? What are the pinouts? Where are tip and ring located?

4. After taking the proper electrical safety precautions, a multimeter can be used to measure the voltages on the line.

Activity 2—Experiment with the Desktop Telephone or VoIP Phone

Though it may seem overly simple, the point of this activity is to get you to think about the signals and features represented by the desktop unit.

Materials: telephone

1. Is it powered locally or by the PBX/central office?
2. What kind of telephone do you have? Why is this significant?
3. Where does the ring come from?
4. What tones can you generate and what are their frequencies? How do they change in pitch?
5. What features are available to you?

Activity 3—Wiring to the PBX or Central Office

Materials: flashlight, perhaps access to spaces

1. Locate the connections for your telephone. How is the cabling run in your building? If you have access to the wiring closet, see if you can trace the pair connecting your endpoint.
2. If you are at home, can you locate the wiring for your neighborhood? Is there a local distribution frame? Where is the central office?

Activity 4—ITU-T Recommendations

Materials: computer with web access

1. Visit the ITU-T website.
2. After becoming familiar with some of the features and site navigation, locate some of the recommendations listed in this chapter.
3. Pay special attention to Rec E.164, E.180, G.703, G.704, Q.700, and Q.931.

CHAPTER 3

Session Initiation Protocol

Introduction

It seems that competition has always been a part of network protocols as vendors, products, or protocols vie for dominance in the market. Appletalk versus TCP/IP and 802.11g versus 802.11a are examples of this conflict. Local area network protocols such as Token Ring, Ethernet, and Fiber Distributed Data Interchange battled it out for quite some time. Smaller examples, such as the selection of a trunking protocol, are sprinkled throughout our decision processes. Usually the competition goes on until one becomes the de facto standard or drops out of the race.

Voice over IP is no different. This book covers several different signaling protocols, all of them handling the same set of functions. But which one is the right choice? A couple of years ago, the choice would not have been clear due to the variety of equipment being deployed, vendors, and legacy equipment. Today, most professionals agree that the Session Initialization Protocol (SIP) will be the right choice for the future.

SIP is an Internet Engineering Task Force protocol standardized in RFC 3261, though there are several companion RFCs. It is a nonproprietary signaling protocol that is now supported by almost all vendors in the VoIP industry. Although there is a significant installed base of systems running Skinny and H.323, newer network builds are likely to adopt SIP over the others. Like the other signaling protocols, SIP relies on the Real-Time Transport Protocol (RTP) to ferry voice packets between source and destination. Additionally, RFC 3261 indicates that other supporting protocols (such as MEGACO for controlling gateway functions to the PSTN) may be part of a SIP deployment. SIP also has a secure version and is used extensively to trunk between systems.

Protocol Description

The early work on SIP dates from 1999 with RFC 2543. SIP operates at the application layer for the purpose of initiating user sessions for multimedia transmissions such as voice, video, chat, gaming, and virtual reality. These sessions can be either unicast or multicast and can operate with or without a call server or gateway. Per the RFC, a session is an exchange of data between participants. SIP supports name mapping and redirection services, features that allow users to be reached or transmit from different locations. For those of us not comfortable with RFC terminology, this means that when VoIP nodes connect to each other, there has to be a mechanism for setting up the communication and establishing some rules. SIP and the Session Descriptor Protocol (SDP) take care of this.

As it supports a similar set of features and codecs, SIP is sometimes deployed along with either H.323 or Skinny in order to serve newer applications or features. It is often said that SIP is much easier to read and use than other nonproprietary signaling protocols. This may be because SIP is very similar in structure to the Hypertext Transfer Protocol, or HTTP. We will see that there is a certain amount of truth to this sentiment. SIP does not do everything offered by the heavyweight H.323 (described in Chapter 6). It is simply designed to set up and tear down media sessions. Other functions include user location and capabilities, availability, and session-handling information. If you read the H.323 chapter, you may have noticed that H.323 is quite complex and often attempts to negotiate or provide information that may not be used.

Since SIP does not handle everything, implementations use another protocol called the Session Descriptor Protocol, or SDP, to negotiate the parameters of the multimedia connection. Beyond this, SIP topologies operate in much the same way as any other VoIP configuration. Our task in this chapter is to understand how. Figure 1-16 in Chapter 1 illustrated a typical VoIP deployment. We will use a similar topology, seen in Figure 3-1, to work through this chapter.

The network is equipped with a VoIP PBX (private branch exchange) in the form of an Asterisk box, a trivial file transfer protocol (TFTP) server, a dynamic host configuration protocol (DHCP) server, and a switch providing power over Ethernet, or PoE. The switch is also configured with mirrored ports for packet capture.

Components

When reading about SIP, it is helpful to understand a couple of SIP-specific terms. The following components are the most common.

User Agent (UA)
> Logical portion that initiates or responds to SIP transactions. The UA can be a client or server and is stateful, so it maintains the session.

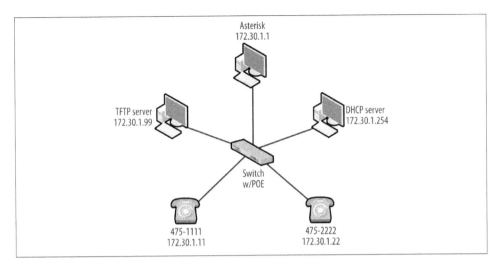

Figure 3-1. SIP topology

User Agent Client (UAC)
> Initiates requests and accepts responses. Typically, it is the SIP phone initiating the call.

User Agent Server (UAS)
> Accepts requests and sends back responses.

 The locations of the UAC and UAS are highly dependent on the operations for a particular node. For example, a node may both accept call requests from others and initiate its own. The topology shown in Figure 3-1 depicts a particular configuration that may change as other nodes or destinations are added.

Proxy
> Intermediate component that forwards requests from a UAC to a UAS or another proxy. This is done primarily for routing but can enforce policies such as authentication. An example of a standard deployment is a web proxy. Clients send web requests to the proxy, which then forwards the requests to the web servers. So the clients never actually communicate with the web server.

Redirect Server
> Sends requests from a UAC to an alternate set of uniform resource IDs, or URIs.

Registrar Server
> UAS that accepts REGISTER messages and updates the location.

Updating the topology with these component labels, we end up with the network shown in Figure 3-2.

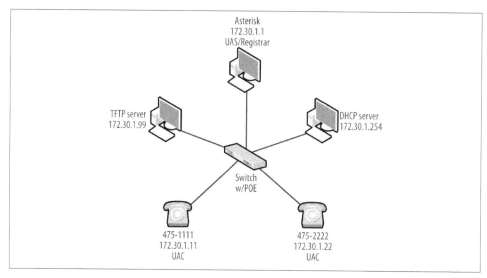

Figure 3-2. Topology updated with labels

This topology now includes the client- and server-side SIP agents. It lacks labels for other components because, at this point, it is an isolated telephony system that does not call outside.

Addressing

SIP conversations can begin by contacting an IP address or username in order to let the UAC communicate with another user or resource on the network. The standard SIP addressing is similar to email, taking one of the following forms (the port is optional, and if it is not specified, 5060 is used):

sip:user@domain:port

sip:user@host:port

sip:phone number@domain

Another example of the SIP addressing is shown in Figure 3-3. The format is the Uniform Resource Identifier, or URI. Per the RFC, your SIP address or identity is your SIP URI. From RFC 3261:

> Alice 'calls' Bob using his SIP identity, a type of Uniform Resource Identifier (URI) called a SIP URI. SIP URIs are defined in Section 19.1. It has a similar form to an email address, typically containing a username and a host name. In this case, it is sip:bob@biloxi.com,

```
Internet Protocol Version 4, Src: 172.30.1.11 (172.30.1.11), Dst: 172.30.1.1 (172.30.1.1)
User Datagram Protocol, Src Port: sip (5060), Dst Port: sip (5060)
Session Initiation Protocol
⊕ Request-Line: INVITE sip:4752222@172.30.1.1 SIP/2.0
⊕ Message Header
⊕ Message Body
```

Figure 3-3. SIP addressing

where biloxi.com is the domain of Bob's SIP service provider. Alice has a SIP URI of sip:alice@atlanta.com. Alice might have typed in Bob's URI or perhaps clicked on a hyperlink or an entry in an address book. SIP also provides a secure URI, called a SIPS URI. An example would be sips:bob@biloxi.com.

The URI is commonly the IP address or fully qualified domain name (FQDN) of the host. Instead of sip, the URI can begin with sips, indicating a Secure SIP URI, which will use port 5061. The type of addressing is dependent upon the network topology and services deployed. For example, the topology used for this chapter does not have an email or domain name server.

RFC 3261 recommends the use of fully qualified domain names (FQDN) for addressing, although they were not used here for the sake of simplicity. Thus, SIP implementations are commonly integrated with the domain name systems, or DNS.

Every URI contains the SIP address of record (AOR), which is sometimes thought of as the public address for a user. The AOR points to the domain for the user. Within that domain, there should be a service that can map the URI to a URI of the user's current location. Another way to think of this is the public address of the user. In other words, it's how someone would contact you.

Basic Operation

Like most VoIP topologies, the operation of the SIP network begins with a series of conversations that do not have anything to do with voice. The first thing nodes have to do is obtain an IP address from the DHCP server, as the updated topology in Figure 3-4 indicates.

Both of the SIP UACs require IP addresses. If we trace and filter the packet captures for the *bootp* process from each node, we can see the conversations (Figure 3-5).

The VoIP phones used in this topology were also used in some of the other chapters. This means they can use a couple different signaling protocols. When switching between these protocols or ensuring that the latest configuration is used, the phones contact the TFTP server, as shown in Figure 3-6.

Taking a close look at the packet numbers and the IP addresses, we can see that for 172.30.1.11, this conversation occurred after the DHCP conversation. For a networking

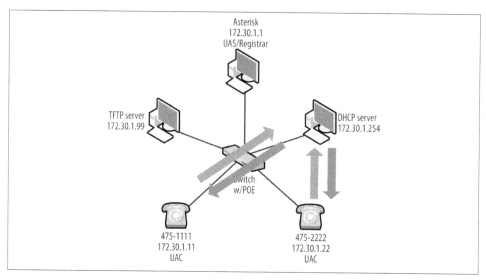

Figure 3-4. Topology with DHCP

No.	Source	Destination	Protocol	Info	
21	0.0.0.0	255.255.255.255	DHCP	DHCP Discover	- Transaction ID 0xc6e01d47
24	172.30.1.254	172.30.1.11	DHCP	DHCP Offer	- Transaction ID 0xc6e01d47
27	0.0.0.0	255.255.255.255	DHCP	DHCP Request	- Transaction ID 0xc6e01d47
28	172.30.1.254	172.30.1.11	DHCP	DHCP ACK	- Transaction ID 0xc6e01d47
No.	Source	Destination	Protocol	Info	
22	0.0.0.0	255.255.255.255	DHCP	DHCP Discover	- Transaction ID 0xc6de1019
26	172.30.1.254	172.30.1.22	DHCP	DHCP Offer	- Transaction ID 0xc6de1019
29	0.0.0.0	255.255.255.255	DHCP	DHCP Request	- Transaction ID 0xc6de1019
30	172.30.1.254	172.30.1.22	DHCP	DHCP ACK	- Transaction ID 0xc6de1019

Figure 3-5. DHCP conversations

	Source	Destination	Protocol	Info
38	172.30.1.11	172.30.1.99	TFTP	Read Request, File: 46xxupgrade.scr
39	172.30.1.99	172.30.1.11	TFTP	Data Packet, Block: 1
40	172.30.1.11	172.30.1.99	TFTP	Acknowledgement, Block: 1
41	172.30.1.99	172.30.1.11	TFTP	Data Packet, Block: 2
42	172.30.1.11	172.30.1.99	TFTP	Acknowledgement, Block: 2

Figure 3-6. TFTP conversation

pro, this only makes sense, but it also underscores another portion of the topology configuration: the TFTP server address is given out by the DHCP server. The basic Cisco router DHCP server configuration follows:

```
ip dhcp pool voip
network 172.30.1.0 255.255.255.0
default-router 172.30.1.254
next-server 172.30.1.99 option
```

```
option 150 ip 172.30.1.99
option 176 ascii "TFTPSRVR=172.30.1.99,MCIPADD=172.30.1.1"
```

The "next-server", "option 176", and "option 150" commands are all used to assign the TFTP address, though only one is required. They are shown here because matching the best method with the phone is not always easy. At this point, the topology has moved on to the phase shown in Figure 3-7.

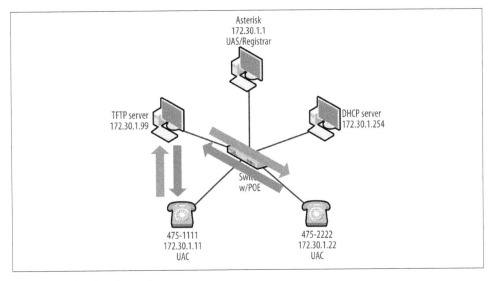

Figure 3-7. Updated topology

The last conversation necessary before a phone can make a call is to register with the call server. This is accomplished, strange as it may seem, via our first SIP message: REGISTER. This message is part of an exchange with the PBX, as depicted in Figure 3-8.

```
110   GiantEle_05:cb:11 Broadcast        ARP   Who has 172.30.1.1?  Tell 172.30.1.11
111   AsustekC_d6:05:9b GiantEle_05:cb:11 ARP  172.30.1.1 is at 00:11:d8:d6:05:9b
112   172.30.1.11       172.30.1.1       SIP   Request: REGISTER sip:172.30.1.1
113   172.30.1.1        172.30.1.11      SIP   Request: OPTIONS sip:4751111@172.30.1.11:5060
114   172.30.1.1        172.30.1.11      SIP   Status: 200 OK   (1 bindings)
115   172.30.1.11       172.30.1.1       SIP   Status: 200 OK
```

Figure 3-8. Registration exchange

Once the phone has the address of the call server, it sends the SIP REGISTER message. The REGISTER message is shown in Figure 3-9. From this packet, we can see that SIP is using port 5060 and the User Datagram Protocol (UDP). In this case, UDP is the layer-4 transport protocol for SIP. However, in other topologies, TCP may be used. TCP is typically the default layer-4 protocol for SIPS. The message also contains the IP address and URI to be used when communicating with this node.

```
Internet Protocol version 4, Src: 172.30.1.11 (172.30.1.11), Dst: 172.30.1.1 (172.30.1.1)
User Datagram Protocol, Src Port: sip (5060), Dst Port: sip (5060)
Session Initiation Protocol
⊟ Request-Line: REGISTER sip:172.30.1.1 SIP/2.0
    Method: REGISTER
  ⊕ Request-URI: sip:172.30.1.1
    [Resent Packet: False]
⊟ Message Header
  ⊕ via: SIP/2.0/UDP 172.30.1.11:5060;branch=z9hG4bK31e7e1cfa
    Max-Forwards: 70
    Content-Length: 0
  ⊕ To: 4751111 <sip:4751111@172.30.1.1>
  ⊕ From: 4751111 <sip:4751111@172.30.1.1>;tag=afec0e2ffae8169
    Call-ID: dd5d67821535446081b1eece5c33e606@172.30.1.11
  ⊕ CSeq: 87753542 REGISTER
  ⊕ Contact: 4751111 <sip:4751111@172.30.1.11:5060>;expires=3600
    Allow: NOTIFY
    Allow: REFER
    Allow: OPTIONS
    Allow: INVITE
    Allow: ACK
    Allow: CANCEL
    Allow: BYE
    User-Agent: Avaya SIP R2.2 Endpoint Brcm Callctrl/1.5.1.0 MxSF/v3.2.6.26
```

Figure 3-9. SIP REGISTER message

We can also see that the communication is now between the phone and the call server (Figure 3-10), as are most of the messages from this point on.

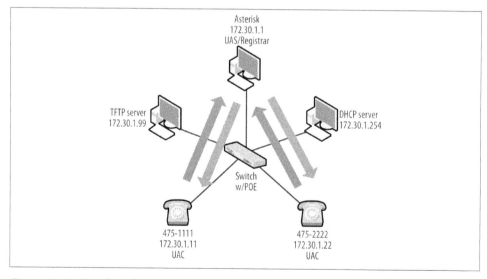

Figure 3-10. Topology during registration

SIP Messages and Message Structure

SIP is described in a lengthy RFC, due in part to the number of messages it defines. Like the other signaling protocols, SIP has messages that are operation-specific, though many of them share similar fields. The SIP RFC also uses the term *METHOD*. A METHOD is a function, and these functions are wrapped in a message type. SIP nodes have rules for each method, although some rules are common to all of them. For example, all SIP requests must contain fields for To, From, CSeq, Call-ID, Max-Forwards, and Via. These fields are described later in this chapter. This section will cover these common components and discuss the messages seen in a standard call sequence. One of the reasons for SIP having a familiar header is that, per RFC 3261, SIP messages follow the general format specified for Internet messages as described in RFC 5322. This is true for both requests and responses. RFC 5322 is focused on text-based communication, and so SIP has broadened to include things that are not specified in RFC 5322.

The general format for SIP messages consists of a start line, message headers, and then an empty line terminated with a carriage return and line feed. Start lines have a couple of types; for request messages, they are request lines and for responses they are statuses. Figure 3-9 shows the start line, which is a request line because this is a REGISTER message. After the start line come the message headers, which vary with the type of message. The last items visible, at least in hexadecimal, are the CR LF characters. Figure 3-11 depicts the same REGISTER message with the fields collapsed to make the basic message components easier to see.

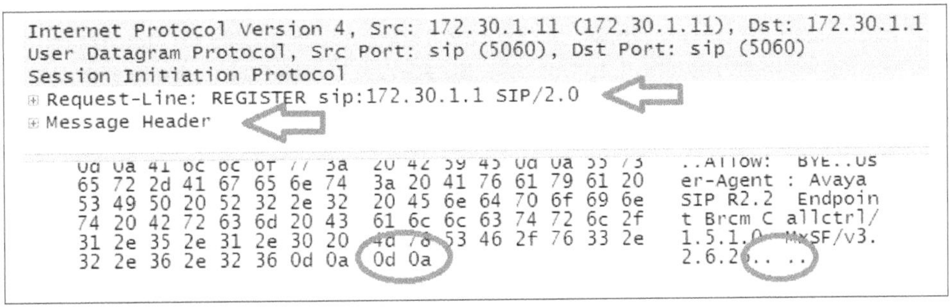

Figure 3-11. Basic SIP headers

The two arrows point to the start line and the message headers. The first circle indicates the hexadecimal values for the carriage return and the line feed (0d 0a), while the second shows their effect.

Requests

To clarify a little bit, for an SIP request message, the start line is actually called a request line. The request line contains the SIP URI and version and terminates with the CR LF characters, as shown in Figure 3-12. In the image, the request line has been highlighted.

```
Internet Protocol Version 4, Src: 172.30.1.11 (172.30.1.11), Dst: 172.30.1.1
User Datagram Protocol, Src Port: sip (5060), Dst Port: sip (5060)
Session Initiation Protocol
  Request-Line: REGISTER sip:172.30.1.1 SIP/2.0
  Message Header

000  00 11 d8 d6 05 9b 00 09   6e 05 cb 11 08 00 45 00    ........ n.....E.
010  02 3c 00 5f 00 00 40 11   1e 0a ac 1e 01 0b ac 1e    .<._..@. ........
020  01 01 13 c4 13 c4 02 28   5f 0f 52 45 47 49 53 54    .......( _.REGIST
030  45 52 20 73 69 70 3a 31   37 32 2e 33 30 2e 31 2e    ER sip:1 72.30.1.
040  31 20 53 49 50 2f 32 2e   30 0d 0a 56 69 61 3a 20    1 SIP/2. 0..via:
050  53 49 50 2f 32 2e 30 2f   55 44 50 20 31 37 32 2e    SIP/2.0/ UDP 172.
060  33 30 2e 31 2e 31 31 3a   35 30 36 30 3b 62 72 61    30.1.11: 5060;bra
070  6e 63 68 3d 7a 39 68 47   34 62 4b 33 31 65 37 65    nch=z9hG 4bK31e7e
```

Figure 3-12. SIP request line as a hex dump

SIP requests minimally must include the following header fields: Via, From, To, Call-ID, CSeq, and Max-Forwards. These contain the information necessary for routing, identification, and ordering.

Responses

SIP responses like the one shown in Figure 3-13 have a status line for the start and a status code for the transaction. In this case, the server (172.30.1.1) returns a status code of 200 to the VoIP phone, indicating success.

```
Internet Protocol Version 4, Src: 172.30.1.1 (172.30.1.1), Dst: 172.30.1.11 (172.30.1.11)
User Datagram Protocol, Src Port: sip (5060), Dst Port: sip (5060)
Session Initiation Protocol
  Status-Line: SIP/2.0 200 OK
  Message Header
    Via: SIP/2.0/UDP 172.30.1.11:5060;branch=z9hG4bK31e7e1cfa;received=172.30.1.11
    From: 4751111 <sip:4751111@172.30.1.1>;tag=afec0e2ffae8169
    To: 4751111 <sip:4751111@172.30.1.1>;tag=as10e6b586
    Call-ID: dd5d67821535446081b1eece5c33e606@172.30.1.11
    CSeq: 87753542 REGISTER
    Server: FPBX-2.10.0rc1(1.8.11)
    Allow: INVITE, ACK, CANCEL, OPTIONS, BYE, REFER, SUBSCRIBE, NOTIFY, INFO, PUBLISH
    Supported: replaces, timer
    Expires: 3600
    Contact: <sip:4751111@172.30.1.11:5060>;expires=3600
    Date: Wed, 15 Aug 2012 16:10:31 GMT
    Content-Length: 0
```

Figure 3-13. SIP response to registration request

Though this was successful, there are a variety of codes that could be returned, each one handling a different general scenario. From RFC 3261:

1xx: Provisional
Request received, continuing to process the request.

2xx: Success
The action was successfully received, understood, and accepted.

3xx: Redirection
Further action needs to be taken in order to complete the request.

4xx: Client Error
The request contains bad syntax or cannot be fulfilled at this server.

5xx: Server Error
The server failed to fulfill an apparently valid request.

6xx: Global Failure
The request cannot be fulfilled at any server.

The response packets also have specific use for the CR LF characters, and, as can be seen from Figure 3-12 and Figure 3-13, both requests and responses contain the SIP version in the start line. Header lines begin with the field name followed by a colon and then the value. For example, in Figure 3-13, the first field begins `Via: SIP/2.0/UDP 172.30.1.11:5060`.

Header Fields

As indicated in the SIP request description, certain fields in the next portion of the packet are mandatory. The following definitions are general, as the fields have special conditions attached or behavior dependent upon the circumstance. Figure 3-14 can be used to compare the packets and discover the header field values. This image is a comparison of packets 112 and 114 from Figure 3-8.

As we move through the definitions, note the field values in the two packets in Figure 3-14.

Via
This field tells the nodes involved where to send the SIP packet. This field has a number of rules, beginning with the requirement to start with SIP/2.0 and the stack communication details. Per the RFC, the branch parameter "must be unique across time and space" except in the case of an ACK, CANCEL, or non-2xx response. In addition, the branch parameter must begin with "z9hG4bk" as a seven-character magic cookie to ensure that older implementations using RFC 2543 will not use these values. This provides an indication that RFC 3261 was used for the transmission.

```
Internet Protocol Version 4, Src: 172.30.1.11 (172.30.1.11), Dst: 172.30.1.1 (172.30.1.1)
User Datagram Protocol, Src Port: sip (5060), Dst Port: sip (5060)
Session Initiation Protocol
⊕ Request-Line: REGISTER sip:172.30.1.1 SIP/2.0
⊖ Message Header
  ⊕ Via: SIP/2.0/UDP 172.30.1.11:5060;branch=z9hG4bK31e7e1cfa
    Max-Forwards: 70
    Content-Length: 0
  ⊕ To: 4751111 <sip:4751111@172.30.1.1>
  ⊕ From: 4751111 <sip:4751111@172.30.1.1>;tag=afec0e2ffae8169
    Call-ID: dd5d67821535446081b1eece5c33e606@172.30.1.11
  ⊕ CSeq: 87753542 REGISTER
Internet Protocol Version 4, Src: 172.30.1.1 (172.30.1.1), Dst: 172.30.1.11 (172.30.1.11)
User Datagram Protocol, Src Port: sip (5060), Dst Port: sip (5060)
Session Initiation Protocol
⊕ Status-Line: SIP/2.0 200 OK
⊖ Message Header
  ⊕ Via: SIP/2.0/UDP 172.30.1.11:5060;branch=z9hG4bK31e7e1cfa;received=172.30.1.11
  ⊕ From: 4751111 <sip:4751111@172.30.1.1>;tag=afec0e2ffae8169
  ⊕ To: 4751111 <sip:4751111@172.30.1.1>;tag=as10e6b586
    Call-ID: dd5d67821535446081b1eece5c33e606@172.30.1.11
  ⊕ CSeq: 87753542 REGISTER
```

Figure 3-14. Header-field comparison

From

> This is the identity of the request initiator in URI format. Typically, this is populated by input from the user or configuration information. For example, the phones know the IP address of the call server, and this is how they will be contacted. In addition, the user logs into the phone with a username or phone number.
>
> The tags are used to specify a dialog. The unique identification is actually a combination of the Call-ID and the two tags in the "To" and "From" fields. For example, the "From" tags for both the registration request (packet 112) and the corresponding response (packet 114) have a value of afec0e2ffae8169 and the same lengthy Call-ID. The response in packet 114 provides the second half of the tagging. Tags are to be unique, with 32 bits of randomness, and not reused.
>
> The Call-ID is a value that groups all of the messages from a dialog together. RFC 3261 states that all of the requests and responses in a dialog must have the same value. This is true in the packets depicted in Figure 3-14. This field has the same uniqueness concern as the branch parameter.

To

> This specifies the recipient of the request, also in URI format. It does not necessarily have to be the name or URI of the ultimate recipient. It is also tied to the display name.

CSeq

> This field provides a value to help identify transactions and to order them. We can see from Figure 3-14 that the CSeq numbers are the same. However, the next packet (113) is a different transaction, and so the values used for this packet are changed.

Figure 3-15 presents the SIP OPTIONS message from the call server to the VoIP phone.

```
Internet Protocol Version 4, Src: 172.30.1.1 (172.30.1.1), Dst: 172.30.1.11 (172.30.1.11)
User Datagram Protocol, Src Port: sip (5060), Dst Port: sip (5060)
Session Initiation Protocol
⊕ Request-Line: OPTIONS sip:4751111@172.30.1.11:5060 SIP/2.0
⊟ Message Header
  ⊕ Via: SIP/2.0/UDP 172.30.1.1:5060;branch=z9hG4bK74fc46f8
    Max-Forwards: 70
  ⊕ From: "Unknown" <sip:Unknown@172.30.1.1>;tag=as0c7400a4
  ⊕ To: <sip:4751111@172.30.1.11:5060>
  ⊕ Contact: <sip:Unknown@172.30.1.1:5060>
    Call-ID: 6769ae784bfb461948c8c8a0733eca09@172.30.1.1:5060
  ⊟ CSeq: 102 OPTIONS
      Sequence Number: 102
      Method: OPTIONS
    User-Agent: FPBX-2.10.0rc1(1.8.11)
    Date: Wed, 15 Aug 2012 16:10:31 GMT
    Allow: INVITE, ACK, CANCEL, OPTIONS, BYE, REFER, SUBSCRIBE, NOTIFY, INFO, PUBLISH
    Supported: replaces, timer
    Content-Length: 0
```

Figure 3-15. SIP OPTIONS message

The CSeq contains not only the sequence number (32-bit unsigned integer less than 231) but also the method (OPTIONS).

Max-Forwards

This value limits the number of hops that a message can traverse on its way to the destination. If the fields reaches zero, the message will not be delivered, and an error code (status) of 483 will be generated. This field is used in requests and the recommendation is that the value be set to 70. From our captures of packets thus far, we can see that the current SIP network is following the rules.

Contact

This field must be present in the request. It is supposed to contain a single URI matching the format used earlier in the header. Examining the header of Figure 3-15, we can see that there is consistency between the fields in terms of the URI structure. "Unknown" was listed as the username, as a user was not tied to this phone number; only an IP address was.

Allow

This is a list of the methods supported by the user agent generating the message. As mentioned earlier, methods are functions performed by the SIP UAC or UAS. Normally, the OPTIONS message is used for this purpose. Operationally, SIP messages may include the Allow fields in order to reduce the overall number of messages required. For example, in the exchange used here, the REGISTER message includes the same fields. Figure 3-15 indicates that there is a wide variety of methods (and therefore messages) supported.

Basic Operation Continued

At this point in our topology, the VoIP phones have been powered up, talked to the DHCP server, connected to the TFTP, server and registered with the call server. This section will cover the transactions that occur when a call is placed between two SIP endpoints. We have to remember that in order to analyze a call, it must be viewed from both sides. In this case, the phone at IP address 172.30.1.11 (475-1111) is calling 475-2222, which is the phone at IP address 172.30.1.22. This is shown in Figure 3-16.

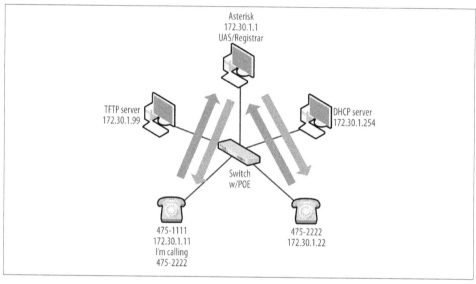

Figure 3-16. Topology with call start

Like the registration, these messages flow to and from the call server (Figure 3-17).

As we examine these messages, we can see that the packets flow up to the call server and back out. In addition, all of the values (tags, CSeq, branch) are different, indicating that these are considered to be different groups of messages. Lastly, the circled content type tells us that SDP is encapsulated within the message body. SDP is the Session Descriptor Protocol.

Session Description Protocol (SDP)

The Session Description Protocol is standardized in RFC 4566, which obsoletes RFC 3266. The purpose of the protocol is to provide a general-purpose protocol that describes the media content to be transferred. In the examples used thus far, the media content type is audio. From RFC 4566:

```
Internet Protocol Version 4, Src: 172.30.1.11 (172.30.1.11), Dst: 172.30.1.1 (172.30.1.1)
User Datagram Protocol, Src Port: sip (5060), Dst Port: sip (5060)
Session Initiation Protocol
⊞ Request-Line: INVITE sip:4752222@172.30.1.1 SIP/2.0
⊟ Message Header
  ⊞ Via: SIP/2.0/UDP 172.30.1.11:5060;branch=z9hG4bK085494974
    Max-Forwards: 70
    Content-Length: 261
  ⊞ To: 4752222 <sip:4752222@172.30.1.1>
  ⊞ From: 4751111 <sip:4751111@172.30.1.1>;tag=980906697d6b2c9
    Call-ID: c3d97bbb99745cbab4252e993de4f49c@172.30.1.11
  ⊞ CSeq: 1324510262 INVITE
    Supported: timer
    Allow: NOTIFY
    Allow: REFER
    Allow: OPTIONS
    Allow: INVITE
    Allow: ACK
    Allow: CANCEL
    Allow: BYE
    Content-Type: application/sdp
  ⊞ Contact: 4751111 <sip:4751111@172.30.1.11:5060>
    Supported: replaces
    User-Agent: Avaya SIP R2.2 Endpoint Brcm Callctrl/1.5.1.0 MxSF/v3.2.6.26
⊞ Message Body

Internet Protocol Version 4, Src: 172.30.1.1 (172.30.1.1), Dst: 172.30.1.22 (172.30.1.22)
User Datagram Protocol, Src Port: sip (5060), Dst Port: sip (5060)
Session Initiation Protocol
⊞ Request-Line: INVITE sip:4752222@172.30.1.22:5060 SIP/2.0
⊟ Message Header
  ⊞ Via: SIP/2.0/UDP 172.30.1.1:5060;branch=z9hG4bK6d33b699
    Max-Forwards: 70
  ⊞ From: "Bruce" <sip:4751111@172.30.1.1>;tag=as4c880664
  ⊞ To: <sip:4752222@172.30.1.22:5060>
  ⊞ Contact: <sip:4751111@172.30.1.1:5060>
    Call-ID: 4f7228bf4152517309c907195fcf9536@172.30.1.1:5060
  ⊞ CSeq: 102 INVITE
    User-Agent: FPBX-2.10.0rc1(1.8.11)
    Date: Wed, 15 Aug 2012 16:15:04 GMT
    Allow: INVITE, ACK, CANCEL, OPTIONS, BYE, REFER, SUBSCRIBE, NOTIFY, INFO, PUBLISH
    Supported: replaces, timer
    Content-Type: application/sdp
    Content-Length: 261
⊞ Message Body
```

Figure 3-17. SIP INVITE messages

SDP is intended for describing multimedia sessions for the purposes of session announcement, session invitation, and other forms of multimedia session initiation.

RFC 3261 (SIP) refers to the use of SDP but does not define it. The important information within the SDP fields will include the reason for the session, duration, media type, and information about the media stream, such as port. Figure 3-18 takes another look at the same INVITE messages seen in Figure 3-17 but this time collapses the message headers and expands the SDP portion. The UDP ports to be used in the subsequent voice data stream are circled.

```
Internet Protocol Version 4, Src: 172.30.1.11 (172.30.1.11), Dst: 172.30.1.1 (172.30.1.1)
User Datagram Protocol, Src Port: sip (5060), Dst Port: sip (5060)
Session Initiation Protocol
⊞ Request-Line: INVITE sip:4752222@172.30.1.1 SIP/2.0
⊞ Message Header
⊟ Message Body
  ⊟ Session Description Protocol
     Session Description Protocol Version (v): 0
   ⊞ Owner/Creator, Session Id (o): MxSIP 0 307545470 IN IP4 172.30.1.11
     Session Name (s): SIP Call
   ⊞ Connection Information (c): IN IP4 172.30.1.11
   ⊞ Time Description, active time (t): 0 0
   ⊞ Media Description, name and address (m): audio 34008 RTP/AVP 0 8 18 2 127
   ⊞ Media Attribute (a): rtpmap:0 PCMU/8000
   ⊞ Media Attribute (a): rtpmap:8 PCMA/8000
   ⊞ Media Attribute (a): rtpmap:18 G729/8000
   ⊞ Media Attribute (a): rtpmap:2 G726-32/8000
   ⊞ Media Attribute (a): rtpmap:127 telephone-event/8000
   ⊞ Media Attribute (a): ptime:20
Internet Protocol Version 4, Src: 172.30.1.1 (172.30.1.1), Dst: 172.30.1.22 (172.30.1.22)
User Datagram Protocol, Src Port: sip (5060), Dst Port: sip (5060)
Session Initiation Protocol
⊞ Request-Line: INVITE sip:4752222@172.30.1.22:5060 SIP/2.0
⊞ Message Header
⊟ Message Body
  ⊟ Session Description Protocol
     Session Description Protocol Version (v): 0
   ⊞ Owner/Creator, Session Id (o): root 1524739687 1524739687 IN IP4 172.30.1.1
     Session Name (s): Asterisk PBX 1.8.11-cert1
   ⊞ Connection Information (c): IN IP4 172.30.1.1
   ⊞ Time Description, active time (t): 0 0
   ⊞ Media Description, name and address (m): audio 16690 RTP/AVP 0 8 101
   ⊞ Media Attribute (a): rtpmap:0 PCMU/8000
   ⊞ Media Attribute (a): rtpmap:8 PCMA/8000
   ⊞ Media Attribute (a): rtpmap:101 telephone-event/8000
   ⊞ Media Attribute (a): fmtp:101 0-16
   ⊞ Media Attribute (a): ptime:20
     Media Attribute (a): sendrecv
```

Figure 3-18. SIP INVITE message body

Wireshark occasionally makes additions to packets in order to describe the content of a field. Some of these are helpful, and some are confusing. With SIP, the differences can impact our perception of the SIP message structure. For this reason, it is sometimes appropriate to view the messages in a raw format. Figure 3-19 depicts the same message shown in the top half of Figure 3-18. For space, only one of the messages is shown. Figure 3-19 demonstrates the marked difference between the two. I am fond of saying "When in doubt, go to the packets." Perhaps I should add, "If doubt persists, go to the raw packet."

```
Session Initiation Protocol
⊞ Request-Line: INVITE sip:4752222@172.30.1.1 SIP/2.0
⊞ Message Header
⊟ Message Body
    ⊞ Session Description Protocol
Session Initiation Protocol (SIP as raw text)
    INVITE sip:4752222@172.30.1.1 SIP/2.0\r\n
    Via: SIP/2.0/UDP 172.30.1.11:5060;branch=z9hG4bK085494974\r\n
    Max-Forwards: 70\r\n
    Content-Length: 261\r\n
    To: 4752222 <sip:4752222@172.30.1.1>\r\n
    From: 4751111 <sip:4751111@172.30.1.1>;tag=980906697d6b2c9\r\n
    Call-ID: c3d97bbb99745cbab4252e993de4f49c@172.30.1.11\r\n
    CSeq: 1324510262 INVITE\r\n
    Supported: timer\r\n
    Allow: NOTIFY\r\n
    Allow: REFER\r\n
    Allow: OPTIONS\r\n
    Allow: INVITE\r\n
    Allow: ACK\r\n
    Allow: CANCEL\r\n
    Allow: BYE\r\n
    Content-Type: application/sdp\r\n
    Contact: 4751111 <sip:4751111@172.30.1.11:5060>\r\n
    Supported: replaces\r\n
    User-Agent: Avaya SIP R2.2 Endpoint Brcm Callctrl/1.5.1.0 MxSF/v3.2.6.26\r\n
    \r\n
    v=0\r\n
    o=MXSIP 0 307545470 IN IP4 172.30.1.11\r\n
    s=SIP Call\r\n
    c=IN IP4 172.30.1.11\r\n
    t=0 0\r\n
    m=audio 34008 RTP/AVP 0 8 18 2 127\r\n
    a=rtpmap:0 PCMU/8000\r\n
    a=rtpmap:8 PCMA/8000\r\n
    a=rtpmap:18 G729/8000\r\n
    a=rtpmap:2 G726-32/8000\r\n
    a=rtpmap:127 telephone-event/8000\r\n
    a=ptime:20\r\n
```

Figure 3-19. SIP INVITE raw view

An SDP header may include not only the mandatory fields such as version, originator, and session ID but also some optional items. One of the important items is the port number to be used in the media stream, as circled in Figure 3-18. Since we are not rewriting the RFC, this section will cover the fields used by the packets seen in the included figures.

Version

This is the version of SDP. RFC 4566 is version 0.

Originator (owner)

This field is actually comprised of several subfields, as shown in Figure 3-20. In this case, the fields were pulled from the INVITE sent directly from the Avaya phone at 172.30.1.11.

```
⊟ Owner/Creator, Session Id (o)  MxSIP 0 307545470 IN IP4 172.30.1.11
    Owner Username: MxSIP
    Session ID: 0
    Session Version: 307545470
    Owner Network Type: IN
    Owner Address Type: IP4
    Owner Address: 172.30.1.11
```

Figure 3-20. Originator subfields

In this case, a username was not present, just the phone itself. The circled session ID is a tuple of the subfields. The version is created by the endpoint with the recommendation that the network time format is used. The text network type (IN) will almost always indicate that this is an Internet type. The address type is also text. The value will typically be either IP4 or IP6. The owner address is the source of the INVITE message.

Session name(s)

This is simply a meaningful name for the exchange. It must not be empty, so it will minimally have the characters "s=" in the space. The characters must be from ISO 10646, which defines the Universal Character Set.

Connection information (c)

The connection info field must be present. Like the originator, it is made up of subfields: the connection network type (IN), the connection address type (IP4), and the connection IP address. One example from Figure 3-18 is IN IP4 172.30.1.11.

Time description

This field specifies the start and stop times for the media session. The value is given in seconds. The field has a start and stop value. A stop value of zero means that the session is not bounded, and a start value of zero means that the session is considered permanent. Unbounded sessions can create utilization problems.

Media description

This field tells us exactly what is to be used by the media stream in terms of ports and codec. The general form is m=VALUE, where the VALUE is registered with the Internet Assigned Number Authority (IANA) and is commonly documented in RFCs. In Figure 3-21, the media description of "m=audio 34008 RTP/AVP 0 8 18 2 127" (followed by the CR and LF) can be read. The hex has been included here so that we can fully understand the line. Note the use of the equals sign and the spaces (hex character 20) in the line. The colon in the decode window can be confusing; this would be cleared up in a raw view similar to the way the output was changed in Figure 3-18 and Figure 3-19.

This line tells us that it is an audio stream that will use port 34008 in the RTP stream. The transport mechanism will be RTP. From RFC 3551 RTP A/V Profiles, we get

```
Session Description Protocol
  Session Description Protocol Version (v): 0
⊞ Owner/Creator, Session Id (o): MxSIP 0 307545470 IN IP4 172.30.1.11
  Session Name (s): SIP Call
⊞ Connection Information (c): IN IP4 172.30.1.11
⊞ Time Description, active time (t): 0 0
⊟ Media Description, name and address (m): audio 34008 RTP/AVP 0 8 18 2 127
    Media Type: audio
    Media Port: 34008
    Media Protocol: RTP/AVP
    Media Format: ITU-T G.711 PCMU
    Media Format: ITU-T G.711 PCMA
    Media Format: ITU-T G.729
    Media Format: ITU-T G.721
    Media Format: DynamicRTP-Type-127
⊞ Media Attribute (a): rtpmap:0 PCMU/8000
⊞ Media Attribute (a): rtpmap:8 PCMA/8000
2e 33 30 2e 31 2e 31 31  0d 0a 74 3d 30 20 30 0a   .30.1.11 ..t=0 0.
0a 6d 3d 61 75 64 69 6f  20 33 34 30 30 38 20 52   .m=audio 34008 R
54 50 2f 41 56 50 20 30  20 38 20 31 38 20 32 20   TP/AVP 0 8 18 2 
31 32 37 0d 0a 61 3d 72  74 70 6d 61 70 3a 30 20   127..a=r tpmap:0 
50 43 4d 55 2f 38 30 30  30 0d 0a 61 3d 72 74 70   PCMU/800 0 a=rtp
```

Figure 3-21. Media description

the numbers 0, 8, 18, 2 and 127. In an audio-only media session like this one, it is usual to see a single codec used. So, this line would have a single codec listed. Where multiple codecs can be used and supported, more may be listed.

Media attribute

Attributes are potential characteristics of the media stream that more fully explain the items listed in the media description. Attributes can apply to either the individual media or the session. The example given in the RFC is a single connection to a conference or the conference as a whole. The general form is a=VALUE. Figure 3-22 provides an example of an attribute from one of the INVITE messages.

The field value is a=rtpmap:0 PCMU/8000 followed by the CR and LF (0d 0a) characters. This particular attribute refers to the G.711 codec, which uses pulse code modulation at 8000 samples per second. The rtpmap value of zero is used here because it is standardized. Chapters 4 and 5 discuss RTP and codecs in depth.

Earlier in this collection of packets, we saw the attribute a=sendrecv. This indicates the directions specified by the attributes. One other attribute that appears in this INVITE is a=ptime. This is the time in milliseconds used by the media in the packet. It may aid in decoding, though it is not necessary. In this case, the value is 20 milliseconds. Codecs require a certain amount of time to generate a voice packet, and the voice packet has a specified length.

After the SIP INVITE has been sent, the destination VoIP phone (475-2222, IP address 172.20.1.22) responds with a TRYING message and a RINGING message back to the call server. The call server also sends TRYING and RINGING messages back to the

```
Session Description Protocol
  Session Description Protocol Version (v): 0
⊕ Owner/Creator, Session Id (o): MxSIP 0 307545470 IN IP4 172.30.1.11
  Session Name (s): SIP Call
⊕ Connection Information (c): IN IP4 172.30.1.11
⊕ Time Description, active time (t): 0 0
⊕ Media Description, name and address (m): audio 34008 RTP/AVP 0 8 18 2 127
⊟ Media Attribute (a): rtpmap:0 PCMU/8000
    Media Attribute Fieldname: rtpmap
    Media Format: 0
    MIME Type: PCMU
    Sample Rate: 8000
⊕ Media Attribute (a): rtpmap:8 PCMA/8000
⊕ Media Attribute (a): rtpmap:18 G729/8000
⊕ Media Attribute (a): rtpmap:2 G726-32/8000
⊕ Media Attribute (a): rtpmap:127 telephone-event/8000
⊕ Media Attribute (a): ptime:20
30 2e 31 2e 31 31 0d 0a   73 50 53 49 50 20 43 01   0.1.11.. s=SIP Ca
6c 6c 0d 0a 63 3d 49 4e   20 49 50 34 20 31 37 32   ll..c=IN  IP4 172
2e 33 30 2e 31 2e 31 31   0d 0a 74 3d 30 20 30 0d   .30.1.11 ..t=0 0.
0a 6d 3d 61 75 64 69 6f   20 33 34 30 30 38 20 52   .m=audio  34008 R
54 50 2f 41 56 50 20 30   20 38 20 31 38 20 32 20   TP/AVP 0  8 18 2
31 32 37 0d 0a 61 3d 72   74 70 6d 61 70 3a 30 20   127..a=r tpmap:0
50 43 4d 55 2f 38 30 30   30 0d 0a 61 3d 72 74 70   PCMU/800 0..a=rtp
6d 61 70 3a 38 20 50 43   4d 41 2f 38 30 30 30 0d   map:8 PC MA/8000.
0a 61 3d 72 74 70 6d 61   70 3a 31 38 20 47 37 32   .a=rtpma p:18 G72
```

Figure 3-22. Media attribute example

originating phone (475-1111, IP address 172.30.1.11). The sequences of the packets up
to this point are shown in Figure 3-23.

```
10   172.30.1.11   172.30.1.1    SIP/SDP   Request: INVITE sip:4752222@172.30.1.1
11   172.30.1.1    172.30.1.11   SIP       Status: 100 Trying
12   172.30.1.1    172.30.1.11   SIP       Status: 180 Ringing
14   172.30.1.1    172.30.1.11   SIP       Status: 180 Ringing
19   172.30.1.1    172.30.1.11   SIP/SDP   Status: 200 OK, with session description
20   172.30.1.11   172.30.1.1    SIP       Request: ACK sip:4752222@172.30.1.1:5060
21   172.30.1.1    172.30.1.11   RTP       PT=ITU-T G.711 PCMU, SSRC=0x895E7E0, Seq=
22   172.30.1.1    172.30.1.11   RTP       PT=ITU-T G.711 PCMU, SSRC=0x895E7E0, Seq=
```

Figure 3-23. Packet list to this point

Another handy way to examine communications of any kind is with a flow or ladder
diagram. These diagrams show a conversation in terms of direction, IP addresses, port
numbers, time stamps, and message type. Figure 3-24 depicts the conversation from
Figure 3-23 in this format.

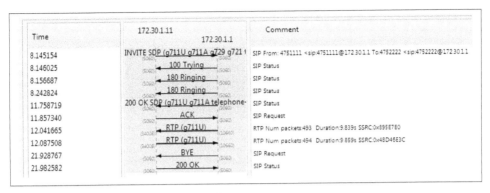

Figure 3-24. Call-flow diagram up to this point

Note that this flow diagram does not show both sides of the conversation. As the call server is placed between the two endpoints, this diagram only shows half of the transmission.

Examples of the TRYING and RINGING messages are shown in Figure 3-25 and Figure 3-26.

```
Internet Protocol Version 4, Src: 172.30.1.1 (172.30.1.1), Dst: 172.30.1.11 (172.30.1.11)
User Datagram Protocol, Src Port: sip (5060), Dst Port: sip (5060)
Session Initiation Protocol
⊞ Status-Line: SIP/2.0 100 Trying
⊟ Message Header
  ⊞ Via: SIP/2.0/UDP 172.30.1.11:5060;branch=z9hG4bK085494974;received=172.30.1.11
  ⊞ From: 4751111 <sip:4751111@172.30.1.1>;tag=980906697d6b2c9
  ⊞ To: 4752222 <sip:4752222@172.30.1.1>
    Call-ID: c3d97bbb99745cbab4252e993de4f49c@172.30.1.11
  ⊞ CSeq: 1324510262 INVITE
    Server: FPBX-2.10.0rc1(1.8.11)
    Allow: INVITE, ACK, CANCEL, OPTIONS, BYE, REFER, SUBSCRIBE, NOTIFY, INFO, PUBLISH
    Supported: replaces, timer
  ⊞ Contact: <sip:4752222@172.30.1.1:5060>
    Content-Length: 0
```

Figure 3-25. SIP TRYING message

Notice that the SIP TRYING message has a provisional code of 100. This code and the message have the effect of preventing the retransmission of the INVITE from the originating UAC—in this case, the VoIP phone at 475-1111 and IP address of 172.30.1.11. In addition, this TRYING message is not to be forwarded by proxies. The provisional code of 100 indicates that the server is in the middle of an action on behalf of the original request. Since TRYING receives a provisional code, it is treated in the same way.

```
Internet Protocol Version 4, Src: 172.30.1.1 (172.30.1.1), Dst: 172.30.1.11 (172.30.1.11)
User Datagram Protocol, Src Port: sip (5060), Dst Port: sip (5060)
Session Initiation Protocol
⊕ Status-Line: SIP/2.0 180 Ringing
⊟ Message Header
  ⊕ Via: SIP/2.0/UDP 172.30.1.11:5060;branch=z9hG4bK085494974;received=172.30.1.11
  ⊕ From: 4751111 <sip:4751111@172.30.1.1>;tag=980906697d6b2c9
  ⊕ To: 4752222 <sip:4752222@172.30.1.1>;tag=as13d5d28a
    Call-ID: c3d97bbb99745cbab4252e993de4f49c@172.30.1.11
  ⊕ CSeq: 1324510262 INVITE
    Server: FPBX-2.10.0rc1(1.8.11)
    Allow: INVITE, ACK, CANCEL, OPTIONS, BYE, REFER, SUBSCRIBE, NOTIFY, INFO, PUBLISH
    Supported: replaces, timer
  ⊕ Contact: <sip:4752222@172.30.1.1:5060>
    Content-Length: 0
```

Figure 3-26. SIP RINGING message

The RINGING message is sent from the SIP endpoint that received the INVITE. The status code of 180 is standard. This provides an indication that the client is attempting to inform the user of an incoming request. In our case, the phone rings. The next packet seen is the response to the INVITE message. Recall that the INVITE contained the SDP packet. Note that when the response comes back (generated from the receiving UAC), the status code is 200, indicating success (Figure 3-27).

```
Internet Protocol Version 4, Src: 172.30.1.22 (172.30.1.22), Dst: 172.30.1.1
User Datagram Protocol, Src Port: sip (5060), Dst Port: sip (5060)
Session Initiation Protocol
⊕ Status-Line: SIP/2.0 200 OK
⊕ Message Header
⊟ Message Body
  ⊟ Session Description Protocol
      Session Description Protocol Version (v): 0
    ⊕ Owner/Creator, Session Id (o): MxSIP 0 612545041 IN IP4 172.30.1.22
      Session Name (s): SIP Call
    ⊕ Connection Information (c): IN IP4 172.30.1.22
    ⊕ Time Description, active time (t): 0 0
    ⊕ Media Description, name and address (m): audio 34008 RTP/AVP 0 8 101
    ⊕ Media Attribute (a): rtpmap:0 PCMU/8000
    ⊕ Media Attribute (a): rtpmap:8 PCMA/8000
    ⊕ Media Attribute (a): rtpmap:101 telephone-event/8000
    ⊕ Media Attribute (a): ptime:20
      Media Attribute (a): sendrecv
```

Figure 3-27. SIP SDP response message

The last SIP packet prior to the exchange of RTP data is the SIP ACK message, like the one shown in Figure 3-28.

```
Internet Protocol Version 4, Src: 172.30.1.1 (172.30.1.1), Dst: 172.30.1.22
User Datagram Protocol, Src Port: sip (5060), Dst Port: sip (5060)
Session Initiation Protocol
⊞ Request-Line: ACK sip:4752222@172.30.1.22:5060 SIP/2.0
⊟ Message Header
  ⊞ Via: SIP/2.0/UDP 172.30.1.1:5060;branch=z9hG4bK3de2e936
    Max-Forwards: 70
  ⊞ From: "Bruce" <sip:4751111@172.30.1.1>;tag=as4c880664
  ⊞ To: <sip:4752222@172.30.1.22:5060>;tag=a8f65563ffc41bb
  ⊞ Contact: <sip:4751111@172.30.1.1:5060>
    Call-ID: 4f7228bf4152517309c907195fcf9536@172.30.1.1:5060
  ⊞ CSeq: 102 ACK
    User-Agent: FPBX-2.10.0rc1(1.8.11)
    Content-Length: 0
```

Figure 3-28. SIP ACK message

Returning to the packet list shown in Figure 3-23, we can see that as soon as the ACK is returned, the RTP stream commences. The RTP stream continues until one end of the connection closes the session. In our example, 475-2222 hangs up the phone, severing the connection. This is accomplished through the SIP BYE message depicted in Figure 3-29.

```
Internet Protocol Version 4, Src: 172.30.1.22 (172.30.1.22), Dst: 172.30.1.1
User Datagram Protocol, Src Port: sip (5060), Dst Port: sip (5060)
Session Initiation Protocol
⊞ Request-Line: BYE sip:4751111@172.30.1.1:5060 SIP/2.0
⊟ Message Header
  ⊞ Via: SIP/2.0/UDP 172.30.1.22:5060;branch=z9hG4bK72aa280bb
    Max-Forwards: 70
    Content-Length: 0
  ⊞ To: "Bruce" <sip:4751111@172.30.1.1>;tag=as4c880664
  ⊞ From: <sip:4752222@172.30.1.22:5060>;tag=a8f65563ffc41bb
    Call-ID: 4f7228bf4152517309c907195fcf9536@172.30.1.1:5060
  ⊞ CSeq: 869553303 BYE
    Supported: timer
    Supported: replaces
    User-Agent: Avaya SIP R2.2 Endpoint Brcm Callctrl/1.5.1.0 MxSF/v3.2.6.26
```

Figure 3-29. SIP BYE message

Upon receipt of the SIP BYE message, the receiving endpoint (475-1111) returns a response with a status code of 200. Remember that the SIP BYE message is actually a request to shut down the connection. The response is shown in Figure 3-30.

```
Internet Protocol Version 4, Src: 172.30.1.11 (172.30.1.11), Dst: 172.30.1.1
User Datagram Protocol, Src Port: sip (5060), Dst Port: sip (5060)
Session Initiation Protocol
⊞ Status-Line: SIP/2.0 200 OK
⊟ Message Header
   Call-ID: c3d97bbb99745cbab4252e993de4f49c@172.30.1.11
   ⊞ CSeq: 102 BYE
   ⊞ From: 4752222 <sip:4752222@172.30.1.1>;tag=as13d5d28a
   ⊞ To: 4751111 <sip:4751111@172.30.1.1>;tag=980906697d6b2c9
   ⊞ Via: SIP/2.0/UDP 172.30.1.1:5060;branch=z9hG4bK78d0499e
   Content-Length: 0
   Supported: replaces
   User-Agent: Avaya SIP R2.2 Endpoint Brcm Callctrl/1.5.1.0 MxSF/v3.2.6.26
```

Figure 3-30. SIP BYE response

Terminating a call is more than simply sending a BYE message. A session (not simply a connection) has been established between the two endpoints upon receipt of the response (status code 200) to the INVITE. So, there is a Call-ID associated with the session or exchange of data. The BYE references a particular INVITE and session. From the RFC, the idea of hanging up is not well defined for SIP, although the desire is clear. But because we do not know when calling or called parties will actually hang up or terminate the call, we are also unsure as to whether the proper status or ACK messages have been received. Thus, it is often up to the developer to ensure that the UAC handles these possibilities. The hope is that when a user or device hangs up by placing the handset on the cradle or by clicking a button that terminates the call, the UAC will generate a SIP BYE request referencing the Call-ID.

 By requiring that a SIP BYE reference a particular session, it prevents additional INVITEs to that session because the Call-IDs would be different. A message related to the BYE is the CANCEL, but its use is slightly different.

This brings us to the close of the SIP conversation. If you review these messages, either in the chapter or using the capture files posted on the book website, you should remember that the conversation can be tracked by the tags and Call-ID fields. In this case, the call server is between the two endpoints for the exchanges, effectively setting up two different sets of messages. This means that the values are different for the two connections.

One other interesting thing to note is the flow of RTP messages. This chapter illustrates one of two possible configurations for the voice streams. The pathways are shown in Figure 3-31.

It is common for the call server to connect the two endpoints and then simply step out of the conversation. At that point, the RTP messages flow directly between the phones,

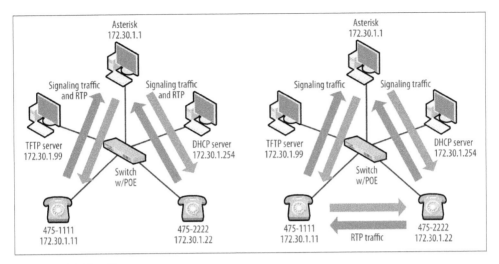

Figure 3-31. Traffic patterns

as shown on the right side. So, the packets would have 172.30.1.11 and 172.30.1.22 as the source and destination addresses. However, with this small topology and the default AsteriskNOW configuration, the call server stays for the entire call, from start to termination, as shown on the left.

Trunks

SIP trunks seem to be all the rage right now, with vendors offering services of all kinds. A challenge for those trying to learn about them is that vendors and service providers have different definitions for a trunk. Lastly, the word "trunk" does not appear anywhere in RFC 3261. In the IETF draft article "What Is a Session Initiation Protocol (SIP) Trunk Anyway?" J. Rosenberg from Cisco made the following proposal to the Internet Engineering Task Force:

> A SIP trunk is a virtual sip entity on a server (UAS, UAC or proxy) constrained by a predefined set of polices and rules that determine how to process requests.
>
> The behavior of the trunk is conditioned on a contract—an agreement between the client and the server, that so long as requests are formatted based on the nature of the contract, the request will receive the specified treatment.

Further, the proposal suggests that the trunk exists an as instance on the server rather than a defined link between switches or offices. From Microsoft, we get the following definition and capability:

A SIP trunk is a direct connection between your organization and an Internet telephony service provider (ITSP). It enables you to extend voice over IP (VoIP) telephony beyond your organization's firewall without the need for an IP-PSTN gateway. ...In addition to VoIP calls, SIP trunks can also carry instant messages, multimedia conferences, user presence information, Enhanced 9-1-1 (E9-1-1) emergency calls, and other SIP-based, real-time communications services.

What these definitions (and many others) share is that a SIP trunk is not a physical connection such as the link running off-site but rather a logical connection to an endpoint that handles a particular set of applications. This relationship is shown in Figure 3-32.

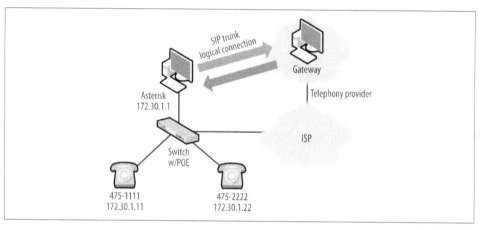

Figure 3-32. SIP trunk logical connections

While this image indicates that the telephony and Internet Service Providers are different entities, this is not necessarily the case. For example, Time Warner provides both connectivity and a VoIP service.

While SIP trunks may initially have been thought of as voice tunnels, they are now part of a larger, unified platform. If you are paying a provider for VoIP service, there is a good chance it is via a SIP trunk.

Security

The problem with VoIP security in general, and SIP security in particular, is that, as VoIP-info.org correctly states:

SIP security is a vast and somewhat challenging field.

But if we boil things down a bit and ignore everything that is not VoIP specific, VoIP security has two general components: securing the signaling traffic and securing the voice data. In securing the signaling traffic, we are seeking to lock down the registrations, invitations, terminations, and so forth. When we target the voice data, we really seek to protect the RTP stream as it transverses the network; doing this becomes particularly challenging for wireless networks. But even focusing our actions on these two areas is not without difficulties. Vendor support and compatibility are not guaranteed, and there are times when securing VoIP components may actually prevent them from operating.

Part of the problem comes from the simplicity and readability of SIP. As pointed out in this chapter, SIP bears a strong resemblance to HTTP and is formatted using many of the same rules. Thus, the messages and their flow are straightforward. Common security attacks on SIP include:

Registration
> Attackers can easily spoof the identity of a valid user. In the calls captured for this chapter, at no point was authentication required.

Call disconnects and denial of service
> A SIP teardown attack is an example of one way to disconnect a valid user. The attacker simply sends a BYE packet with the proper IDs.

Man in the middle
> Man-in-the-middle attacks are all-purpose attacks used to capture traffic and credentials for valid network nodes. There are several forms of this attack (e.g., ARP poisoning, ICMP redirect, rogue APs), and the shared strategy between the various forms is to place the attacker between the node and the server or network. The attacker fools the client into sending traffic to it. After receiving the traffic from the valid node, the attacker forwards the traffic to the server. This is repeated for traffic flowing in the opposite direction. In this way, the endpoints are not aware that the attacker is there and reading all of the data.

The mitigation for these attacks includes a combination of authentication and encryption mechanisms offered by Secure SIP and Secure RTP.

 Though it simplifies the security conversation, to focus on VoIP-specific security is dangerous. For example, attacks against network equipment or trunk lines can expose network conversations to eavesdroppers. Wireless networks dependent upon WPA-PSK with short passphrases are vulnerable to an attacker with modest skills. The call server itself and the clients must be protected. For these reasons, VoIP security is necessarily part of a much larger discussion.

Secure SIP provides what is called a secure URI (SIPS URI) and uses port 5061 instead of 5060. The format is similar to the addressing identified earlier in this chapter, except that it begins with sips instead of sip. For example, sips:4751111@172.30.1.1. The idea is that a call made using a SIPS URI would be secured using transport layer security, or TLS. TLS is described in RFC 5246. If TLS is used, the entire connection is secured via certificates. But managing these certificates, especially in the context of a larger network that may have additional security infrastructure, is not always a simple task. The other element for reducing attacks is to encrypt the voice data itself using secure RTP (SRTP), which ignores the signaling traffic and is covered in RFC 5506. Though the two components are described in different RFCs, typically they go hand in hand. However, implementations are often vendor specific, and there are significant challenges to interoperation.

But where should the encryption be implemented? If users are connecting via the wired network, one could argue that no encryption is necessary. Protecting wireless users is an important task, but are they already using stronger (or equal) encryption via something like 802.1x? External connectivity is often established via a virtual private network (VPN), and thus encrypting the voice stream may be redundant, not to mention the potential performance degradation it might cause. So, there are options for securing the voice traffic, but it is important to determine exactly what is to be protected and why.

Summary

The infrastructure necessary to support a VoIP deployment is composed of both non-VoIP and VoIP-specific components. In the VoIP-specific category, there are a collection of signaling and transport protocols. The signaling protocols are used to handle setup, accounting, session characteristics, and tear down. Examples of these signaling protocols include SIP, H.323, and Skinny. Of these three, SIP has the greatest amount of support and is emerging as the protocol of choice for the future. SIP is standardized in RFC 3261 but is dependent upon many other protocols. This chapter covered the operation of SIP from startup through a VoIP call. Understanding SIPs characteristics, fields, and security concerns simplifies deployment and troubleshooting. This chapter addresses these along with the content captured from an operating SIP deployment.

Standards and Reading

RFC 3261
> SIP: Session Initiation Protocol (*http://tools.ietf.org/html/rfc3261*)

RFC 3986
> Uniform Resource Identifier (URI): General Syntax (*http://tools.ietf.org/html/rfc3986*)

RFC 4566
> SDP: Session Description Protocol (*http://tools.ietf.org/html/rfc4566*)

RFC 5322
> Internet Message Format (*http://tools.ietf.org/html/rfc5322*)

RFC 5630
> The Use of the SIPS URI Scheme in the Session Initiation Protocol (SIP) (*http://tools.ietf.org/html/rfc5630*)

Review Questions

1. What port is used by SIP?
2. What message is used to contact another user for a call?
3. What is the status-code value that indicates success?
4. What is the purpose of SDP?
5. How is RFC 5322 related to SIP?
6. True or false: SIP is an ITU-T recommendation.
7. True or false: the recommended way to protect SIP transmissions is with transport layer security based on IPSec VPNs.
8. True or false: URIs are the same thing as the AOR.
9. What status codes indicate failure?
10. True or false: SIP trunks are used to multiplex traditional telephony connections to the VoIP provider over a single physical line.

Review Question Answers

1. 5060.
2. INVITE.
3. 200.
4. The Session Description Protocol (SDP) provides the characteristics of the media connection such as codec and direction.
5. RFC 5322 provides the format for general Internet text-based messages. SIP follows and expands on this format.
6. False—SIP is standardized in IETF RFC 3261.
7. False—TLS is transport layer (layer-4) security. Though it and IPSec can use certificates, it operates at layer 4.

8. False—the SIP address of record (AOR) is a public URI that can be redirect to a URI where the user is located. So, the AOR is a URI, but not all URIs are AORs.

9. Codes 4xx through 6xx indicate failure of either the client or the many servers that might be part of the connection.

10. False—the SIP trunk is not tied to a physical line or traditional telephony connections.

Lab Activities

This chapter is supported by the book website. So, if the activity lists equipment or software that you do not have, go to the book website for additional content.

Activity 1—Build the Topology Shown

This is the topology that was used in this chapter. Most of the materials are available free of charge.

Materials: Ethernet switch, AsteriskNow, computers capable of acting as the DHCP and TFTP servers, SIP endpoints

The goal for this topology (Figure 3-33) is to have a couple of VoIP nodes running SIP. Other components include DHCP, TFTP, and a switch. The topology in this chapter used AsteriskNOW as the call server and a pair of Avaya VoIP phones. The VoIP endpoints do not have to be desktop phones. They can be softphones. A very nice list based on operating system has been compiled by voip-info.org (*http://bit.ly/153TiKO*).

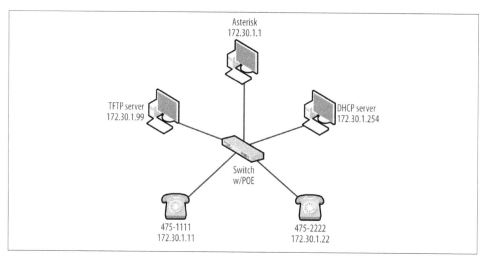

Figure 3-33. Activity 1 topology

1. Download the AsteriskNOW iso, an Asterisk virtual machine, or your favorite Linux distribution. While this may seem a bit heavy-handed for a lab exercise, the GUI is straightforward to work with and will provide a good basis for future VoIP studies. Once you have the install completed, create a couple of SIP stations.

2. The TFTP server is only necessary if you wish to support desktop phones or complete the topology used in the chapter.

3. Connect all of the nodes to a switch and add a DHCP server. A home gateway can serve as the switch and the DHCP server; however, power over Ethernet (PoE) may be an issue depending on the type of phones used.

4. Test the phones by making a call.

Activity 2—Packet Capture

Materials: the topology from Activity 1 and Wireshark

The goal of this activity is to understand how SIP and the phones operate. To this end, at least one capture machine will be required. Depending on the type of VoIP endpoint, the capture may be accomplished on the same node. A mirrored port may also be configured on the switch.

Activity 3—Packet Capture Analysis

Materials: same as above

Answer the following questions.

1. What happens when the phone is registered? Hung up?

2. What are the conversations?

3. Are your services such as DHCP and TFTP accessed?

4. Are there any other services requested by the phone that are not on the network? For ex. NTP

Activity 4—Phone-Call Analysis

Materials: same as above

Start a capture and make a phone call between your endpoints. Complete the steps and answer the following questions.

1. Open the SIP INVITE. Analyze the fields. Pay special attention to the tags and IDs.

2. Can you find the response to this packet? Can you match the sequence and ID numbers?

3. Locate the URI. What values from your network are used?

Activity 5—SDP

Materials: same as above

Locate the SDP components in the capture. Answer the following questions.

1. What are the parameters used for the call?

2. What codecs are listed? What codec is used?

CHAPTER 4

The Real-Time Transport Protocol and the Real-Time Control Protocol

> *RTP is a protocol framework that is deliberately not complete. This document specifies those functions expected to be common across all the applications for which RTP would be appropriate. Unlike conventional protocols ... RTP is intended to be tailored through modifications and/or additions to the headers as needed.*
>
> —RFC 1889

VoIP endpoint registration, setup, number dialing, media sessions and features are all governed by the VoIP signaling protocol. Probably the most common signaling protocols in use today are the Session Initialization Protocol (SIP), H.323 from the International Telecommunications Union–Telecom (ITU-T), and the Skinny Client Control Protocol (Skinny) from Cisco. These three protocols could not be more different from each other. But, despite these differences, they share the need to transport voice data from one phone to another, and they all use the same method—the Real-Time Transport Protocol, or RTP. While RTP is used on almost every standardized Voice over IP deployment, its malleable nature allows it to be expanded or modified to suit future media streams and codecs.

This chapter will describe the operation of RTP and provide several examples of packets captured on an operating VoIP network. Mixed in with the RTP packets, we will also see another protocol—the real-time control protocol (RTCP), which provides feedback regarding the quality or performance of the RTP stream. One challenge in writing a chapter like this is that vendors do not implement these protocols in the same way, so the chapter will review captures taken from different deployments to illustrate the ideas. Thus, the packets shown in this chapter will come from a collection of Cisco, Avaya, and Polycom topologies.

RTP and RTCP were originally defined in RFC 1889. This RFC was made obsolete by RFC 3550. This chapter will use the latter as the primary resource. The companion document to RFC 3550 is RFC 3551 (3551 obsoletes RFC 1890), which defines an RTP profile for audio and video conferencing. Much of the information required to fully understand the operation of RTP (and its malleability) is also contained in RFC 3551, so this will be an integral part of the discussion.

Protocol Description

If you have read the previous chapters, you know that there are many components required to support a VoIP deployment, such as a signaling protocol, and infrastructure, such as the trivial file transfer protocol (TFTP) server and dynamic host configuration, or DHCP. These conversations occur before the RTP stream starts. The signaling protocol only returns for termination of the call. So, the signaling protocol (H.323, SIP, Skinny) and the transport protocol (RTP) handle different aspects of the communication. Per RFC 3550, RTP does the following:

> Provides end-to-end delivery services for data with real-time characteristics, such as interactive audio and video.

In this context, delivery service means that RTP is the container for the voice or video data or both. The data is the result of the codec operation. So, voice and/or video is sampled per the codec and then placed inside an RTP packet. An example of this is shown in Figure 4-1.

```
Internet Protocol Version 4, Src: 192.168.16.4 (192.168.16.4), Dst: 192.168.16.16 (192.168.16.16)
User Datagram Protocol, Src Port: clearvisn (2052), Dst Port: btpp2audctrl (2536)
Real-Time Transport Protocol
  [Stream setup by H245 (frame 22700)]
  10.. .... = Version: RFC 1889 Version (2)
  ..0. .... = Padding: False
  ...0 .... = Extension: False
  .... 0000 = Contributing source identifiers count: 0
  0... .... = Marker: False
  Payload type: ITU-T G.711 PCMU (0)
  Sequence number: 2
  [Extended sequence number: 65538]
  Timestamp: 320
  Synchronization Source identifier: 0x07fff4aa (134214826)
  Payload: 9d96929192969dabe92e1e18141214181e2c54b4a49d9998...
```

Figure 4-1. Sample RTP packet

This packet indicates that the payload was created via the G.711 codec, as indicated by the top arrow. G.711 is an audio codec used to generate voice frames (the process is described in chapter 5) that constitute the payload; this is indicted by the bottom arrow. The receiver of audio data has to know exactly what codec was used to create the packet and how to put the stream back together. While there are several fields in an RTP packet, the protocol has two main focal points: payload identification and sequencing.

At layer 4 of our networking models, RTP is encapsulated in a UDP header. UDP provides very little in the way of priority handling or sequencing. This is common for real-time data simply because a lost or significantly delayed packets might create problems if the application at the destination has to wait for them. But this is not true of the TCP-based signaling protocol. The signaling protocol handles the other operations, such as registration and call setup. However, once data starts to flow, it is placed in an RTP wrapper. Thus, RTP is often built into an application. One other feature of RTP is that it is expandable and flexible. For example, payload types can be added to the RFC, and security additions such as secure RTP need not rewrite the entire header.

 While RFC 3550 obsoletes RFC 1889, it does not mean that there have been major changes to the structure or operation. The major aspects of RTP and RTCP actually change very little. From RFC 3550:

> Most of the text in this memorandum is identical to RFC 1889 which it obsoletes. There are no changes in the packet formats on the wire, only changes to the rules and algorithms governing how the protocol is used.

> So, when reviewing RTP packets, we might expect headers defined by the most recent RFC. However, most transmissions use RFC 1889.

Profiles

The idea of a profile must now be introduced. While RFC 3550 describes the general structure and operation of both RTP and RTCP, there are some items that can be modified through the use of a profile. A type of transmission may desire an additional function outside of the fixed header defined in the RFC. Both the marker and payload fields (defined later in this chapter) can be slightly modified to suit these needs. In addition, a collection of fixed fields can be added immediately before the payload field. This is described by an extension to the header.

Section 5.3 of RFC 3550 provides more information about the profile modifications and the header extensions. RFC 3551 contains the profile for audio and video in a conferencing application. Importantly, this RFC contains the RTP payload-field values used by the common audio and video codecs.

Basic Operation

RTP is used to convey the real-time data. Typically this will be voice and/or video. So, the signaling protocol (H.323, Skinny, or SIP) will be used to handle the messages used to establish calls or connections. Part of this is the negotiation of the method used to encode the data. Chapters 3, 6, and 7 show how SIP, H.323, and Skinny handle this.

Once a media session has been established, the RTP packets begin to flow between the endpoints in both directions. The packets from each source are tied together via an identification number.

Since the performance of real-time data is critical with latency, packet loss, and jitter resulting in poor perceived call quality, RTP has a control protocol used to measure some of these values. Thus, RTCP packets are also sent along with the RTP stream although they are much fewer in number. The point of RTCP is to keep track of the RTP stream and provide this information to the endpoints. Specifically, RTCP counts the number of packets and bytes sent. It also measures the transmission times for the RTP packets. When RTP and RTCP are together, the UDP port used by RTCP is supposed to be the next highest odd numbered port.

To help with the explanation of these ideas, we will use the topology shown in Figure 4-2.

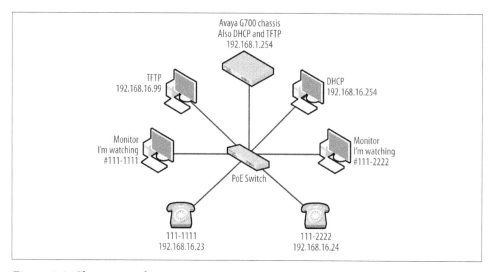

Figure 4-2. Chapter topology

An Avaya G700 chassis will be our call server. This topology happens to use the H.323 suite of protocols. Like the other topologies discussion in this book, a dynamic host configuration protocol (DHCP) server and trivial file transfer protocol (TFTP) servers will also be present. The two VoIP phones have been given the numbers 111-1111 (192.168.16.23) and 111-2222 (192.168.16.24), and there are management stations observing traffic flowing to and from the two phones via monitor sessions running on the switch. The following sections will describe the structure of the RTP and RTCP protocols using this topology.

Protocol Structure

The nice thing about RTP is that it is a fairly straightforward protocol with a small set of header fields. In this section, we will discuss what are called the fixed-header fields. The text version of the header is taken from RFC 1889 and can be seen in Figure 4-3.

```
 0                   1                   2                   3
 0 1 2 3 4 5 6 7 8 9 0 1 2 3 4 5 6 7 8 9 0 1 2 3 4 5 6 7 8 9 0 1
+-+-+-+-+-+-+-+-+-+-+-+-+-+-+-+-+-+-+-+-+-+-+-+-+-+-+-+-+-+-+-+-+
|V=2|P|X|  CC   |M|     PT      |       sequence number         |
+-+-+-+-+-+-+-+-+-+-+-+-+-+-+-+-+-+-+-+-+-+-+-+-+-+-+-+-+-+-+-+-+
|                           timestamp                           |
+-+-+-+-+-+-+-+-+-+-+-+-+-+-+-+-+-+-+-+-+-+-+-+-+-+-+-+-+-+-+-+-+
|           synchronization source (SSRC) identifier            |
+=+=+=+=+=+=+=+=+=+=+=+=+=+=+=+=+=+=+=+=+=+=+=+=+=+=+=+=+=+=+=+=+
|            contributing source (CSRC) identifiers             |
|                             ....                              |
+-+-+-+-+-+-+-+-+-+-+-+-+-+-+-+-+-+-+-+-+-+-+-+-+-+-+-+-+-+-+-+-+
```

Figure 4-3. Header from RFC 3550

The next section will provide details, but first let's compare the RFC header in Figure 4-3 with an actual RTP packet as shown in Figure 4-4. The first couple of fields are very small and include information regarding the content of the packet. But some of the most important fields will be PT or Payload Type (G.711), the sequence number (11639), timestamp (998248329), and the SSRC, or synchronization source identifier. As the fields are defined, the following section will refer to both diagrams for clarification.

```
Internet Protocol Version 4, Src: 192.168.16.23 (192.168.16.23), Dst: 192.168.16.24
User Datagram Protocol, Src Port: tsb2 (2742), Dst Port: acc-raid (2800)
Real-Time Transport Protocol
⊞ [Stream setup by H245 (frame 597)]
  10.. .... = Version: RFC 1889 Version (2)
  ..0. .... = Padding: False
  ...0 .... = Extension: False
  .... 0000 = Contributing source identifiers count: 0
  0... .... = Marker: False
  Payload type: ITU-T G.711 PCMU (0)
  Sequence number: 11639
  [Extended sequence number: 77175]
  Timestamp: 998248329
  Synchronization Source identifier: 0x196d27c5 (426584005)
  Payload: cec4e14b60cb61f8684a70febfcd5f51494d70c1cdde3f4a...
```

Figure 4-4. Actual RTP packet for comparison

Header first octet

The first octet of the RTP header is a collection of small fields. The binary value of 1000 0000 (80 in hexadecimal) can easily be broken down into these subfields. The high-lighted line of Figure 4-5 begins the first octet, and this is reflected in the hexadecimal at the bottom. This particular packet is only a portion of the one we've been using in this section. It has been edited for space but not for content. The three periods a the very end of the decoded portion (3f4a...) simply indicate that there is more payload than would fit on the screen.

```
Internet Protocol Version 4, Src: 192.168.16.23 (192.168.16.23), Dst: 192.168.16.24
User Datagram Protocol, Src Port: tsb2 (2742), Dst Port: acc-raid (2800)
Real-Time Transport Protocol
 ± [Stream setup by H245 (frame 597)]
  10.. .... = Version: RFC 1889 Version (2)
  ..0. .... = Padding: False
  ...0 .... = Extension: False
  .... 0000 = Contributing source identifiers count: 0
  0... .... = Marker: False
  Payload type: ITU-T G.711 PCMU (0)
  Sequence number: 11639
  [Extended sequence number: 77175]
  Timestamp: 998248329
  Synchronization Source identifier: 0x196d27c5 (426584005)
  Payload: cec4e14b60cb61f8684a70febfcd5f51494d70c1cdde3f4a...

)00  00 09 6e 05 cb 12 00 09  6e 05 cb 11 08 00 45 b8   ..n..... n.....E.
)10  00 c8 02 77 00 00 40 11  d5 76 c0 a8 10 17 c0 a8   ...w..@. .v......
)20  10 18 0a b6 0a f0 00 b4  55 65 ▒▒ 00 2d 77 3b 80   ........ Ue▒.-w;.
)30  0f 89 19 6d 27 c5 ce c4  e1 4b 60 cb 61 f8 68 4a   ...m'... .K`.a.hJ
```

Figure 4-5. RTP header first octet

Subfield Descriptions

Version (V)

This is a 2-bit field indicating the protocol variant. Possible values include:

0

Pre-RTP; indicates the vat audio tool

1

First draft version of RTP

2

Current version of RTP

An interesting note is that both RFC 1889 and 3550 use the phrase "version defined by this specification" when the value in this field two. The fact that both RFCs use the same value in this field is another indication that there is not much difference between them. From Figure 4-5, we can see that the value is 10 in binary and that Wireshark considers this compliant with RFC 1889.

Padding (P)

This single-bit field tells us whether or not the packet contains octets that are not part of the audio or video payload making up the stream. A zero indicates that this padding is not included. Should padding be part of the packet, the last octet of the padding provides the number of padded octets. Some implementations use fixed block sizes that may not be filled by the samples and so require padding.

Extension (X)

This is another single-bit field indicating the status of the current packet. As mentioned earlier, RTP is an extendable protocol; this allows functions that were defined after the current RFCs to be integrated smoothly into the protocol. Should an extension be required, the header will be enlarged once to contain the function defined by the extension, which happens in a fixed manner described by RFC 3550.

Contributing Source Identifiers Count (CC)

RTP has the ability to carry several samples, and these may be from different sources, as would happen in conference calling with multiple participants. To handle this case, RTP must provide a method to separate the samples and the source for each so that the streams can be reconstructed at the receiving end. If the value of this 4-bit field is set to zero (0000 in binary), then there is a single source associated with this packet. If the value is nonzero, it contains the number of other sources present.

Header second octet

The next octet is also broken into two subfields: marker and payload type. Clicking on the marker bit locates this second octet for us. The second octet of the header begins with the highlighted field in Figure 4-6.

```
Internet Protocol Version 4, Src: 192.168.16.23 (192.168.16.23), Dst: 192.168.16.24
User Datagram Protocol, Src Port: tsb2 (2742), Dst Port: acc-raid (2800)
Real-Time Transport Protocol
⊕ [Stream setup by H245 (frame 597)]
   10.. .... = Version: RFC 1889 Version (2)
   ..0. .... = Padding: False
   ...0 .... = Extension: False
   .... 0000 = Contributing source identifiers count: 0
   0... .... = Marker: False
   Payload type: ITU-T G.711 PCMU (0)
   Sequence number: 11639
   [Extended sequence number: 77175]
   Timestamp: 998248329
   Synchronization Source identifier: 0x196d27c5 (426584005)
   Payload: cec4e14b60cb61f8684a70febfcd5f51494d70c1cdde3f4a...

)00   00 09 6e 05 cb 12 00 09   6e 05 cb 11 08 00 45 b8    ..n..... n.....E.
)10   00 c8 02 77 00 00 40 11   d5 76 c0 a8 10 17 c0 a8    ...w..@. .v......
)20   10 18 0a b6 0a f0 00 b4   55 65 80 00 2d 77 3b 80    ........ Ue..-w;.
)30   0f 89 19 6d 27 c5 ce c4   e1 4b 60 cb 61 f8 68 4a    ...m'... .K`.a.hJ
```

Figure 4-6. RTP header second octet

Following are the second octet field descriptions.

Marker (M)

The simple definition of this single-bit field is that the marker allows important event such as a frame boundary to be marked. But the use of a marker is defined by a profile. RFC 3551 provides the following guidance:

For applications which send either no packets or occasional comfort-noise packets during silence, the first packet of a talkspurt, that is, the first packet after a silence period during which packets have not been transmitted contiguously, SHOULD be distinguished by setting the marker bit in the RTP data header to one. The marker bit in all other packets is zero.

As discussed earlier, not all aspects of the protocol are implemented in the same way. So, some vendors may have a reason for delimiting the RTP stream by setting the marker bit to one, but it is common for the bit to be unused and therefore set to zero. The example shown in Figure 4-7 comes from a Cisco topology. For the packets beginning the sample voice conversation, we can see that both of the "talkspurts" have the marker bit set.

```
40 192.168.1.1      192.168.1.254    RTP    PT=ITU-T G.729, SSRC=0x165F61D9, Seq=2627, Time=407040, Mark
41 192.168.1.1      192.168.1.254    RTP    PT=ITU-T G.729, SSRC=0x165F61D9, Seq=2628, Time=407200
42 192.168.1.1      192.168.1.254    RTP    PT=ITU-T G.729, SSRC=0x165F61D9, Seq=2629, Time=407360
43 192.168.1.1      192.168.1.254    RTP    PT=ITU-T G.729, SSRC=0x165F61D9, Seq=2630, Time=407520
44 192.168.1.254    192.168.1.1      RTP    PT=ITU-T G.729, SSRC=0x1AFB02FE, Seq=330, Time=46048, Mark
```

Figure 4-7. RTP stream with marker bit set

Payload Type (PT)

This is a 7-bit field that tells the receiver the format of the data contained in the packet. This value gives us the numerical value of the source codec used for the samples. Low values (0-23) are for the audio codecs, and the higher values are commonly for video, although other payload types may also be present. For example, RFC 4733 (RFC 2833) describes several DTMF payloads using a variety of IDs. We can see from the collection of packets in Figure 4-7 that the RTP packets contain data that was encoded with G.729. The packet shown in Figure 4-6 is encoded with the G.711 codec. RFC 3551 provides a list of the codecs defined up to the time of its writing. Some examples from Table 4 of RFC 3551 include the following (Figure 4-8):

As an example, PT 0 (PCMU) is for the G.711 codec, which encodes via pulse code modulation μ-law, and these can be seen in both the table and the previous packets. From RFC 3551 Table 5, we get the list of video codec types (Figure 4-9):

Specifying the value provides the receiver with the exact codec used. Other values can be used for dynamic, or source-defined, codecs. At the bottom of Figure 4-9, we can see the values assigned to dynamic codecs. Of course, using a dynamic RTP payload value like the one seen in Figure 4-10 from a Polycom endpoint can make it more difficult on the receiver because it must know the code. This also means that this information must be negotiated prior to the beginning of the RTP stream.

```
PT    encoding      media type    clock rate    channels
      name                        (Hz)

0     PCMU          A             8,000         1
1     reserved      A
2     reserved      A
3     GSM           A             8,000         1
4     G723          A             8,000         1
5     DVI4          A             8,000         1
6     DVI4          A             16,000        1
7     LPC           A             8,000         1
8     PCMA          A             8,000         1
9     G722          A             8,000         1
10    L16           A             44,100        2
11    L16           A             44,100        1
12    QCELP         A             8,000         1
13    CN            A             8,000         1
14    MPA           A             90,000        (see text)
15    G728          A             8,000         1
16    DVI4          A             11,025        1
17    DVI4          A             22,050        1
18    G729          A             8,000         1
dyn   G726-40       A             8,000         1
dyn   G726-32       A             8,000         1
dyn   G726-24       A             8,000         1
dyn   G726-16       A             8,000         1
dyn   G729D         A             8,000         1
dyn   G729E         A             8,000         1
```

Figure 4-8. RFC 3551 audio payload examples

```
PT        encoding      media type    clock rate
          name                        (Hz)

24        unassigned    V
25        CelB          V             90,000
26        JPEG          V             90,000
27        unassigned    V
28        nv            V             90,000
29        unassigned    V
30        unassigned    V
31        H261          V             90,000
32        MPV           V             90,000
33        MP2T          AV            90,000
34        H263          V             90,000
35-71     unassigned    ?
72-76     reserved      N/A           N/A
77-95     unassigned    ?
96-127    dynamic       ?
dyn       H263-1998     V             90,000
```

Figure 4-9. Video codec types

```
Ethernet II, Src: D-Link_ce:90:78 (00:05:5d:ce:90:78), Dst: D-Link_c4:2e:04 (00:50:ba:c4:2e:04)
Internet Protocol Version 4, Src: 10.210.200.112 (10.210.200.112), Dst: 10.210.200.111 (10.210.
User Datagram Protocol, Src Port: sftdst-port (3230), Dst Port: sftdst-port (3230)
Real-Time Transport Protocol
  [Stream setup by SDP (frame 17)]
  10.. .... = Version: RFC 1889 Version (2)
  ..0. .... = Padding: False
  ...0 .... = Extension: False
  .... 0000 = Contributing source identifiers count: 0
  0... .... = Marker: False
  Payload type: SIREN14 (99)
  Sequence number: 0
  [Extended sequence number: 65536]
  Timestamp: 1045536
  Synchronization Source identifier: 0xb7e91701 (3085506305)
  Payload: d0b3e1262e7ea15550aab360d0a609249406fa86414a0124...
```

Figure 4-10. RTP dynamic payload type 99

In this case, the payload type was negotiated via the Session Description Protocol (SDP), a portion of which is shown in Figure 4-11. SDP is a part of the SIP protocol, and the circled value of 99 tells the parties involved that the SIREN codec is to be used. On a separate topology, this value might be used again but for a completely different codec.

```
Session Initiation Protocol
  Status-Line: SIP/2.0 200 OK
  Message Header
  Message Body
    Session Description Protocol
      Session Description Protocol Version (v): 0
      Owner/Creator, Session Id (o): Administrator 17446 0 IN IP4 10.210.200.111
      Session Name (s): -
      Connection Information (c): IN IP4 10.210.200.111
      Bandwidth Information (b): AS:384
      Time Description, active time (t): 0 0
      Media Description, name and address (m): audio 3230 RTP/AVP 99 98 97 102 101 103 9 15 18 0 8
      Media Attribute (a): rtpmap:99 SIREN14/16000
      Media Attribute (a): fmtp:99 bitrate=48000
      Media Attribute (a): rtpmap:98 SIREN14/16000
      Media Attribute (a): fmtp:98 bitrate=32000
      Media Attribute (a): rtpmap:97 SIREN14/16000
      Media Attribute (a): fmtp:97 bitrate=24000
```

Figure 4-11. SDP payload type definition

Packet fields beyond the first two octets

Now that the first couple of octets are out of the way, let's move on to the rest of the fields.

Sequence numbers

This 2-byte field contains the number referencing a particular packet and can help in detecting lost packets and placing the packets in the correct order. However, we have to remember that these are part of a UDP stream, and so sequencing is not tightly controlled by the host. These numbers increase by one for each packet sent by the same source. RFC 3550 recommends that these numbers start at a random value to make them less predictable. The packets shown in Figure 4-5 and Figure 4-6 is part of a much larger collection of packets in the audio stream, and the sequence numbers can be followed by looking at them together.

To make this discussion a little easier to follow, I'll use the same series of packets. Remember that a call has been made from 111-1111 (192.168.16.23) to 111-2222 (192.168.16.24). Figure 4-12 starts us off.

```
192.168.16.23    192.168.16.24    RTP    PT=ITU-T G.711 PCMU, SSRC=0x196D27C5, Seq=11644, Time=998249129
192.168.16.23    192.168.16.24    RTP    PT=ITU-T G.711 PCMU, SSRC=0x196D27CA, Seq=11645, Time=998249289
192.168.16.23    192.168.16.24    RTP    PT=ITU-T G.711 PCMU, SSRC=0x196D27C5, Seq=11646, Time=998249449
192.168.16.23    192.168.16.24    RTP    PT=ITU-T G.711 PCMU, SSRC=0x196D27C5, Seq=11647, Time=998249609
192.168.16.24    192.168.16.23    RTP    PT=ITU-T G.711 PCMU, SSRC=0x49FF2367, Seq=15712, Time=635392464
```

Figure 4-12. RTP sequence numbers

The sequence numbers for the first four RTP packets begin with 11644 as the random number and progress to 11647. Note that a voice call consists of two unidirectional streams, and the sequence numbers for the two streams have a different base value. The last packet contains a sequence number that is part of a stream heading in the opposite direction. As can be see by examining the Polycom captures in Figure 4-13, not every vendor follows the randomizing rules, as the sequence numbers in this particular packet stream begin with zero.

```
10.210.200.112    10.210.200.111    RTP    PT=SIREN14, SSRC=0xB7E91701, Seq=0, Time=1045536
10.210.200.112    10.210.200.111    RTP    PT=SIREN14, SSRC=0xB7E91701, Seq=1, Time=1045696
10.210.200.112    10.210.200.111    RTP    PT=SIREN14, SSRC=0xB7E91701, Seq=2, Time=1045856
10.210.200.112    10.210.200.111    RTP    PT=SIREN14, SSRC=0xB7E91701, Seq=3, Time=1046016
```

Figure 4-13. Polycom RTP sequence numbers

Timestamp

The timestamp is the clock value at the sampling time of the packets' first octet. The accuracy of this 32-bit field is entirely dependent on the clock. The clock used is not the system clock but a timing function of the codec sampling. The requirements for the clock are stringent, as it is used in the calculations regarding the data stream, most notably the voice (or video) data packets and jitter. For example, per RFC 3551 a G.729, voice frame is 10 milliseconds and contains 80 bits. The default packetization is 20 milliseconds, or two G.729 frames per RTP packet. G.711 is always transmitted in 8-bit samples, each one an eight-thousandth of a second in duration. The RTP clock is based on the number of samples per second. Thus, a 20-millisecond frame contains 160 G.711 samples. Examining the timestamps for the same packets, as in Figure 4-14, shows us that the timestamp increases along these lines.

```
192.168.16.23    192.168.16.24    RTP    PT=ITU-T G.711 PCMU, SSRC=0x196D27C5, Seq=11644, Time=998249129
192.168.16.23    192.168.16.24    RTP    PT=ITU-T G.711 PCMU, SSRC=0x196D27C5, Seq=11645, Time=998249289
192.168.16.23    192.168.16.24    RTP    PT=ITU-T G.711 PCMU, SSRC=0x196D27C5, Seq=11646, Time=998249449
192.168.16.23    192.168.16.24    RTP    PT=ITU-T G.711 PCMU, SSRC=0x196D27C5, Seq=11647, Time=998249609
192.168.16.24    192.168.16.23    RTP    PT=ITU-T G.711 PCMU, SSRC=0x49FF2367, Seq=15712, Time=635392464
```

Figure 4-14. RTP timestamps

Whatever the method, packets or time periods, the size of the data chunks must fit into the payload and break across whole-number octets. The timestamp can also be used to calculate arrival times. Jitter measures variation in arrival time.

Synchronization Source Identifier (SSRC)

This field is a random identifier for the source of the real-time stream. It is not based on the network address. This 4-byte value groups the packets for playback. The idea is that sources involved in the RTP stream(s) will not be given the same value. RFC 3550 even provides a sample algorithm that might be used to generate the random number. From the same packet list, all of the packets from 192.168.16.23 have the same synchronization source identifier (Figure 4-15).

```
192.168.16.23    192.168.16.24    RTP    PT=ITU-T G.711 PCMU, SSRC=0x196D27C5, Seq=11644, Time=998249129
192.168.16.23    192.168.16.24    RTP    PT=ITU-T G.711 PCMU, SSRC=0x196D27C5, Seq=11645, Time=998249289
192.168.16.23    192.168.16.24    RTP    PT=ITU-T G.711 PCMU, SSRC=0x196D27C5, Seq=11646, Time=998249449
192.168.16.23    192.168.16.24    RTP    PT=ITU-T G.711 PCMU, SSRC=0x196D27C5, Seq=11647, Time=998249609
192.168.16.24    192.168.16.23    RTP    PT=ITU-T G.711 PCMU, SSRC=0x49FF2367, Seq=15712, Time=635392464
```

Figure 4-15. RTP synchronization source identifiers

We can see that as soon as the source IP address changes, the synchronization source does too (Figure 4-16).

```
192.168.16.23    192.168.16.24    RTP    PT=ITU-T G.711 PCMU, SSRC=0x196D27C5, Seq=11644, Time=998249129
192.168.16.23    192.168.16.24    RTP    PT=ITU-T G.711 PCMU, SSRC=0x196D27C5, Seq=11645, Time=998249289
192.168.16.23    192.168.16.24    RTP    PT=ITU-T G.711 PCMU, SSRC=0x196D27C5, Seq=11646, Time=998249449
192.168.16.23    192.168.16.24    RTP    PT=ITU-T G.711 PCMU, SSRC=0x196D27C5, Seq=11647, Time=998249609
192.168.16.24    192.168.16.23    RTP    PT=ITU-T G.711 PCMU, SSRC=0x49FF2367, Seq=15712, Time=635392464
```

Figure 4-16. SSRC value change

Contributing Source Identifier (CSRC)

If there are any other data sources in the current RTP stream, their identifiers are listed here. Earlier in this chapter we saw the "contributing source identifiers count" field. With a single source, that field would be zero. Multiple sources are used when mixing or multiplexing sessions.

When audio and video are coming from the same node, different synchronization source identifiers are used to prevent confusion between the data formats. This also allows conversion from one codec to another. So, even if two nodes are communicating via audio and video stream through a single application, as is the case when Skyping with a webcam and microphone, it is likely that different synchronization sources will be used. Figure 4-17 depicts an example.

```
31 192.168.16.112        192.168.16.113        RTP     PT=SIREN14, SSRC=0x5C4FEF01, Seq=11, Time=1760
33 192.168.16.112        192.168.16.113        RTP     PT=SIREN14, SSRC=0x5C4FEF01, Seq=12, Time=1920
34 192.168.16.112        192.168.16.113        H264    PT=H264, SSRC=0x8D0BC001, Seq=0, Time=24464   NAL
35 192.168.16.112        192.168.16.113        H264    PT=H264, SSRC=0x8D0BC001, Seq=1, Time=24464   NAL
36 192.168.16.112        192.168.16.113        H264    PT=H264, SSRC=0x8D0BC001, Seq=2, Time=24464   NAL
```

Figure 4-17. RTP packet with double SSRC

In Figure 4-17, the packets come from a Polycom videoconferencing client, and we can see that all of these packets are coming from 192.168.16.112 but two codecs are being used. Thus, the two source identifiers, timestamps, and sequence numbers separate the streams.

RTP extension header

As mentioned earlier in this chapter, the RTP header has an extension bit. Should this bit be set, the RTP header expands to include the information required by the application. Only one extension header is permitted. The extension header from RFC 3550 is shown in Figure 4-18.

```
    0                   1                   2                   3
    0 1 2 3 4 5 6 7 8 9 0 1 2 3 4 5 6 7 8 9 0 1 2 3 4 5 6 7 8 9 0 1
   +-+-+-+-+-+-+-+-+-+-+-+-+-+-+-+-+-+-+-+-+-+-+-+-+-+-+-+-+-+-+-+-+
   |      defined by profile       |            length             |
   +-+-+-+-+-+-+-+-+-+-+-+-+-+-+-+-+-+-+-+-+-+-+-+-+-+-+-+-+-+-+-+-+
   |                        header extension                       |
   |                             ....                              |
```

Figure 4-18. RTP extension header

However, the use of this extension header is unusual, as the profile document (RFC 3551) provides the methodology normally used to manipulate the header based on the needs of the application. In fact, none of the topologies used in the writing of these chapters included an extension header. This is not to say that an RTP fixed header is limited to what we have seen so far. Other documents provide additional mechanisms for handling signals and sounds that may be needed on communication systems. For example, RFC 4733 outlines what must be done to send dual-tone multifrequency (DTMF) signals on VoIP systems. An example of this encapsulation is shown in Figure 4-19.

```
User Datagram Protocol, Src Port: alchemy (3234), Dst Port: alchemy (3234)
Real-Time Transport Protocol
⊞ [Stream setup by SDP (frame 8)]
  10.. .... = Version: RFC 1889 Version (2)
  ..0. .... = Padding: False
  ...0 .... = Extension: False
  .... 0000 = Contributing source identifiers count: 0
  0... .... = Marker: False
  Payload type: DynamicRTP-Type-100 (100)
  Sequence number: 0
  [Extended sequence number: 65536]
  Timestamp: 5081566
  Synchronization Source identifier: 0xe2a51901 (3802470657)
RFC 2833 RTP Event
  Event ID: DTMF Zero 0 (0)
  0... .... = End of Event: False
  .1.. .... = Reserved: True
  ..10 0001 = Volume: 33
  Event Duration: 768
```

Figure 4-19. RTP header for DTMF

This packet references RFC 2833, which was superseded by RFC 4733. RFC 4733 describes how to carry traditional signaling in RTP packets. For example, instead of sending a packet to the call server that includes the number to be dialed, a telephone might take the DTMF sounds and convert them to RTP packets in the same way voice is captured.

RTP Control Protocol

RTCP packets and their identifiers are separate from the RTP values because the RTP synchronization source IDs may change. Instead, RTCP uses a canonical name, or CNAME. All of the participants are supposed to send RTCP packets, but if you have read through this book, you know that this is not reality. For example, Skinny-based deployments do not use RTCP at all. Additionally, vendors implement both RTP and RTCP differently, and so network behavior is not as predictable as we might wish.

The RTP control protocol (sometimes referred to as the real-time control protocol), has the primary goal of feedback on the quality of the RTP stream. It is common for VoIP to be described as simply another application running on the network. But it is a critical application, and so it is just as common to allocate network resources to handle real-time data. RTCP can provide information regarding the success of these network settings. The packet capture from the call indicates that RTCP packets are mixed in with the RTP packets, as shown in Figure 4-20.

```
192.168.16.23    192.168.16.24    RTP     PT=ITU-T G.711 PCMU, SSRC=0x196D27C5, Seq=12068, Time=998316969
192.168.16.24    192.168.16.23    RTP     PT=ITU-T G.711 PCMU, SSRC=0x49FF2367, Seq=16133, Time=635459824
192.168.16.24    192.168.16.23    RTCP    Sender Report   Source description
192.168.16.23    192.168.16.24    RTP     PT=ITU-T G.711 PCMU, SSRC=0x196D27C5, Seq=12069, Time=998317129
192.168.16.24    192.168.16.23    RTP     PT=ITU-T G.711 PCMU, SSRC=0x49FF2367, Seq=16134, Time=635459984
```

Figure 4-20. RTP and RTCP packets

The idea is that the senders provide information about the RTP stream, and the receivers provide feedback to the sender. This is accomplished via the sender and receiver report messages, which are sent as often as the bandwidth will allow. The whole point of this exchange is to provide feedback on the quality of the call. Senders and receivers can exchange the number of bytes or packets along with the timing values to obtain the current performance metrics.

RTCP is also encapsulated in UDP. The port used by RTCP is dependent upon RTP; the two protocols are supposed to use sequential ports, as indicated in Figure 4-21.

```
Internet Protocol Version 4, Src: 192.168.16.24 (192.168.16.24), Dst: 192.168.16.23
User Datagram Protocol, Src Port: acc-rait (2800), Dst Port: tsb2 (2742)
Real-Time Transport Protocol

Internet Protocol Version 4, Src: 192.168.16.24 (192.168.16.24), Dst: 192.168.16.23
User Datagram Protocol, Src Port: igcp (2801), Dst Port: murx (2743)
Real-time Transport Control Protocol (Sender Report)
Real-time Transport Control Protocol (Source description)
```

Figure 4-21. RTP and RTCP ports

One of the other functions of RTCP is to give each participant a canonical name, or CNAME. This is separate from the synchronization source ID (SSRC) because the SSRC can change over the course of a transmission. The CNAME does not. The Source Description message contains the CNAME. All told, there are five different RTCP message types: Sender Report, Receiver Report, Source Description, BYE, and Application Specific. From the RFC (Table 4-1):

Table 4-1. RTCP messages

Abbreviation	Name	Value
SR	Sender Report	200
RR	Receiver Report	201
SDES	Source Description	202
BYE	Goodbye	203
APP	Application-defined	204

Like RTP, RTCP messages begin with a fixed header. RTCP packets are also stackable, which allows them to be compounded. An example can be seen in the Sender Report packets, which also include the Source Description. Based on the requirements of knowing the CNAMEs and obtaining performance information, RFC 3550 requires the RTCP messages to be compounded packets. The first packet in the compound packet must be a report. Let's take a closer look at the individual messages.

Sender Report (SR) and Receiver Report (RR)

These messages contain transmission and reception statistics from an active sender or an inactive receiver. Examples can be seen in Figure 4-22 and Figure 4-23. The arrows in the packet capture indicate the packet type (200 for the Sender Report and 201 for Receiver Report) as well as the Synchronization Source ID. Note that both of these packets came from the same IP address: 192.168.16.23. Since this was a bidirectional conversation, both phones act as a sender and receiver. Each of the SR and RR packets contains the values helpful to determining the quality of the call. Timestamps, packet count, octet count, lost packets, and jitter values are all present.

```
Internet Protocol Version 4, Src: 192.168.16.23 (192.168.16.23), Dst: 192.168.16.24
User Datagram Protocol, Src Port: murx (2743), Dst Port: igcp (2801)
Real-time Transport Control Protocol (Sender Report)
  [Stream setup by H245 (frame 597)]
    10.. .... = Version: RFC 1889 Version (2)
    ..0. .... = Padding: False
    ...0 0001 = Reception report count: 1
    Packet type: Sender Report (200)
    Length: 12 (52 bytes)
    Sender SSRC: 0x196d27c5 (426584005)
    Timestamp, MSW: 81 (0x00000051)
    Timestamp, LSW: 3380122050 (0xc97891c2)
    [MSW and LSW as NTP timestamp: Not representable]
    RTP timestamp: 1025641874
    Sender's packet count: 599
    Sender's octet count: 95840
  Source 1
Real-time Transport Control Protocol (Source description)
[RTCP frame length check: OK - 140 bytes]
```

Figure 4-22. RTCP sender report

Figure 4-23 also happens to contain an RTCP BYE message coded with type 203.

Source Description Items (SDES)

The packets shown in Figure 4-22 and Figure 4-23 are compound packets. In case you missed the headers, Figure 4-24 points them out. In the case of the Sender Report, the second packet is the Source Description, or SDES. Figure 4-24 also depicts an expansion of this section from the same message seen in Figure 4-22. This time the Sender Report portion has been collapsed. The CNAME is circled.

With the SDES message, all receivers will know the CNAME of the endpoint, its phone number, and the actual endpoint unit being used in the transmission. Table 4-2 lists SDES types from the RFC.

```
Internet Protocol Version 4, Src: 192.168.16.23 (192.168.16.23), Dst: 192.168.16.24
User Datagram Protocol, Src Port: murx (2743), Dst Port: igcp (2801)
Real-time Transport Control Protocol (Receiver Report)
 [Stream setup by H245 (frame 597)]
   10.. .... = Version: RFC 1889 Version (2)
   ..0. .... = Padding: False
   ...0 0000 = Reception report count: 0
   Packet type: Receiver Report (201)
   Length: 1 (8 bytes)
   Sender SSRC: 0x196d27c5 (426584005)
Real-time Transport Control Protocol (Source description)
Real-time Transport Control Protocol (Goodbye)
 [Stream setup by H245 (frame 597)]
   10.. .... = Version: RFC 1889 Version (2)
   ..0. .... = Padding: False
   ...0 0001 = Source count: 1
   Packet type: Goodbye (203)
   Length: 4 (20 bytes)
   Identifier: 0x196d27c5 (426584005)
   Length: 8
   Text: Teardown
[RTCP frame length check: OK - 116 bytes]
```

Figure 4-23. RTCP receiver report

```
Internet Protocol Version 4, Src: 192.168.16.23 (192.168.16.23), Dst: 192.168.16.24
User Datagram Protocol, Src Port: murx (2743), Dst Port: igcp (2801)
Real-time Transport Control Protocol (Sender Report)
Real-time Transport Control Protocol (Source description)
 [Stream setup by H245 (frame 597)]
   10.. .... = Version: RFC 1889 Version (2)
   ..0. .... = Padding: False
   ...0 0001 = Source count: 1
   Packet type: Source description (202)
   Length: 21 (88 bytes)
 Chunk 1, SSRC/CSRC 0x196D27C5
   Identifier: 0x196d27c5 (426584005)
   SDES items
     Type: CNAME (user and domain) (1)
     Length: 29
     Text: ext1111111@192.168.16.23:2742
     Type: PHONE (phone number) (4)
     Length: 7
     Text: 1111111
     Type: TOOL (name/version of source app) (6)
     Length: 35
     Text: Avaya IP Telephone (a10d01b2_8.bin)
     Type: END (0)
[RTCP frame length check: OK - 140 bytes]
```

Figure 4-24. RTCP SDES section

Table 4-2. SDES Types

Abbreviation	Name	Value
END	End of SDES list	0
CNAME	Canonical name	1
NAME	Username	2
EMAIL	User's electronic mail address	3

Abbreviation	Name	Value
PHONE	User's phone number	4
LOC	Geographic user location	5
TOOL	Name of application or tool	6
NOTE	Notice ab out this source	7
PRIV	Private extensions	8

BYE

Figure 4-23 also includes the Receiver Report with the compounded BYE (Good-bye) message. The requirement here is that the BYE message be the last message sent with a particular SSRC or CSRC. Upon receipt of the BYE packet, the synchronization source ID is removed from the participant list.

APP

This particular RTCP message is called the Application Defined packet. It is intended for experimental use.

Detailed Operation

RFC 3550 spends a good amount of time discussing the proper rate at which RTCP packets should be generated. Added challenges to selecting the proper rate include questions about affecting the performance of the RTP stream, getting the CNAME information to all participants, scaling of the connections when there are many users, and multicasting. From the RFC:

> It is RECOMMENDED that the fraction of the session bandwidth added for RTCP be fixed at 5%. It is also RECOMMENDED that 1/4 of the RTCP bandwidth be dedicated to participants that are sending data so that in sessions with a large number of receivers but a small number of senders, newly joining participants will more quickly receive the CNAME for the sending sites.

According to the RTCP Sender Report (Figure 4-22) from the phone at 192.168.16.23 (extension 111-1111), a total of 599 RTP packets were sent. The phone at 192.168.16.24 (extension 111-2222) sent a total 427 RTP packets; this packet is not shown here. By contrast, each node only about 14 RTCP packets, well below the RFC 3550 recommendation. However, this is just one topology and a small one at that. RFCs 3550 and 3551 also leave room for the profile to specify the report interval. On an Avaya system like the one used in this network, the RTCP report interval is commonly set to five seconds. Other than the percentage of session bandwidth noted above, the recommended transmission rate recommended by the RFC is a minimum of every five seconds.

Security

Certainly one of the objects of an attack is a replay of VoIP-based transmissions. In order to accomplish this, attackers would need access to the RTP stream. Unfortunately, the same mechanism that allows a receiver to understand the encoding mechanism used by the sender also allows the attacker to decode the stream. Each packet contains the payload ID, which identifies the codec. The synchronization source identifier allows the receiver (and attacker) to collect packets from the same source, and the sequence numbers keep them in order.

Once the packets are collected and ordered, it is a simple matter to play them back. Figure 4-25 displays the player built into Wireshark. The player is activated after selecting a single RTP packet and performing an RTP-stream analysis from the Telephony menu.

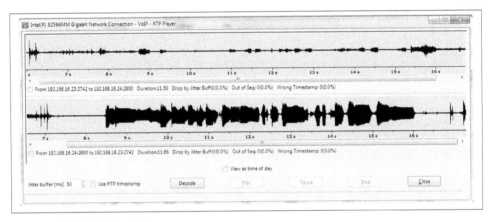

Figure 4-25. Wireshark player

The BackTrack distributions and Wildpackets Omnipeek also have the ability to collect packets and play them back.

Vectors

How does an attacker get access to the RTP stream? The proliferation of wireless networks also leads to the proliferation of wireless endpoints, such as phones. Attacking a wireless network is straightforward: capture the traffic. The same tools that provide a player also have the ability to capture wireless frames. But even without access to the wireless network, or if the wireless network is encrypted, an attacker can sometimes gain access to the RTP streams by attacking infrastructure devices. Two popular methods are overflowing the source address table on a switch and spoofing a trunk port on a switch.

With source address table flooding (also known as MAC address table flooding), the switch memory is constantly filled with MAC addresses such that valid addresses cannot be added to the table. Traffic destined for these valid MAC addresses must be flooded out of all ports. Spoofing a trunk port is an attack in which the target switch is fooled into believing that a trunk line is connected. Traffic destined for unknown MAC addresses is flooded down trunk ports like broadcast traffic. The attacker can also send traffic to specific destinations by tagging traffic and VLAN hopping. Attacks against hosts can trick them into sending traffic to the attacker or allowing the attacker to act as a man in the middle.

In the face of these challenges, RTP streams must be encrypted in order to protect their privacy. RFC 3711 describes the Secure Real-Time Transport Protocol, or SRTP. RFC 3711 also defines SRTCP and therefore has provisions for the privacy and authentication of both RTP and RTCP messages.

SRTP Operation

Secure RTP is considered a profile of RTP. Thus, it modifies RTP slightly to suit its purposes. SRTP and SRTCP use the same structure as RTP and RTCP, with the addition of the information allowing the additional functions. Figure 4-26 depicts the packet structure.

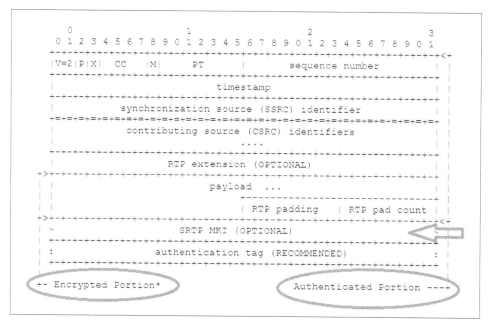

Figure 4-26. SRTP header

The SRTP packet shares the entire RTP header, adding the fields indicated by the arrow. We can also see that while the entire packet is authenticated, only a part is encrypted. STP fields include:

Master Key Index
This is an optional field that can be used to provide information about which master key is to be used.

Authentication Tag
The field is used to provide the value calculated by the authentication algorithm.

RFC 3711 has predefined keys and algorithms (though others are supported) for use in a secure deployment. For encryption, the "default cipher" is the Advanced Encryption Standard, or AES. For authentication, the Hashed Message Authentication Code – Secure Hash Algorithm 1 (HMAC-SHA1) is specified. There are two keys used: a master and session key. Endpoints and the call server use the master key to derive the session. The session keys are those actually used to encrypt the voice or video data. The RFC does not specify key distribution. This is often handled by the signaling protocol.

The idea is that the endpoints maintain what is called the "cryptographic context," or information about the algorithms, keys, and the current state of the connection. But endpoints also keep track of rollover counters (which count the reuse of sequence numbers), replay lists, and any salt keys. Salting adds extra material to the session generation process in order to make the session key more difficult to derive externally. SRTP and SRTCP share the same master key and cryptographic context but typically do not use the same session keys. Figure 4-27 depicts the SRTCP structure described by RFC 3711.

Again, we can see the shared structure of the packet. The entire message is authenticated, but only the data about the stream is encrypted. The MKI and authentication tag fields serve the same purpose as they did in SRTP.

Not all vendors support SRTP and SRTCP. Even for those that do, it is often the case that in a mature environment, endpoint devices have varying levels of support for features or encryption requirements. Lastly, some of these items differ between vendors. If you want to encrypt media transmissions in real-time streams, you should thoroughly examine the planned deployment with an eye toward the SRTP profile. An argument can be made that encryption is not necessary because most VoIP endpoints are wired and internal. This is necessarily a local decision, but the presence of wireless networks, hosted solutions, guest access, telecommuters, or other situations in which the RTP streams may be exposed argue for a close examination of the network specifications.

```
 0                   1                   2                   3
 0 1 2 3 4 5 6 7 8 9 0 1 2 3 4 5 6 7 8 9 0 1 2 3 4 5 6 7 8 9 0 1
+-+-+-+-+-+-+-+-+-+-+-+-+-+-+-+-+-+-+-+-+-+-+-+-+-+-+-+-+-+-+-+-+<+
|V=2|P|   RC   | PT=SR or RR   |             length            | |
+-+-+-+-+-+-+-+-+-+-+-+-+-+-+-+-+-+-+-+-+-+-+-+-+-+-+-+-+-+-+-+-+ |
|                         SSRC of sender                       | |
+>+=+=+=+=+=+=+=+=+=+=+=+=+=+=+=+=+=+=+=+=+=+=+=+=+=+=+=+=+=+=+=+ |
| ~                        sender info                       ~ |
| +-+-+-+-+-+-+-+-+-+-+-+-+-+-+-+-+-+-+-+-+-+-+-+-+-+-+-+-+-+-+-+ |
| ~                      report block 1                      ~ |
| +-+-+-+-+-+-+-+-+-+-+-+-+-+-+-+-+-+-+-+-+-+-+-+-+-+-+-+-+-+-+-+ |
| ~                      report block 2                      ~ |
| +-+-+-+-+-+-+-+-+-+-+-+-+-+-+-+-+-+-+-+-+-+-+-+-+-+-+-+-+-+-+-+ |
| ~                           ...                            ~ |
| +-+-+-+-+-+-+-+-+-+-+-+-+-+-+-+-+-+-+-+-+-+-+-+-+-+-+-+-+-+-+-+ |
| |V=2|P|   SC   | PT=SDES=202   |             length          | |
| +=+=+=+=+=+=+=+=+=+=+=+=+=+=+=+=+=+=+=+=+=+=+=+=+=+=+=+=+=+=+=+ |
| |                        SSRC/CSRC_1                        | |
| +-+-+-+-+-+-+-+-+-+-+-+-+-+-+-+-+-+-+-+-+-+-+-+-+-+-+-+-+-+-+-+ |
| ~                        SDES items                        ~ |
| +=+=+=+=+=+=+=+=+=+=+=+=+=+=+=+=+=+=+=+=+=+=+=+=+=+=+=+=+=+=+=+ |
| ~                           ...                            ~ |
+>+=+=+=+=+=+=+=+=+=+=+=+=+=+=+=+=+=+=+=+=+=+=+=+=+=+=+=+=+=+=+=+ |
| |E|                      SRTCP index                        | |
| +-+-+-+-+-+-+-+-+-+-+-+-+-+-+-+-+-+-+-+-+-+-+-+-+-+-+-+-+-+-+-+<+
| ~                   SRTCP MKI (OPTIONAL)                    ~ |
| +-+-+-+-+-+-+-+-+-+-+-+-+-+-+-+-+-+-+-+-+-+-+-+-+-+-+-+-+-+-+-+ |
| :                   authentication tag                     : |
| +-+-+-+-+-+-+-+-+-+-+-+-+-+-+-+-+-+-+-+-+-+-+-+-+-+-+-+-+-+-+-+ |
|                                                             |
+--- Encrypted Portion              Authenticated Portion -----+
```

Figure 4-27. SRTCP header

Summary

VoIP signaling protocols handle such items as registration, address signaling, establishing logical channels, and call termination. However, they do not transport voice or video (real-time) data. Most VoIP communication systems rely on RTP for this purpose. RTP provides encapsulation for this data, sequencing, time-stamps, and identification for all of the packets that are part of the real-time stream.

In order to better understand the quality and performance of the connection, RTCP is part of the RTP deployment. RTCP carries data about information such as timing and packet count between the senders and receivers. Both of these protocols are described in RFC 3550. A companion document to RFC 3550 is RFC 3551, which describes the profiles used in conjunction with RTP. Profiles allow media streams to provide additional fields to the RTP header that may contain flow-specific parameters.

RTP's cleartext nature can open it up to attacks such as replay, meaning that attackers can collect the RTP packets and play back the conversation. In order to help defend against this, Secure RTP (SRTP) and Secure RTCP (SRTCP) were defined in RFC 3711. This RFC provides for the encryption of the real-time data and authentication of the messages.

This chapter explains the structure and operation of RTP and RTCP through the use of packets caught on a VoIP network.

Standards and Reading

RFC 3550 (obsoletes RFC 1889)
> RTP: A Transport Protocol for Real-Time Applications (*http://tools.ietf.org/html/rfc3550*)

RFC 3551 (obsoletes RFC 1890)
> RTP Profile for Audio and Video Conferences with Minimal Control (*http://tools.ietf.org/html/rfc3551*)

RFC 3711
> The Secure Real-Time Transport Protocol (SRTP) (*http://tools.ietf.org/html/rfc3711*)

RFC 4733
> RTP Payload for DTMF Digits, Telephony Tones, and Telephony Signals (*http://tools.ietf.org/html/rfc4733*)

RFC 5506
> Support for Reduced-Size Real-Time Transport Control Protocol (RTCP): Opportunities and Consequences (*http://tools.ietf.org/html/rfc5506*)

RFC 5761
> Multiplexing RTP Data and Control Packets on a Single Port (*http://tools.ietf.org/html/rfc5761*)

RFC 6051
> Rapid Synchronisation of RTP Flows (*http://tools.ietf.org/html/rfc6051*)

RFC 6222
> Guidelines for Choosing RTP Control Protocol (RTCP) Canonical Names (CNAMEs) (*http://tools.ietf.org/html/rfc6222*)

Review Questions

1. True or false: most communication systems use RTP when transporting voice and video data.

2. True or false: RTP has a build in quality of service mechanism.

3. How are RTP streams differentiated from each other?

4. True or false: the ports for RTP and RTCP are random.

5. What is the payload type for a G.729 encoded packet?

6. What are the five RTCP message types?

7. What is the primary purpose of RTCP?

8. In what packet can the canonical name be found?

9. True or false: RTCP is tied to the RTP stream by using the same synchronization source ID.

10. What is a common rate at which RTCP packets are transmitted?

Review Answers

1. True.

2. False.

3. Using the synchronization source identifier.

4. The selection of the RTP port is random, but the RTCP port is supposed to be the next highest odd-numbered port.

5. 18.

6. Source Report, Receiver Report, Source Description, Bye, and APP.

7. To provide performance feedback on the RTP streams.

8. Source Description.

9. False.

10. Every five seconds.

Lab Activities

This chapter is supported by the book website. So, if the activity lists equipment or software that you do not have, go to the book website for additional content.

Activity 1—Topology Build

The point of this activity is to build a topology capable of generating RTP and RTCP packets. This can be done via a topology with a call manager at its center or via point-to-point connections using VoIP soft clients. For example, this book typically uses topologies with a call server but occasionally uses captures done with just a pair of Polycom soft clients (Figure 4-28).

Materials: two VoIP endpoints (software or hardware), call server (optional), Wireshark

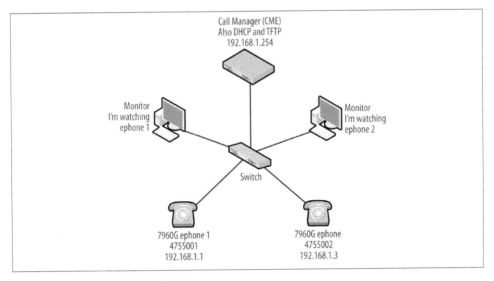

Figure 4-28. Activity 1 topology

1. Once the topology is built, start a capture on either the soft-client endpoints or the monitor stations watching the VoIP phones.

2. Make a phone call between the VoIP endpoints.

3. Ensure that the capture obtains the packets necessary for the next couple of activities.

Activity 2—Analysis of the RTP Stream

Materials: captures from the previously built topology

1. Within Wireshark, filter the packets using RTP (Figure 4-29).

2. From the RTP stream, identify the following items:

   - Payload type
   - Sequence numbers
   - Timestamps
   - Synchronizing Source Identifier

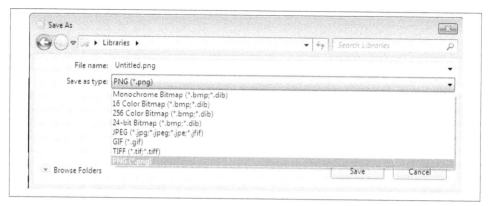

Figure 4-29. Activity 2 tools

3. How do the sequence numbers advance? Are there contributing sources? How do the timestamps advance? Do any of the packets have markers?

Activity 3—The Codec

Materials: captures from the previously built topology.

1. Identify the hexadecimal value of the payload type from these captures.
2. To what codec does the payload type correspond?
3. How does this codec work?
4. What are the bandwidth requirements of this codec?
5. What are the uses of this particular codec?

Activity 4—Analysis of the RTCP Stream

Materials: captures from the previously built topology.

1. Filter the packet captures for RTCP in the same way that you filtered for RTP.
2. Analyze the RTCP packets for the four basic message types: Source Report, Receiver Report, Source Description, and APP.
3. Open each of these packets and identify the fields in each. What are the packets trying to tell you?

CHAPTER 5

Codecs

Audio and video streams such as those created when we speak into a computer microphone or use a digital camera start off as analog signals. There was a time when the voice signal traversed the entire telephone network in this form. However, this architecture is limited and cumbersome. Today, voice or video conversations, whether on a traditional telephony system or one based on Voice over IP, start off as analog but then are converted to a digital format. The digital representation of the voice or video is transmitted to the receiver and then converted back to analog in order to be understood by the human at the other end. For the most part, this process of analog-to-digital and digital-to-analog conversion is handled by a codec, or coder-decoder.

There are many different techniques used to handle these audio and video streams. Most of the popular codecs used today are standardized in the ITU-T (International Telecommunications Union–Telecom) recommendations, though there are many others. Much of the work done with codecs has been in an effort to reduce the amount of bandwidth consumed by the voice stream through the use of compression. Voice over IP, or VoIP, deployments require the same conversion processes to occur, though they do not always have the bandwidth concerns of more traditional topologies. Understanding common codecs and their basic operation can help with initial deployment and troubleshooting problems. In this chapter, communication frequencies and common audio and video codecs will be examined. In addition, the reader will gain some insight into codec selection and call quality.

Audio Frequencies

There are very good reasons for structuring the telephone network as described in Chapter 2. As humans, we have limited capabilities in terms of hearing and generating sounds. The human ear can hear frequencies as low as 20Hz (hertz) and those up to about 20,000Hz, or 20KHz. You may have a sense of your own hearing range based on the hearing tests given in school. Hearing ranges for a variety of animals, including humans, is shown in Figure 5-1. As we can see, compared to other animals, we humans do not have anything to brag about.

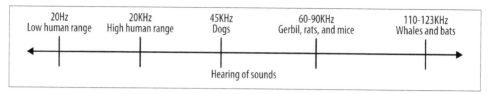

Figure 5-1. Hearing ranges

We can also generate sounds, but the range is much less than what we can hear. According to the *Guinness Book of World Records*, the lowest frequency generated by a human was just above 0Hz, and the highest was just a little bit less than 5000Hz. Figure 5-2 gives us an idea of how we fare compared to other mammals.

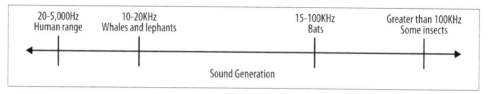

Figure 5-2. Ranges for hearing and sound generation

While the full range for human speech is not functional (you're not likely to have a conversation at 5000Hz), it does provide a basis for our discussion regarding the size of the voice channel on traditional telephony systems. Since most of the sounds we create are low frequencies, the standard local loop connection is allocated 0–4000Hz. For transmission systems, this range is actually reduced to a 300–3400Hz as outlined by documents such as the ITU-T Recommendation G.107. This recommendation provides the computational model for transmission planning.

If this is the range of frequencies allocated to each circuit, then any other signals using the same channel must also fall with the same range of frequencies. Thus, all of the tones and sounds heard on your telephone handset fall within this range. In fact, band-pass filters prevent frequencies outside of this range.

Voice Signals

An audio or voice signal is an analog waveform. A basic analog waveform is shown in Figure 5-3. This image provides a three second glimpse of a tone generated at 500Hz. It would appear as though it is a continuous block of analog information. At a rate of 500Hz, there are 500 cycles, or full waveforms, per second. A single wave can be transmitted in a five-hundredth of second, or .002 seconds. This is also called the period of the wave. Stated another way, in the three seconds seen in Figure 5-3, there are actually 1500 waves.

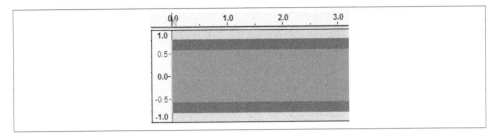

Figure 5-3. 500Hz continuous tone

With Figure 5-4, zooming in to examine what is happening in one one-hundredth of a second (.01 seconds), the waveform can be seen. In fact, there are five cycles present if we measure from the first to the last zero crossing.

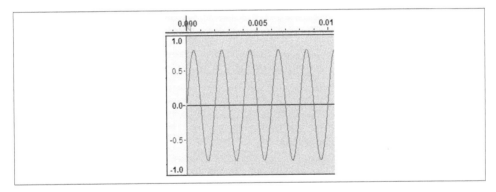

Figure 5-4. Waveform viewed over a fraction of a second

Analog waveforms have three primary characteristics: frequency, amplitude, and phase. Phase (relationship with respect to time or another point in time) does not play much of a role in our discussion, but the amplitude (strength) of the wave and the frequency (cycles per second) do. Because it is a single sound that does not change volume, as the tone is generated, the frequency and amplitude remain constant. Five hundred hertz is within the range of human hearing and would fall within the frequencies allowed on the telephone circuit. But listening to this tone would be rather boring, as there is no variation; however, an MP3 of the tone is available on the book website. Human speech is a collection of frequencies that vary. Even the simplest signal contains a wide variety of these frequencies.

An example of a voice signal is shown in Figure 5-5. In this case, the four-second analog wave represents the word "Hello" said three times.

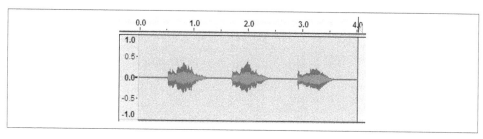

Figure 5-5. Hello

Though we can see some variation in the signal even when the same word is repeated, what is not clear from the image is just how complex the signal actually might be. Expanding the time base of the waveform and focusing on a smaller portion, we can see some of the details. Figure 5-6 depicts a quarter of a second of the first "Hello."

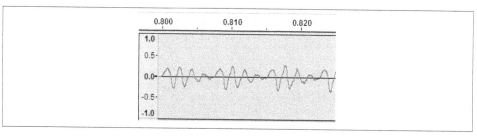

Figure 5-6. Hello waveform expanded

Unlike the expanded section of the 500Hz tone, there are variations in the frequency and in the amplitude. This is because the sounds we generate, even within the same word, vary in strength and tone. Signals like these are sent down the telephone wires to the line card in the switch or central office. The challenge for a codec is to capture all of this variation in a series of samples that can be put back together at the other end in a meaningful way.

Audio Coders and Decoders

A codec has the task of turning the analog wave into a series of samples and then providing a binary value for that sample. This is done so that the voice data can be transferred through the digital portions of the public switched telephone network, or PSTN. But this is only half of the story. At the receiver, these samples must be reassembled and converted back into an analog waveform that can be interpreted properly. This process is called pulse code modulation (PCM), and it serves as the base method used on the PSTN and many VoIP deployments for encoding voice data. It is defined by ITU-T Recommendation G.711. Let's take a more detailed look.

Sampling

Recall that both ends of the connection are typically analog, and the analog wave must first be sampled. With PCM, a sample is simply an evaluation of the signal strength at sample time. Figure 5-7 depicts a much-enlarged version of Figure 5-6. The vertical lines are the locations, or the times, of the individual samples, and the dots are the locations on the waveform.

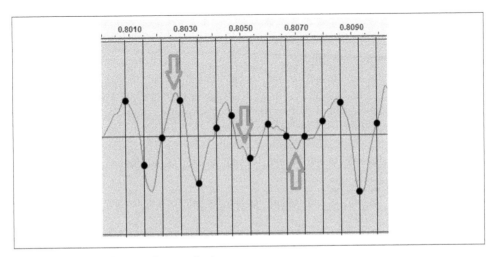

Figure 5-7. Waveform with sample times

The trick with the samples is to take enough of them to provide an accurate reproduction of the original while not sampling too much. As we can see from the arrows in Figure 5-7, a low sampling rate may cause details of the original signal to be lost. In addition, the low sampling rate may result in aliasing. This occurs when a transmitted signal appears to be of a lower frequency than the actual signal. Sampling at too great a frequency results in unnecessary bandwidth consumption.

Quantizing

Samples without an assigned value are not worth much. So, once the samples are taken, a value must be assigned to each in a process called quantization. Every codec provides a limited number of values for these samples, as shown in Figure 5-8. The horizontal lines represent the amplitude, and therefore the value, of the sample.

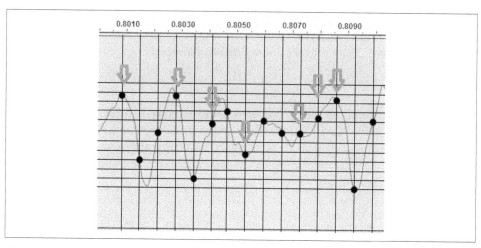

Figure 5-8. Quantizing the samples

As we can see from this image, some of the PCM samples fall on the line and some, indicated by the arrows, do not. When the sample amplitude does not fall on a line, the actual value is converted to one of the allowed values. This clearly has an impact on the accuracy of the signal when it is reproduced at the receiver. The difference in the quantized and actual values shown in Figure 5-9 will result in distortion.

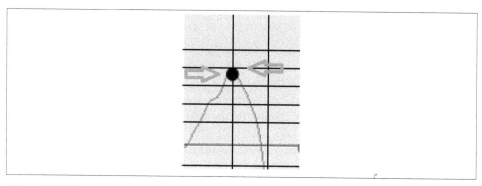

Figure 5-9. Quantizing error

This distortion from quantizing error is not unanticipated. It is a factor that is planned for in transmission systems carrying voice and even has its own variable. To quote from ITU-T Rec. G.113:

> A quantization distortion unit (qdu) was defined in 1982 as equivalent to the distortion that results from a single encoding (A/D) and decoding (D/A) by an average G.711 codec. Such a device has a signal/distortion ratio of 35 dB when measured according to [ITU-T O.132]. Conceptually, the number of qdus assigned to a particular PCM process should

reflect the effect of only the quantization noise produced by the PCM process on speech. In practice, the qdus must be determined from subjective measurements of real or simulated processes, where subjects will be exposed to not only the quantization noise but to other impairments produced by the digital process tested, including the departures from ideal frequency response in the anti-aliasing and reconstruction filters.

Another problem with this error is that the lower the volume or amplitude, the greater the effect of the distortion. A high-amplitude signal may ignore this level of quantizing error because it represents a smaller percentage of the whole. Codecs such as G.711 require amplitude granularity at lower amplitudes to be greater than at the higher ones. In other words, there is greater accuracy at the lower amplitudes.

Summarizing, we know that sampling rates that are too small or too great create problems. We also know that improper quantizing levels can affect the accuracy of signal creation at the receiver. What then are the proper sampling and amplitude levels to use? For example, G.711 PCM creates 8000 samples per second. The rationale for this value is most often attributed to Harry Nyquist. The premise is that to accurately reproduce a signal, you must sample it at a rate equal to twice the original bandwidth. In this way, all of the frequency variations can be accounted for. With 4000Hz (the actual transmission uses 3.1kHz) assigned to each local loop, the sample rate should be 8000 samples per second. In other words, the sampling frequency is 8000Hz.

To determine the quantizing value, start by asking the number of possible values that would need to be assigned. For example, if you have a thermometer that can provide readings only in increments of ten, how would you describe thirty-five degrees? Conversely, there is no reason to provide readings for one-tenth of a degree if we only care about whole numbers. If the possible number of values are too great, the bandwidth required by the channel may exceed allowable capacity. For G.711 PCM, each sample is assigned a value based on eight bits. This provides for 256 possible values, which means that a signal like the one shown in Figure 5-8 could have as many as 256 possible lines of resolution.

The capacity of the channel is the product of the two. For a G.711 PCM-encoded channel, the data rate equals the sampling rate times the bits per sample.

```
8000 samples × 8 bits per sample = 64000 bit per second
```

G.711 is the most successful codec in terms of the mean opinion score (MOS) and resilience in the presence of packet loss, but it does have a cost. The 64Kbps allocated for a G.711 voice channel is the greatest amount of bandwidth consumed by an audio codec in most systems. This does not sound like all that much, but when there is a bandwidth concern, particularly on wide area network (WAN) links, 64Kbps can seem like an awful lot for a single call. For this reason, other methods have been developed to provide greater compression and a reduction in resources consumed. But even with various types of compression, pulse code modulation provides the basis for the most commonly used codecs.

ITU-T G Series Specifications

The most popular audio and video codecs are standardized in the ITU-T G series. Generally, these codecs are divided into two types: waveform and source codecs. Waveform codecs sample and compress the analog waveform, quantizing as they go. The quantization values are transmitted to the receiver and are decoded directly into the original waveform. Waveform codecs are easy to recognize, as they are typically based on PCM. Source codecs such as G.729 attempt to determine a value that describes the data (metadata) and send this instead. For example, G.729 analyzes voice samples for predictive coefficients. These parameters are then encoded and transmitted. The most common waveform and source codecs and their basic techniques are outlined here.

G.711 Pulse Code Modulation (PCM) of Voice Frequencies

This recommendation dates from 1972. As previously stated, this codec defines 64Kbps PCM voice coding and puts voice data in the proper format for PSTN- and PBX-based transmission. This is accomplished by sampling the voice stream 8000 times per second (once every 125μsec) and assigning 8 bits per sample. The 8 bits are divided into the polarity bit (bit one), followed by the segment bits and amplitude level. There are actually two different versions of G.711: G.711 μLaw (Mu-Law) and G.711 A-Law. They are similar but have slight differences in the detail of the signal. μ-Law is deployed in North America and Japan, while A-Law is used in Europe and elsewhere. The ITU-T recommendation also states that when in doubt, A-Law is to be supported. The codec provides tables that outline the values for samples in both versions.

The practical side: This codec provides the best overall performance in both traditional and VoIP settings, even in the presence of latency and packet loss. However, it also consumes the greatest amount of network bandwidth at 64Kbps. This is typically not a concern for LANs, but it can stress WAN connections.

G.722 7kHz Audio Coding within 64Kbps

G.722 uses a technique called Subband Adaptive Differential PCM (SB-ADPCM) encoding over a range of 50–7000Hz. It has three modes of operation that result in transmission rates of 48, 56, and 64Kbps. But the codec uses a higher sampling rate of 16kHz and 14 bits per sample. The subbands divide the channel into the lower (0–4000Hz) and upper (4000–8000Hz) bands. The lower subband results in a 48Kbps signal and 16Kbps for the upper.

Regardless of the mode, the base encoding is 64Kbps. Downstream from the PCM-based audio encoder (the preliminary stage of the codec), one or two bits of the subband may be used for what is called an "auxiliary data channel" of either 8Kbps or 16Kbps. The number of bits allocated to the data channel is dependent on the mode determination. The recommendation indicates that it should be able to interoperate with G.721 (32Kbps) and that G.725 provides some detail on handshaking and mode control. It was approved in 1988.

The practical side: This codec is not expected to outperform G.711; however it gets close. One of the real benefits of G.722 is that it has the ability to perform packet loss concealment, or PLC. PLC is covered in greater detail later in this chapter, but essentially it is the ability to predict what the voice sample should have looked like if it were not missing.

G.723.1 Dual-Rate Speech Coder for Multimedia Communications
This 2006 codec uses speech and audio compression techniques at very low bit rates (5.3Kbps and 6.3Kbps) as part of the H.324 standards.

- 5.3Kbps—Algebraic Code Excited Linear Prediction (ACELP)
- 6.3 Kbps—Multipulse Maximum Likelihood Quantization (ML-MLQ)

Unlike the 20-millisecond frame size used by G.711, G.723 uses a 30-millisecond frame and a 7.5-millisecond "look-ahead," for a total of 37.5-millisecond delay in frame creation. Like most streams, the voice data is first sampled in a fashion compatible with G.711 and then converted to the 16-bit linear PCM required by the encoder, which works on blocks of 240 (30ms) samples. The idea is that linear prediction and pitch estimation are used to eventually construct a "short-term perceptual weighting filter," which is used in turn to build the "perceptually weighted speech signal." The final stages differ based on the desired bit rate.

The practical side: These are very low-bit-rate codecs and as such have a significance only where bandwidth is at a real premium. So they are not recommended for VoIP.

G.726 Adaptive Differential PCM encoding at 16, 24, 32, and 40Kbps
Approved in 1990, the codec converts the standard 64Kbps channel to one of the speeds listed above. The individual data rates have different applications ranging from use in multiplexing equipment to modems. The recommendation goes on to say that the assignment, signaling, and multiplexing of G.726 channels are left to recommendations from the G.76x series.

The codec operates on a difference signal resulting from subtracting the estimated input from the actual input signal. Quantization for the difference signal is based on the desired bit rate, assigning two to five binary digits. For example, at 40Kbps, five bits are assigned, one for the polarity and four for the amplitude.

The practical side: G.726 provides good performance, although the processing delay is greater than G.711. So, the question for deployment would be, is the increase in latency worth the reduction in bandwidth usage?

G.729 Coding of Speech at 8Kbps Using Conjugate Structure ACELP
G.729 and G.729 Annex A provide quality similar to 32Kbps ADPCM. G.729 is arguably one of the more popular codecs next to G.711. For example, some Cisco devices use this as the default codec. Developed in 1996, G.729 uses the same linear prediction described earlier, but the voice frames used are 10 milliseconds and

therefore 80 samples in size. Samples are taken every 125 microseconds, or one-eight thousandth of a second. With the look-ahead of five microseconds, the total delay for frame construction is fifteen microseconds.

For comparison, most codecs build a voice packet every 20 microseconds. Each packet may contain a couple of voice frames. In fact, RFC 3551 states that frame-oriented codecs should be able to encode a couple of frames per second, although perhaps different numbers of frames. For G.729, frame creation takes 10 milliseconds, and packets contain two frames. The prediction algorithm adds time to the frame creation, delaying packet construction.

The practical side: G.729 performs well, especially in the LAN environment. For WAN links, G.729 would have the same reservation as G.726. Is the exchange of latency increase and bandwidth conservation worth it? How does the connection perform when the codecs are changed?

Codec Selection and Performance

Historically, the choice as to which codec to use has been based on terms of quality and cost. If money and bandwidth were not impediments, organizations would probably use G.711 exclusively. Even though it is expensive in terms of bandwidth (G.711 requires 64Kbps), it behaves very well in the presence of network problems such as latency, packet loss, and jitter. All real-time streams are adversely affected by these, but no matter how you slice it, G.711 always seems to perform the best given the same network conditions.

However, outside connectivity does cost money, and many of the codecs and compression algorithms described earlier were developed in order to obtain quality similar to that of G.711 PCM while using less capacity. This is because calls to the outside travel over links that have much less bandwidth, so codec selection has greater impact. For example, an organization connected to the outside world via a T-1 link is limited to 1.544Mbps. Using G.711, each call would consume one twenty-fourth of this capacity. A codec such as G.729 uses half of that. Of course, at some point, increasing compression to conserve bandwidth does start to affect call quality.

One common measurement of call quality is the Mean Opinion Score, or MOS, from ITU-T Recommendation. P.800. The scale range is from 1 to 5 with 5 being the best. There are actually several measurements that might go into the MOS value, as shown in Table 5-1.

Table 5-1. MOS components

Quality of Speech	Score
Excellent	5
Good	4
Fair	3
Poor	2
Bad	1

Another part of the picture is how hard you have to work in order to understand the caller. This is shown in Table 5-2.

Table 5-2. Listening effort scale

Effort Required to Understand the Meaning of Sentences	Score
Complete relaxation possible; no effort required	5
Attention necessary; no appreciable effort required	4
Moderate effort required	3
Considerable effort required	2
No meaning understood with any feasible effort	1

Scores of 3.9–4.1 are considered very good, with scores less than 3 reading as poor to unacceptable. The idea is that a person listening to a caller makes a determination of the clarity of the call. Software can attempt to emulate the human-based MOS, but sometimes it's best to simply pick up the phone and listen. A related measurement is the Perceptual Evaluation of Speech Quality (PESQ) score. PESQ is described in ITU-T Recommendation P.862. The scaling is similar to MOS. It is important to understand that these are scores based on human experience. In other words, a person listens to the call and, based on that experience, picks a quality value from 1 to 5. It is not a measurement such as latency or jitter. However, software packages such as Omnipeek attempt to assign an MOS value to VoIP calls.

It is sometimes said that measurements like MOS and PESQ do not have much value in a VoIP or unified communications setting because of the bandwidth available for each connection. Internal link speeds for data network nodes often exceed 100Mbps, and a 64Kbps demand for a connection is not even 1 percent of the bandwidth. Thus, the codec doesn't often affect performance for internal calls. It is probably more accurate to say that we use an informal MOS scale without realizing it. When making changes to a system, adding nodes (especially soft clients), combining systems, or comparing alternate or backup pathways, it is natural to pick up the phone to see if it works. Part of this process is, or at least should be, a comparison of the quality. The MOS scale can be used to compare connections between different systems or connections made over difference pathways. Understanding the factors that affect the connection (such as the codec) enable the VoIP administrator to troubleshoot and repair problems.

So, what values can we expect?

It turns out that while codecs vary in performance, they usually are separated by no more than 20 to 40 percent on the MOS scale. Cisco has an evaluation of many of these codecs published in the Cisco Press book titled *VoIP: An In-depth Analysis*. This evaluation, using the MOS scale, reveals that while almost all common audio codecs have an MOS score above 3.6, the top performers (G.726, G.729, and G.711) range from 3.85 to 4.1. This is consistent with other reports examining codec performance.

Another analysis from Broadcom uses the PESQ scale and can be found here (*http://bit.ly/XjjJtF*). As part of this evaluation, Broadcom includes delay values and the performance when different languages are transmitted. Again, G.711 performs very well, as do many of the other codecs from ITU-T. However, I'm not sure that I would want to count on G.723 if clarity were an issue.

Transcoding

Transcoding is a process that occurs when voice or video data encoded with one codec is transformed so that an endpoint using another codec can understand it. For example, if a voice endpoint uses G.711 to encode the data, it cannot be directly received and decoded by a system using G.729. So, a device such as a gateway must convert the G.711 stream to G.729. When this occurs, there will be transcoding errors or distortion. This distortion is very similar to the encoding distortion discussed earlier in this chapter. The problem is that after a codec samples and quantizes the data, it has a certain value. Another codec performing the same process will use different values. Thus, when handing these values to each other for decoding, the result is necessarily different. Thus, the sampling data may not be converted easily by the connected system, which results in a different value for the voice sample. Distortion or completely lost voice samples erode the quality of the call.

Given the number of codecs available, it seems reasonable to assume that the amount of transcoding error will be different depending on the codec combination between the two ends. From the proceedings of the First IP Telephony Workshop (2000), Alcatel presented a graphic comparing several codecs; this can be seen in Figure 5-10.

CODEC	G.711 (64kb/s)	G.726 (40kb/s)	G.726 (32kb/s)	G.726 (24kb/s)	G.726 (16kb/s)	G.728 (16kb/s)	GSM-FR (13kb/s)	G.728 (12.8kb/s)	GSM-EFR (12.2kb/s)	G.729 (8kb/s)	G.723.1 (6.3kb/s)	GSM-HR (5.6kb/s)	G.723.1 (5.3kb/s)
G.711 (64kb/s)	94.3	92.3	87.3	69.3	44.3	87.3	74.3	74.3	89.3	84.3	79.3	71.3	75.3
G.726 (40kb/s)	92.3	90.3	85.3	67.3	42.3	85.3	72.3	72.3	87.3	82.3	77.3	69.3	71.3
G.726 (32kb/s)	87.3	85.3	80.3	62.3	37.3	80.3	67.3	67.3	82.3	77.3	72.3	64.3	68.3
G.726 (24kb/s)	69.3	67.3	62.3	44.3	19.3	62.3	49.3	49.3	64.3	59.3	54.3	46.3	50.3
G.726 (16kb/s)	44.3	42.3	37.3	19.3	0	37.3	24.3	24.3	39.3	34.3	29.3	21.3	25.3
G.728 (16kb/s)	87.3	85.3	80.3	62.3	37.3	80.3	67.3	67.3	82.3	77.3	72.3	64.3	68.3
GSM-FR (13kb/s)	74.3	72.3	67.3	49.3	24.3	67.3	54.3	54.3	69.3	64.3	59.3	51.3	55.3
G.728 (12.8kb/s)	74.3	72.3	67.3	49.3	24.3	67.3	54.3	54.3	69.3	64.3	59.3	51.3	55.3
GSM-EFR (12.2kb/s)	89.3	87.3	82.3	64.3	39.3	82.3	69.3	69.3	84.3	79.3	74.3	66.3	70.3
G.729 (8kb/s)	84.3	82.3	77.3	59.3	34.3	77.3	64.3	64.3	79.3	74.3	69.3	61.3	65.3
G.723.1 (6.3kb/s)	79.3	77.3	72.3	54.3	29.3	72.3	59.3	59.3	74.3	69.3	64.3	56.3	60.3
GSM-HR (5.6kb/s)	71.3	69.3	64.3	46.3	21.3	64.3	51.3	51.3	66.3	61.3	56.3	48.3	52.3
G.723.1 (5.3kb/s)	75.3	73.3	68.3	50.3	25.3	68.3	55.3	55.3	70.3	65.3	60.3	52.3	56.3

Figure 5-10. Transcoding matrix

In this image, with higher numbers being better, we can see that G.711, G.726, and G. 729 perform very well, with little performance degradation from transcoding. However, the lower-bit-rate codecs using a different method to quantize the voice data have significant losses. It is interesting to note that endpoints using the same codec have some transcoding problems simply because there is some distortion or loss in the coding and quantizing process.

For video, the same encoding problems exist but have additional complications, such as format. But in a low-level example, imagine three images taken of the same picture. One of them uses variations in red, green, and blue; another uses cyan, magenta, and yellow; and the third uses luminance, color saturation, and color hue. The colors are close but not the same. When trying to covert from one set of the colors to another, some information must be "closest value," causing a loss of fidelity to the original image. In a real-life example, Kodak struggled with the famous Kodak yellow "K." The company spent a lot of time and money ensuring that people the world over knew the logo, only to find that the color varied from computer to computer and browser to browser.

Because of the difficulties presented by transcoding, most organizations involved with creating or deploying codecs (such as the ITU-T) have guidance on creating tests for codecs, including their performance in transcoding.

Packet Loss and Packet Loss Concealment (PLC)

Packet loss is another problem that can have a significant impact on codec performance and the ability of the receiver to understand the transmission. For waveform codecs, it amounts to lost quantized samples. For source codecs, which rely on numerical values about the data and high compression, packet loss may cause significant errors. So much so that ITU-T Recommendation G.113 (quoted earlier in this chapter) describes a packet-loss robustness factor for codecs, as shown in Table 5-3. Higher values are better. VAD is an acronym for Voice Activity Detection, which determines if a voice signal is present.

Table 5-3. *Provisional planning value for the equipment impairment factor, Ie, and for packet-loss robustness factor, Bpl*

Codec	Packet Size	PLC Type	Ie	Bpl
G.723.1+VAD	30 ms	Native	15	16.1
G.729Δ+VAD	20 ms (2 frames)	Native	11	19.0
GSM-EFR	20 ms	Native	5	10.0
G.711	10 ms	None	0	4.3
G.711	10 ms	Appendix I of [ITU-T G.711]	0	25.1

While many of these numbers are "currently under study," including the maximum and minimum values, it is clear that G.711 performs well. It is also clear that codec success varies in the presence of packet loss.

Because packet loss can cause significant problems, codecs have been expanded to include techniques such as packet loss concealment (PLC) or frame erasure concealment (FEC) to mitigate some of the damage. When the codec recognizes that a packet is missing, there are a couple of things that can be done to mask the loss. For example, a codec may fill in all zeros or scale down the current signal to zero until the next packet arrives. Codecs can also simply repeat the last packet in order to fill in the gap. However, these approaches are not considered packet loss concealment algorithms. PLC algorithms attempt to determine what the signal should or would have been had the packet not been lost. An example can be seen in G.722 Appendix III. This addition to the codec relies on periodic waveform extrapolation (PWE) and pitch estimation to fill in the gaps left by lost frames. The technique it uses for stretching and shrinking a signal along the time axis is called time warping. This codec appendix does such a good job at hiding the loss that it is actually superior to some of the changes that came later. In fact, G.722 claims that while there is an increase in complexity or processing with the appendix, in cases where this is not an issue, it can be implemented without an increase in delay over standard G.722.

And this brings us to the problem associated with implementing packet loss concealment—delay. PLC works in part by understanding the before and after of the voice-data packet stream. This means that there is necessarily some level of delay in performing the packet loss concealment. So the double-edged sword is that to combat problems due to packet loss, we implement packet loss concealment, which can cause increased delay.

What Codec Are You Using?

When problems with voice or video crop up, knowing exactly what codec is in use can be helpful. Looking at settings or capabilities does not always tell the whole story, particularly if we do not control the entire pathway. Fortunately, we can take a look at the packets in the voice or video stream for this information. The Real-Time Transport Protocol (RTP) is used by most VoIP and videoconferencing systems for data transport. Chapter 4 provides greater detail on the protocol, but we can see from Figure 5-11 that the codec is identified in the header.

```
Internet Protocol Version 4, Src: 192.168.16.23 (192.168.16.23), Dst: 192.168.16.24
User Datagram Protocol, Src Port: tsb2 (2742), Dst Port: acc-raid (2800)
Real-Time Transport Protocol
⊕ [Stream setup by H245 (frame 597)]
   10.. .... = Version: RFC 1889 Version (2)
   ..0. .... = Padding: False
   ...0 .... = Extension: False
   .... 0000 = Contributing source identifiers count: 0
   0... .... = Marker: False
   Payload type: ITU-T G.711 PCMU (0)
   Sequence number: 11639
   [Extended sequence number: 77175]
   Timestamp: 998248329
   Synchronization Source identifier: 0x196d27c5 (426584005)
   Payload: cec4e14b60cb61f8684a70febfcd5f51494d70c1cdde3f4a...
```

Figure 5-11. RTP packet with G.711 codec

The payload of this packet was encoded using G.711 μ-Law. Using this value, endpoints understand which codec must be used to decode the same data. In fact, anyone capturing these packets will be able to decode the data. Video is identified the same way as shown in Figure 5-12.

Video Signals

The challenge when moving from audio to video is that not only do codecs have to convey information about a picture or series of pictures, but also they include information about color and movement between the images. In addition, there is the challenge associated with processing all of this data in a timely fashion. Some applications such as videoconferencing require that the codecs and the transmission of the data be reasonably fast so that the conversation is viable. For example, the delay experienced

```
Internet Protocol Version 4, Src: 192.168.16.113 (192.168.16.113), Dst: 192.168.16.112
User Datagram Protocol, Src Port: mdtp (3232), Dst Port: mdtp (3232)
Real-Time Transport Protocol
⊞ [Stream setup by SDP (frame 13)]
   10.. .... = Version: RFC 1889 Version (2)
   ..0. .... = Padding: False
   ...0 .... = Extension: False
   .... 0000 = Contributing source identifiers count: 0
   0... .... = Marker: False
   Payload type: H264 (10?)
   Sequence number: 63
   [Extended sequence number: 65599]
   Timestamp: 140614
   Synchronization Source identifier: 0x77f61001 (2012614657)
H.264
```

Figure 5-12. RTP packet with H.264 payload

when watching a news broadcast with an overseas correspondent can be tedious. At the opposite end of the spectrum, we have one-way viewing of video, such as DVDs. In this case, a high amount of processing can be used to compress the video because those watching it are not waiting for the compression to be completed; it was done before the movie was copied to the disc. Video over IP is considered a real-time application, so the codecs must complete their tasks quickly.

Generally speaking, video is also an analog signal. Many video codecs start with the idea of PCM and then apply predictive or differential techniques. This allows them to encode only the difference, which saves bandwidth. Much of the standards work is dedicated to decoding the incoming streams. Video streams typically have an audio track as well, so an audio codec is also used. In addition to handling data rate, type of technique, and compression, video codecs must also worry about image resolution and frame-rate variables. This can make the choice of codec very important for compatibility and performance.

Selecting the codec that provides the greatest quality video may actually be a mistake because it may require more resources, both from the network and processing. As resources are used up, performance suffers. Oddly enough, in these cases, selecting a lower quality setting may result in better performance and therefore a higher-quality conference.

The common video conferencing target is 384Kbps. This data rate corresponds to low resolution (about 352x288 pixels) and 30 frames per second. For comparison, high-definition video can consume more than ten times this bandwidth. Some codecs can negotiate the data rate and capabilities at connection time and may even be able to adapt to changing conditions. However, transmissions are typically capped at a maximum rate.

Sending a Series of Pictures

Most video codecs, with the exception of some of the early work, send pictures or frames based on the Common Intermediate Format, or CIF. CIF images start with a resolution of 352x288 and an aspect ratio of 4:3. Some of the difference between the resolution and the ratio can be attributed to the pixel aspect ratio (PAR), the type of scanning, and the encoding of the data. There are several variations on the basic CIF format. Related terms include standard definition (SD) at 704x480 and high definition (HD) at 1920x1080. HD has a 16:9 aspect ratio. The "p" or one following the video resolution indicates either progressive or interlaced scanning. For example, 1080p60 means 1080 vertical lines of resolution, progressive scan with 60 frames per second. Horizontal measurements are in pixels.

After the image format, the color must be determined. The traditional method is with red, green, and blue (RGB) colors with a value for each. So, a pixel could be described by these three numbers. As codecs progress, we see the use of the Y, CB, CR scheme referring to luminance, color saturation, and color hue instead. Mapping a relationship between these values and the actual image provides a vector for reducing the data required to represent the image. Various color levels can be seen in Figure 5-13. Both RGB and Y, CB, CR are depicted.

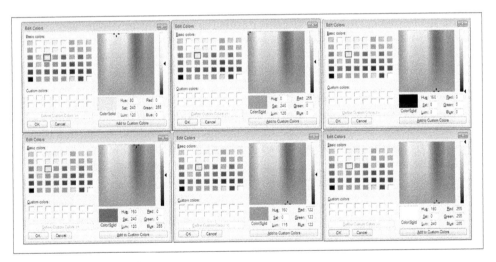

Figure 5-13. Color levels

Now that the format and color of the frame have been determined, the next task is to send the frames with as little data as possible while preserving as much quality as possible. Fortunately, the human eye is an imperfect machine, so codecs can get away with changing the image data a bit. One method used to reduce bandwidth consumed is to simply use black and white. The only values required will be the grayness levels and the locations of the pixels. We can also reduce the number of possible colors used for the images to be transmitted. Figure 5-14 depicts two bitmap images. The one on the left was saved using 24 bits per pixel. The one on the right was saved using 8 bits. Obviously, there is a difference in color quality, with the image on the left being preferred. However, the file size for the left image is also three times larger.

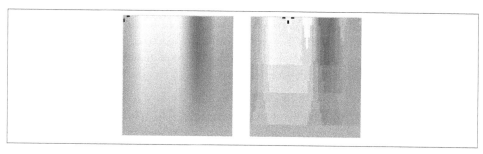

Figure 5-14. Color quality differences

Video Encoding

Let's start this section with a quote from the *Digital Consumer Electronics Handbook*:

> The ultimate goal of video source coding is the bit-rate reduction for storage and transmission by exploring both statistical and subjective redundancies and to encode a "minimum set" of information using entropy coding techniques. This usually results in a compression of the coded video data compared to the original source data.

When encoding a series of frames, the approach might be to simply encode each image as it comes, send it across the network, and then decode the frames at the receiver in the same way. This is called intracoding. If the encoding method results in an image that is exactly like the original, we call that lossless. Otherwise, it would be a lossy codec. Losses occur for the same reason discussed earlier in the chapter—codecs attempt to represent data efficiently but cause distortion when they do so. Take the simple series of images shown in Figure 5-15. The receiver would decode these in the same order they were received. Lossy encoding may result in color changes, loss in resolution for the sword, or missing movements.

Pixels come to the encoder with an indication of physical location within the image. They are converted or transformed onto a format that can be acted on by the compression algorithm. An example of a transformation algorithm is the discrete cosine transform, or DCT. DCT is used by H.261, H.263, and MPEG-4; the incoming image is broken into image sections. Once the encoder divides the image into sections (based on CIF), it is quantized. In the encoding process, the bit rate is reduced by looking for redundancy and repeated patterns. Run length coding (RLC)—also known as runlength encoding (RLE)—and variable-length coding (VLC) are variations in this

| Frame 3 - encode third | Frame 2 - encode second | Frame 1 - encode first |

Figure 5-15. Intraframe encoding

approach. RLC looks for repeated patterns, such as a series of pixels with the same color. This series might be represented by a number followed by the pixel color, this eliminating the need to transmit all of the pixels. However, RLC efficiency is directly proportional to the number of repeated items. VLC seeks to represent data points with another, smaller value. For example, the amount of red in a single pixel might vary between 0–255, such as the color levels shown in Figure 5-13. Normally we might represent these values with 8 bits. But the values of 00000000 might be compressed to 0. Lastly, we might assign a commonly repeated red level to zero, thus reducing the data required to match this common value. Another type of compression is arithmetic coding, which seeks to discover values that can represent the actual data. Figure 5-16 has some examples of frames where these techniques might be helpful.

Figure 5-16. Sectioned images with some repeated patterns

If the frames are divided into sections, some of the sections have more motion than others. In a section having little or no action, as in those on the left side of the figure, there may be little need to transmit the same information. Where RLC or VLC might significantly reduce the amount of data sent, comparing the activity in the section might reveal that we need not transmit any data at all, suggesting the possibility of using another technique—interframe coding.

Intercoding depends on a frame-to-frame correlation using motion vectors to approximate actual object motion. Motion vectors describe how the decoder should manipulate the decoded image to match the original current image. In other words, the encoding of the current frame is done relative to another frame in the sequence. A simple example is shown in Figure 5-17.

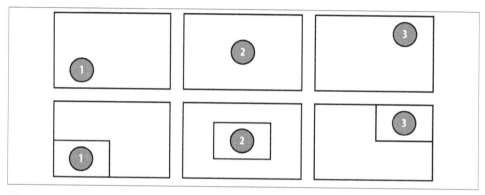

Figure 5-17. Moving images

Imagine a ball moving across the screen. Other than the ball, not much is happening in the frame, and the size and shape of the ball does not change. Now, place the ball in a container and track the movement of the container or section. This requires that you pay attention to the previous location of the section. Typically, codecs combine these ideas, so hybrid encoding uses of both intraframe and interframe techniques.

 H.262 Information Technology—Generic Coding of Moving Pictures and Associated Audio Information: Video provides the detailed description for hybrid-encoding video for data network transmission. It dates from 1995. Many of the ideas expressed in this section are more fully explained in this recommendation.

Standards Groups for Video

There have been two groups involved in the development of video codecs: the ITU-T Video Coding Experts Group (VCEG) and the Moving Picture Experts Group (MPEG), from the International Standards Organization and International Electrotechnical Commission. Recognizing the increased demand for video run over data networks, these two groups formed a Joint Video Team (JVT) in 2001 with the goal of creating a new recommendation or standard.

While all of the video codecs have been updated from time to time, with the exception of H.264, they all started before 2001. The next couple of sections will provide some details on the various codecs, although anyone wishing for greater details should refer to the ITU-T recommendations or ISO standards.

Profiles

As we saw in Chapter 4 during the discussion regarding Real-Time Transport Protocol (RTP), modifications to the operation and payload of RTP can be made through a profile. This idea is also present in codecs. All of the codecs discussed in this chapter have had several versions, additions, or annexes created to address deficiencies, make changes, or add functions. For example, G.729 has been expanded by annexes A through I and has several appendices. These offer variations in compression calculation and data rates.

After these changes are made part of the codec, it is important to note that they do not replace what occurred in a previous generation. Instead, these changes are simply another profile for the codec. This is particularly true in the case of features and functions. In this way, deployments are always compliant even though they may not support a particular object or capability. Differences are addressed during session negotiation.

ITU-T Video Recommendations

The H series of video codecs are summarized below. Of this list, H.120, H.261, H.263, and H.264 have been commonly deployed, especially H.263. H.262 is a generic recommendation for the encoding of video and serves as a good reference document.

H.120 Codecs for Videoconferencing Using Primary Digital Group Transmission (1984)

> This was the very first standard and was amended in 1993. At the time, videoconferencing was also called visual telephone service. This codec is almost never seen today, but it does provide some insight into the demand for and the issues associated with transmitting video over the data network. It is a codec designed to transmit 625 lines (576 visible) and 50 fields/second using a maximum bandwidth of 2Mbps. There is also a version that handles 525 lines and 60 fields/sec. Field rates refer to the frequency of color changes. Other values for these parameters are included in the recommendation. The frames use the same structure defined for T-1s and E-1s.

> The codec includes a 64Kbps voice or audio channel using G.711 A-Law. Several color standards for the image were supported. Here are the basic rules per the recommendation:

> - 256 picture samples/active line, 320 samples/complete line
> - Sampling rate of 5MHz (5,000,000 samples per second)

- Uniformly quantized PCM with 8 bits/sample (black value – 16(00010000), white – 239 (11101111))

- The final picture element in each line was 128 (10000000) as a marker.

A movie is a series of pictures or frames. Each frame (based on ITU-T H.100) has 625 vertical lines. Each frame is actually comprised of two fields that are interlaced to complete a single image (Figure 5-18).

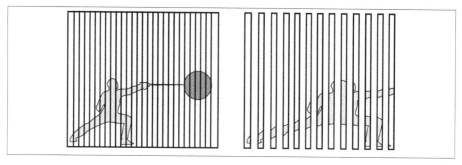

Figure 5-18. Vertical picture elements

Leaving interlacing aside, each line can be thought of as a slice (much thinner than shown here) of the image. Now, each slice is sampled 256 times in much the same way that the audio signals were sampled earlier in this chapter. The samples (the circles in Figure 5-19) are each given their quantized value. For monochrome, these quantized values are essentially the levels of black and white. For color images, the codec uses a color-difference component format.

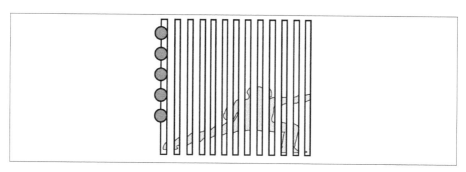

Figure 5-19. Potential samples

A movement detector is used to determine which parts of the picture appear to be moving. Since each line has 256 possible addressable points, the areas that move are transmitted via differential PCM with 16 quantization levels. So, the entire image is not transmitted with each field or frame, and the output is kept to about 2Mbps.

H.261 Video Codec for Audiovisual Service at p x 64Kbps (1988)

This is often considered the first practical success for encoding video. It is the base standard for low data rates and motion. Forming the basis for other codecs, it is employed for data rates up to 2Mbps (the "p" in the title ranges from 1–30) but is more at home at much lower speeds. It is largely obsolete having been replaced by H.263. This recommendation specifies that the encoding is for pictures based on the common intermediate format or CIF.

Some of the other details specified by the codec include 30 frames per second (29.97 FPS), and Y, CB, CR for luminance and color difference. The quantization values for black and white are 16 and 235, respectively. H.261 makes use of both the intraframe and interframe encoding described earlier. The interframe prediction can work with the optional motion compensation, which adds horizontal and vertical motion vectors.

H.263 (1996)

This was a much-improved version and has seen heavy deployment for web content and videoconferencing, where it dominates. It uses H.261 as its base but has 18 options that can be negotiated to improve performance and functionality. To quote from the recommendation:

> A hybrid of inter-picture prediction ... The decoder has motion compensation capability, allowing optional incorporation of this technique in the coder. Half pixel precision is used for the motion compensation, as opposed to ITU-T Rec. H.261 where full pixel precision and a loopfilter are used. Variable length coding is used for the symbols to be transmitted.

H.264/MPEG-4 Advanced Video Coding for generic audiovisual devices (2003)

This was part of the Advanced Video Coding Project (AVC) that led to improvements in coding efficiency. It had the goals of greater resolution and more bits per sample. It was also designed to be network friendly, with some concern for integration with the real-time protocol, or RTP. As stated in the recommendation, it represents the evolution of the H series of codecs; however, as it's a joint work, it was published as both H.264 and ISO/IEC 14496-10.

As stated on the MPEG site, this is the standard for fixed and mobile web multimedia. Generally, this standard starts with H.263 but adds many features and improvements to coding efficiency. MPEG-4 includes a DMIF (delivery multimedia integration framework), which insulates the developer from having to worry about transport. MPEG-4 also provides greater detail and control over the video stream and descriptive elements within the images or scenes. Images are still based on variations in CIF although the compression algorithms are more efficient and include the ability to adjust desired quality. In fact, much of the codec improvement comes from its ability to perform adjustments based on content. For example, in addition to rectangular shape movement, H.264/MEPG-4 also handles movement of arbitrary shapes. Data rates top out at more than 1 Gbps.

ISO/IEC Video Standards

The Moving Picture Expert Group set of standards are primarily associated with video and most commonly with entertainment video. But it is important to remember that there are also MPEG audio standards. For example, MP3 (MPEG-1 level 3) and AAC (advanced audio coding based on MPEG-2) are both heavily used. Recall also that the joint work of the two bodies (MPEG and ITU-T) resulted in H.264/MPEG-4.

MPEG-1 ISO/IEC 11172-1 (1993)
This standard is considered better than H.261 at higher data rates. It shares some ideas with H.261 but added more motion prediction. If fact, it was designed with the H.261 recommendation in mind and uses many of the same techniques, such as DCT. However, since it was targeted at multimedia CD-ROM content, functions that were not part of H.261 had to be added. This includes forward and reverse, editing, random media search, and playback.

MPEG-2/H.262/ISO 13818 (1994)
MPEG-2 builds upon MPEG-1 but approaches the problem from the opposite direction. Most video codecs provide a maximum rate, while MPEG-2 starts at a minimum, choosing to start at the 29.97 FPS, or 50 fields/second rates go up to the ITU-T Rec. BT.601 Y, CB, CR encoding discussed earlier. This was joint work between the two groups and saw wide use in DVDs and digital broadcasting. For a while, it was the most popular video coding standard using the hybrid approach of DCT and Differential PCM. It is a higher speed standard with greater precision. Its maximum data rate is 15Mbps at 30 FPS.

MPEG-4/ISO 14496 (1998)
See H.264

Summary

Voice over IP and its close cousin, Video over IP, have performance metrics that are determined in part by the operation of the codec. In some cases, codec selection is one of the few tools we have to affect call quality. Codecs utilize a variety of compression techniques in order to reduce the resources required to process voice data. Audio codecs for packetized traffic are standardized in the ITU-T G-series. Of this group, G.711 is generally recognized as being the most reliable because it performs well even with adverse network conditions. However, codecs such as G.729 and G.722 certainly have their place, and in cases where bandwidth or network reliability is a problem, they may be good solutions.

Video codecs face many of the same network-based challenges and must also encode images or frames. While the field started with competing groups, efforts to develop video encoders and decoders have largely centered on a single standard: H.264, also known as MPEG-4. Predecessors such as H.263 are still extremely popular, but they will eventually be replaced.

Codec selection is an important part of a successful VoIP deployment because network administrators have to take into account variables such as latency, jitter, packet loss, performance of the codec itself, available bandwidth, and costs. Codecs have well-established performance characteristics for a variety of networking environments. This data should be consulted when choosing codecs to deploy.

Standards and Reading

MPEG website
http://www.mpeg.org/

The MPEG Homepage
http://mpeg.chiariglione.org/

ITU-T Recommendations G.710—G.729
Coding of Voice and Audio Signals (*http://bit.ly/12JvNsa*)

ITU-T Recommendations H.260—H.279
Coding of Voice and Audio Signals (*http://bit.ly/UF1CP3*)

ITU-T Recommendations P.800—P.899
Methods for objective and subjective assessment of speech quality (*http://bit.ly/11VmCFK*)

Review Questions

1. True or false: Pulse Code Modulation forms the basis of most audio and video codecs.

2. In PCM, how many times in the waveform sampled and how many bits are allocated for the quantizing values?

3. What causes distortion when encoding audio?

4. What is the most popular audio codec?

5. True or false: red, green, and blue levels are most often used to describe video pixel data.

6. What is the standard format for an image used for frames?

7. True or false: when predicting movement, algorithms typically target movement across the entire image in order to reduce processing.

8. True or false: the codec is negotiated before transmission and so is not visible during transmission.

9. What codec has a very effective packet loss concealment algorithm?

10. What is transcoding?

Review Question Answers

1. True. While the stream is often converted, most start off in PCM.

2. PCM samples at 8000 times per second, and each sample is allocated 8 bits.

3. Distortion is caused by the difference in quantizing value and the actual value of the waveform at sample time.

4. G.711.

5. False—video codecs and images use Y, CB, and CR.

6. Common Intermediate Format, or CIF.

7. False—images are typically broken down into sections for movement tracking.

8. False—the codec in use is visible in the RTP header during the transmission.

9. G.722.

10. Transcoding is most commonly associated with the process of encoding audio or video with one codec and decoding with another.

Lab Activities

This chapter is supported by the book website. So, if the activity lists equipment or software that you do not have, go to the book website for additional content.

Activity 1—Colors

Materials: drawing program such as MS Paint, computer

1. Open MS Paint or an equivalent program.

2. Go to the Edit Colors toolbar item and, using the cursor in the right-hand section or the color levels, experiment with the RGB and Hue, Saturation, and Luminosity values.

3. Compare the values to the color displayed—can you predict what will happen (Figure 5-20)?

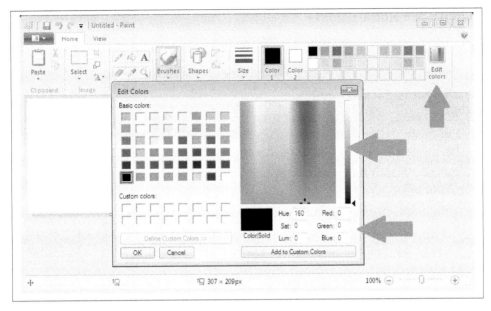

Figure 5-20. Activity 5-1

Activity 2—File Sizes

Materials: drawing program such as MS Paint, computer

1. Using MS Paint or an equivalent program, create or open an image.
2. Save the image using the various formats permitted by the program.
3. Experiment with the detail permitted by the file format.
4. Compare the file sizes with the format used (Figure 5-21).

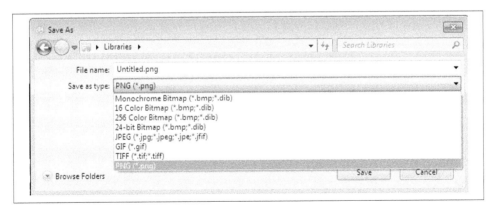

Figure 5-21. Activity 5-2

Activity 3—Audio Quality

Materials: communications program such as Skype, computer

1. Open up your favorite voice software, for example, Skype.

2. Navigate to the audio settings.

3. Place several calls to a partner or to an answering machine. For each call, adjust the call-quality settings. Adjusting these settings is similar to changing the codec. If you have access to or can select a codec, even better.

4. Can you identify the codec used by your software? How could you do this? Settings? Capture?

5. How do the changes you make affect the quality?

6. Advanced—capture the traffic and compare the number and size of the packets that correspond to each settings change. Examine any RTP traffic. Is the codec identified (Figure 5-22)?

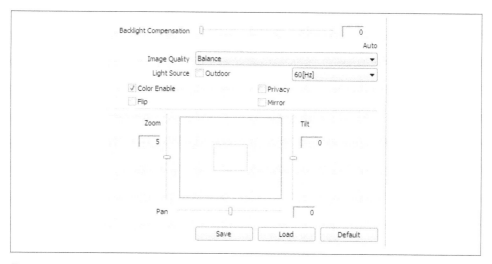

Figure 5-22. Activity 5-3

Activity 4—Video Quality

Materials: program or accessory with video capability, computer

1. Open up your favorite video conferencing or VoIP software. Skype works for this as well.

2. Navigate to the video settings.

3. Place several calls to a partner or an answering machine. For each call, adjust the video settings. Note that some settings will affect quality and some will not.

4. Can you identify the video codec used by your software?

5. What changes have the greatest impact on quality?

6. Advanced—capture the traffic and compare the number and size of the packets that correspond to each settings change. Examine any RTP traffic. Is the codec identified (Figure 5-23)?

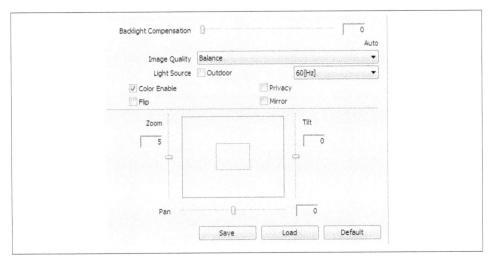

Figure 5-23. Activity 5-4

CHAPTER 6

H.323 ITU-T Recommendation for Packet-Based Multimedia Communications Systems

The 1990s spawned many changes to the ways in which we communicate. Among them were videoconferencing and the idea that voice might actually be encapsulated in a data packet. The International Telecommunications Union–Telecom (ITU-T) H.323 recommendation dates from this time period. While it has been updated many times, most of the ideas have carried forward. The very basic problem addressed by the recommendation is the conversion of the signaling used on a traditional telecommunications network to Internet Protocol (IP) based techniques. Rather than reinvent the wheel, many of the ideas were retained, though the packaging was quite a bit different. Thus H.323 uses as its basis many of the protocols and standards associated with the public switched telephone network, or PSTN, encapsulated in protocols such as TCP (transmission control protocol), UDP (user datagram protocol), and IP. In addition, we see the recommendation leveraging messages from the Integrated Service Digital Network (ISDN), such as call signaling.

This recommendation was the standard for videoconferencing, which includes voice, video, and data. Because it addresses such things as call control and management for point-to-point and multipoint conferences, gateway administration of media traffic, bandwidth parameters, and user participation, it also became the defacto standard for Internet Telephony and VoIP. While this is no longer the case due to the emergence of the Session Initiation Protocol (SIP), a large number of vendors still deploy the H.323 suite because its operation is well understood. There is also a significant amount of installed equipment still using the protocol and interoperability is important.

H.323 is actually part of the later H.3XX series of recommendations from the ITU-T and constitutes a collection of subprotocols that can be seen in packet captures. H.323 can be deployed over either TCP or UDP and uses ports 1719 and 1720, depending on the operation. A VoIP deployment of this kind will use the Real-Time Transport Protocol (RTP) to carry the voice and video data between endpoints. RTP is described in Chapter 4.

H.323 is built upon a telephony background and, in the true style of the ITU-T recommendations, is a very complex set of protocols. When wading through the documentation, one gets the sense of something that is very dense and monolithic. Recommendations from the ITU-T that describe structure and operation tend to discuss every possibility and have a huge number of fields. The fields, in turn, have many combinations that can make things very confusing. This chapter will work through the ideas expressed in the standard, protocol structure, operation, and the packets used when transmitting Voice over IP (VoIP) on an H.323 based system. The information for this chapter was gathered on a pair of operating networks featuring both Avaya and Polycom devices. Using these two topologies, we can gain a more complete picture of the protocol behavior, though there are other deployment models.

We will see that while the topologies in Figure 6-1 use the same protocols, they are markedly different. The Avaya topology also contains the supporting architecture, while the Polycom devices illustrate a stand-alone, point-to-point configuration.

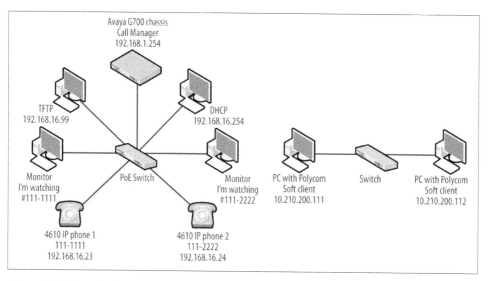

Figure 6-1. Topologies

Recommendation Description

The ITU-T recommendations are organized alphabetically; according to the ITU-T site (*http://bit.ly/XnqmrO*), there are over 3000 still in force today. VoIP and video use many of these recommendations, but this chapter is primarily concerned with the H series, covering audiovisual and multimedia systems. Drilling down a little further, we find that H.200 through H.499 are concerned with infrastructure of a Audiovisual services. The subprotocols of H.323, especially H.225 and H.245, perform tasks such as registration, call setup, and termination. These are part of H.220 through H.229, Transmission Multiplexing and Synchronization, and H.240 through H.259, Communication Procedures. Lastly, the H.300 through H.349 group is concerned with systems and terminal equipment. Specifically, H.323 does the following:

> Describes terminals and other entities that provide multimedia communications services over Packet-Based Networks (PBN) which may not provide a guaranteed Quality of Service.

There are many different types of terminals that can be supported by this protocol, including those based in ISDN and more traditional, generalized switched telephone network devices.

The original standard dates from 1996 and was entitled "Visual telephone systems and equipment for local area networks which provide a non-guaranteed quality of service." Version 2 of the standard changed to the name that has carried on to this day. Thus, there are a couple of versions, with version 7 being the latest. Each packet indicates compliance with a particular version with the protocol identifier field. This field is also an indicator of which version of H.225 and H.245 will be in use. Figure 6-2 depicts H.225 messages indicating the ports and version numbers.

As can be seen, the messages are using ports 1719 and 1720. The current implementation on our lab Avaya G700 chassis is compliant with version 5 of the recommendation.

There are several components that comprise an H.323 system, including terminals, gateways, gatekeepers, multipoint controllers that communicate via video, voice (audio), data, communication, and call-control messages. These are called the information streams. More details on the physical components follow.

Terminals
> Also known as endpoints with H.225 and H.245 signaling, systems control units, media transmission, audio codec (video), and the packet-based network interface.

Gateway
> Handles the communication and translation between the H.323 terminal on an IP network and a switched-circuit network such as the Public Switched Telephone Network. It handles call setup, termination, and possibly translation between codecs via H.225.

```
User Datagram Protocol, Src Port: 49301 (49301), Dst Port: h323gatestat (1719)
H.225.0 RAS
⊟ RasMessage: gatekeeperRequest (0)
  ⊟ gatekeeperRequest
     requestSeqNum: 2
     protocolIdentifier: 0.0.8.2250.0.5 (Version 5)
   ⊞ nonStandardData
   ⊞ rasAddress: ipAddress (0)
   ⊞ endpointType
   ⊞ endpointAlias: 1 item
   ⊞ tokens: 1 item
   ⊞ authenticationCapability: 2 items
   ⊞ algorithmOIDs: 2 items
   ⊞ featureSet
Transmission Control Protocol, Src Port: 4296 (4296), Dst Port: h323hostcall (1720)
TPKT, Version: 3, Length: 1367
Q.931
H.225.0 CS
⊟ H323-UserInformation
  ⊟ h323-uu-pdu
    ⊟ h323-message-body: setup (0)
      ⊟ setup
         protocolIdentifier: 0.0.8.2250.0.5 (Version 5)
       ⊞ sourceInfo
         ...0 .... activeMC: False
         conferenceID: 00000000-0000-1000-0000-0000c0a81017
       ⊞ conferenceGoal: callIndependentSupplementaryService (4)
       ⊞ callType: pointToPoint (0)
       ⊞ callIdentifier
       ⊞ fastStart: 36 items
         1... .... mediaWaitForConnect: True
         1... .... canOverlapSend: True
        0... .... h245Tunnelling: False
```

Figure 6-2. H.225 version numbers and ports

Gatekeeper

This is an optional component that can handle call-control services such as location requests and confirmation, name resolution, admission, and bandwidth control, also via H.225.

Multipoint controller

The controller supports conferences between three or more H.323 endpoints. It also handles the capabilities exchange for the communicating nodes. This occurs through the use of H.245.

Other components are the multipoint processor and multipoint control unit.

As we know from Chapter 4, a big part of any audio and/or video conversation will be the codec. The most common audio codecs are standardized in the ITU-T G.7XX series, and video codecs can be found in the H.26X series. Per the recommendation, to be H.323 compliant, all terminals are required to support G.711u-Law and A-Law. They may support other audio codecs, the use of which would be negotiated using H.245 messages. Video is optional, but if supported, it must be according the H.261 quarter intermediate format, or QCIF. The same is true of any support for H.263. Other codecs may be supported and negotiated using H.245.

Big Picture Warning

By any measure, H.323 is complicated. You are about to go through quite a number of packets and a lot of fields. In order to understand the basics, we do not really need to understand all of the minute details we're about to see. The phones and the call server go through a number of important steps that are good points of interest to remember.

- Dynamic Host Configuration Protocol (DHCP)—More detail and packet captures regarding this protocol can be found in Chapter 1.
- Trivial File Transfer Protocol (TFTP)—More detail and packet captures regarding this protocol can be found in Chapter 1.
- Gatekeeper discovery and registration via H.225 RAS.
- Establishing a connection to the other endpoint via H.225.
- Negotiating the communication parameters for the call or session via H.245 or H. 245 tunneling.
- Transmission of voice data via RTP.
- Tracking the performance of the voice data via RTCP.
- Termination of the media session via H.245.
- Termination of the connection via H.225.

If you can pick these out as we go, you are in good shape, especially since I'll be using two topologies to get through it all. But, understanding the fields and individual messages is what makes you an H.323 ninja.

Subprotocols

Now that we have a little better understanding of the H.323 umbrella recommendation, let's take a little closer look at H.225 and H.245. H.225 is entitled "Call signalling protocols and media stream packetization for packet-based multimedia communication systems" and has as its primary function the management of audio, video, and control information in order to provide "conversational services" for H.323 equipment.

Like H.323, there are several versions of the standard; version 7 is the latest at the time of this writing. Q.931 is another subprotocol often associated with call signaling in H. 323 environments. It is actually called the "ISDN user-network interface layer 3 specification for basic call control." H.225 makes use of the packetized version of this recommendation. Figure 6-3 reflects this relationship.

```
Ethernet II, Src: D-Link_c4:2e:04 (00:50:ba:c4:2e:04), Dst: D-Link_ce:90:78 (00:05:5d:ce:90:78)
Internet Protocol Version 4, Src: 10.210.200.111 (10.210.200.111), Dst: 10.210.200.112 (10.210.200.112)
Transmission Control Protocol, Src Port: h323hostcall (1720), Dst Port: mdtp (3232), Seq: 1, Ack: 649, Len: 103
TPKT, Version: 3, Length: 103
Q.931
H.225.0 CS
```

Figure 6-3. Q.931 and H.225

TPKT is a subprotocol that exists for the purpose of "porting" a non-TCP/IP application to what we now refer to as IP-based environments. International Standards Organization (ISO) transport services or transport protocols are not IP-based. The ISO transport protocol unit of information is called a transport protocol data unit (TPDU), which is encapsulated in a transport packet, or TPKT. Both H.225 and H.245 use TPKT. The encapsulation is covered by RFC 1006. If it seems a little outdated, you may be responding to the fact that RFC 983, which first described this protocol and the need to provide a means for interoperation between layered models, was first written in 1986 with few updates since that time.

H.323 also states the layer-4, or transport, protocols to be used within the architecture; specifically, it states that the reliable Transport Control Protocol (TCP) shall be used to support both H.225 and H.245. The unreliable UDP is mandatory for the audio, video, and RAS channels. RAS is short for registration, admissions, and status signaling. It is referred to as H.225 pre-call control in an H.323 environment with a gatekeeper.

H.245 is the "Control protocol for multimedia communications" and handles capabilities exchange between H.323 endpoints and the configuration of the logical channels between them. The most up-to-date version is number 16, which includes greater "harmonization" with the Session Initiation Protocol, or SIP, especially with respect to the dynamic payload types. These are described in Chapter 4.

Another subprotocol that can be implemented within the H.323 architecture is H.235, which describes security configurations.

Basic Operation and Message Structure

A portion of a typical H.323-based connection is shown in Figure 6-4. This particular list comes from a default Polycom topology that is not using a call manager, meaning that the nodes contact each other directly.

Note that in this list both H.225 and H.245 messages can be seen. This is not always the case, as H.245 is sometimes tunneled inside H.225. A call-flow diagram for the same H.225 and H.245 packets is shown in Figure 6-5.

The Polycom topology is depicted in Figure 6-6.

```
10   10.210.200.112   10.210.200.111   H.225.0   CS: setup
12   10.210.200.111   10.210.200.112   H.225.0   CS: alerting
18   10.210.200.111   10.210.200.112   H.225.0   CS: connect
25   10.210.200.112   10.210.200.111   H.245     terminalCapabilitySet
27   10.210.200.112   10.210.200.111   H.245     masterSlaveDetermination
31   10.210.200.111   10.210.200.112   H.245     terminalCapabilitySet
33   10.210.200.111   10.210.200.112   H.245     masterSlaveDetermination
38   10.210.200.112   10.210.200.111   H.245     terminalCapabilitySetAck
39   10.210.200.111   10.210.200.112   H.245     masterSlaveDeterminationAck
41   10.210.200.111   10.210.200.112   H.245     terminalCapabilitySetAck
42   10.210.200.112   10.210.200.111   H.245     masterSlaveDeterminationAck
44   10.210.200.112   10.210.200.111   H.245     openLogicalChannel (generic)
46   10.210.200.112   10.210.200.111   H.245     openLogicalChannel (genericVideoCapability)
```

Figure 6-4. H.225 and H.245 packet list

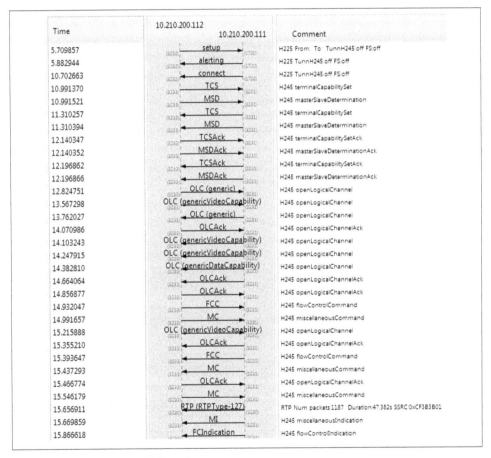

Figure 6-5. Packet list call-flow diagram

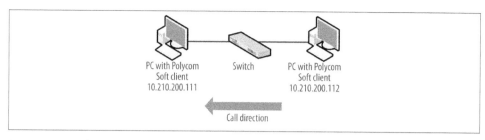

Figure 6-6. Polycom topology

Both H.225 and H.245 have a number of different message types, and each message is quite complex, having many fields. For this reason, this chapter will cover the set of messages commonly seen on H.323 topologies. Some of these messages will also have to be shown in chunks due to their sheer size.

 Although they have not been shown here, in a typical deployment, RTP and RTCP are used for transport, with the Trivial File Transfer Protocol (TFTP) and the Dynamic Host Configuration Protocol (DHCP) handling the overhead processes that are not VoIP specific. If you have been reading this book from start to finish, you have already seen implementations of this type. We will return to the more complex configuration later in this chapter.

H.225 Messaging

While there are five H.225 message categories and twenty-nine messages, not all of them are seen or implemented. For example, in the call-flow diagram for the basic Polycom topology, the only H.225 types seen were the SETUP, ALERTING, and CONNECT messages. Each message has the same basic header, which eventually indicates the message type. Once the message type is determined, the message is constructed accordingly. The basic message header is shown in Figure 6-7.

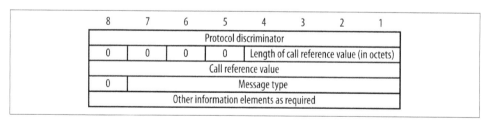

8	7	6	5	4	3	2	1
Protocol discriminator							
0	0	0	0	Length of call reference value (in octets)			
Call reference value							
0	Message type						
Other information elements as required							

Figure 6-7. ITU-T Q.931 basic header format

Expanding the first couple of packets from the list seen in Figure 6-8, we can see the Q.931 message types defined in the packets.

```
Internet Protocol Version 4, Src: 10.210.200.112 (10.210.200.112), Dst: 10.210.200.111 (10.210.200.111)
Transmission Control Protocol, Src Port: mdtp (3232), Dst Port: h323hostcall (1720), Seq: 509, Ack: 1,
TPKT, Version: 3, Length: 648
Q.931
   Protocol discriminator: Q.931
   Call reference value length: 2
   Call reference flag: Message sent from originating side
   Call reference value: 689f
   Message type: SETUP (0x05)
 ⊞ Bearer capability
 ⊞ Display  'Administrator'
 ⊞ User-user
H.225.0 CS
Internet Protocol Version 4, Src: 10.210.200.111 (10.210.200.111), Dst: 10.210.200.112 (10.210.200.112)
Transmission Control Protocol, Src Port: h323hostcall (1720), Dst Port: mdtp (3232), Seq: 1, Ack: 649,
TPKT, Version: 3, Length: 103
Q.931
   Protocol discriminator: Q.931
   Call reference value length: 2
   Call reference flag: Message sent to originating side
   Call reference value: 689f
   Message type: ALERTING (0x01)
 ⊞ User-user
H.225.0 CS
```

Figure 6-8. Q.931 packet types

Q.931 Fields

The fields in this packet are defined in ITU-T Recommendation Q.931 and include:

Protocol Discriminator
> This 1-byte field is set to 08 per the ITU-T Recommendation H.225. This indicates that it is a Q.931 message.

Call Reference Value Length
> This is a 4-bit field, and it specifies the number of octets used for the call reference value. The default maximum length is three octets.

Call Reference Flag
> This is a single-bit flag indicating the direction of a particular message. Originators always set this to zero, and destinations set this to one. The message shown in Figure 6-9 is on its way back to the originator, so the flag is set to one. This flag is the first bit of the 8-bit call reference value. In this case, the bits of the field are 1110 1000 1001 1111 (e89f in hex), with the very first bit being the flag. Without the flag, it would be 110 1000 1001 1111, or 689f in hex.

Call Reference Value
> This field identifies the call or request and is valid for the duration of the call. It is the second part of every message. This value is set by the originator of the call. From the decode we can see that the value determined by Wireshark is 689f. Remember that the reference value and flag are part of the same series of bits. The last three

characters (89f) will be the same, but the first will change (incremented by 8) based on the presence of the flag.

Message Type

This is a 1-byte field (7 bits for the code and 1 bit for future use) specifying the kind of message. ALERTING has a code of 01. Other examples include CALL PROCEEDING (02) and CONNECT (07).

Information Element

The next set of fields are called the information elements and can be either single octet or variable length, depending on the fit bit in the octet. The current value is 7e, or 0111 1110 in binary. The table from ITU-T Recommendation Q.931 indicates that this value is user-user. Other examples include Calling Party Number (0110 1100) and Keypad Facility (0010 1100). It is important to note that each one of these message types causes the header to expand with all of the options for that type.

Length

This is the amount of information in bytes for the element.

This packet has a last field called the protocol discriminator of X.208 and X.209 in the last field. This is specific to the user-user type. X.208 and X.209 are Abstract Syntax Notation rules defined by the ITU-T.

Remember that H.225 is making use of the packetized signaling of Q.931. Figure 6-9 depicts the same ALERTING message but includes the hexadecimal values as another way of seeing the encapsulation. The Q.931 portion of the packet begins with the circled 0x08 and ends with circled 0x05. The next hex value of 0x23 is the start of the H.225-specific information.

The following is a list of mandatory and optional H.225 message types for an H.323 implementation using Q.931. Conditional mandatory means that it is required if the option is supported. With each message type, nodes may be required to transmit, receive, act upon, or all three (Table 6-1).

Table 6-1. Mandatory and optional H.225 messages types for an H.323 implementation using Q.931

	Transmit	Receive and Act Upon
Call Establishment Messages		
Alerting	mandatory	mandatory
Call Proceeding	optional	conditional mandatory
Connect	mandatory	mandatory
Progress	optional	conditional mandatory
Setup	mandatory	mandatory
Setup Acknowledge	optional	optional

```
Internet Protocol Version 4, Src: 10.210.200.111 (10.210.200.111), Dst: 10.210.200.112
Transmission Control Protocol, Src Port: h323hostcall (1720), Dst Port: mdtp (3232), Se
TPKT, Version: 3, Length: 103
Q.931
  Protocol discriminator: Q.931
  Call reference value length: 2
  Call reference flag: Message sent to originating side
  Call reference value: 689f
  Message type: ALERTING (0x01)
⊟ User-user
    Information element: User-user
    Length: 91
    Protocol discriminator: X.208 and X.209 coded user information
H.225.0 CS

  00 05 5d ce 90 78 00 50  ba c4 2e 04 08 00 45 00    ..]..x.P  ......E.
  00 8f f2 52 40 00 80 06  61 92 0a d2 c8 6f 0a d2    ...R@... a....o..
  c8 70 06 b8 0c a0 ec 90  9e 4e 47 4f f4 01 50 18    .p...... .NGO..P.
  fd 77 02 b6 00 00 03 00  00 67 08 02 e8 9f 01 7e    .w.... ..g....~
  00 5b 05 23 80 06 00 08  91 4a 00 04 22 c0 b5 00    .[.#.... .J.."...
  23 31 0f 50 6f 6c 79 63  6f 6d 20 56 69 61 56 69    #1.Polyc om ViaVi
  64 65 6f 16 52 65 6c 65  61 73 65 20 38 2e 30 3a    deo.Rele ase 8.0:
  20 38 2e 30 2e 30 2e 30  35 32 32 01 b0 d8 00 11     8.0.0.0 522....
  00 02 28 5a 75 30 0d 90  10 11 14 e3 e0 99 5e 3f    ..(ZuO.. ......^?
  0d 01 00 01 80 01 00 01  40 10 80 01 00             ........ @....
```

Figure 6-9. Q.931 ALERTING message fields

	Transmit	Receive and Act Upon
Call Clearing (Termination) Messages		
Release complete	mandatory	mandatory
Call Information Phase Messages		
User Information	optional	optional
Miscellaneous Messages		
Information	optional	conditional mandatory
Notify	optional	optional
Status	mandatory	mandatory
Status inquiry	optional	mandatory

H.225 Message Format

H.225 has a couple of stages that are not used by a small, point-to-point topology. For this reason we will be shifting to a more standard call server topology for our examples. In this section, we will be using the topology shown in Figure 6-10.

Central to this topology is the Avaya G700 chassis with an S8300 media gateway. The VoIP endpoints are Avaya 4610 IP phones. This topology also has DHCP and TFTP servers along with monitor stations watching traffic from the two IP phones. As the topology is established, the behavior typical of most VoIP deployments (and the ones seen in the other chapters) can be observed:

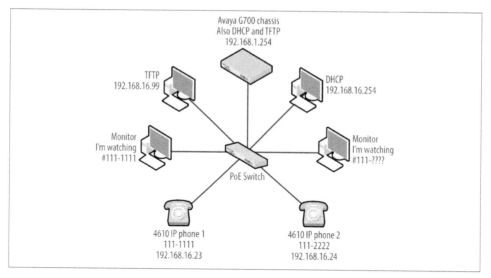

Figure 6-10. Avaya topology

1. Phones power up and look for an IP address via DHCP.

2. Phones look to update their software via the TFTP server. This process varies a little between vendors, but it is present on this Avaya based topology.

3. Phones contact the call server in order to register themselves and allow a user to log in to the phones. This gives the phone its phone or dial number.

We can verify that these processes took place by applying a couple of filters to the captures obtained by the monitor stations (Figure 6-11).

Filter: bootp || tftp.opcode==1 || h225 && eth.addr ==00:09:6e:05:cb:11	▾ Expression... Clear Apply			
No.	Source	Destination	Protocol	Info
28	0.0.0.0	255.255.255.255	DHCP	DHCP Discover - Transaction ID 0xc6e03148
33	0.0.0.0	255.255.255.255	DHCP	DHCP Request - Transaction ID 0xc6e03148
46	192.168.16.23	192.168.16.99	TFTP	Read Request, File: 46xxupgrade.scr, Trans
76	192.168.16.23	192.168.16.99	TFTP	Read Request, File: 46xxsettings.txt, Tran
568	192.168.16.23	192.168.16.1	H.225.0	RAS: gatekeeperRequest
569	192.168.16.1	192.168.16.23	H.225.0	RAS: gatekeeperConfirm
570	192.168.16.23	192.168.16.1	H.225.0	RAS: registrationRequest
571	192.168.16.1	192.168.16.23	H.225.0	RAS: registrationConfirm
576	192.168.16.23	192.168.16.1	H.225.0	CS: setup OpenLogicalChannel
578	192.168.16.1	192.168.16.23	H.225.0	CS: callProceeding
579	192.168.16.1	192.168.16.23	H.225.0	CS: connect OpenLogicalChannel

Figure 6-11. Packet list from phone startup

The filter rule shown at the top of the display in Figure 6-11 allows us to see the conversations that the phone has in trying to join the network. These packets were from Phone 1, so the IP address obtained from the DHCP server was 192.168.16.23. For right now, let's take the very first H.225 packet and go through the header shown in Figure 6-12. There are a couple of things to notice right off the bat.

```
Internet Protocol Version 4, Src: 192.168.16.23 (192.168.16.23), Dst: 192.168.16.1
User Datagram Protocol, Src Port: 49301 (49301), Dst Port: h323gatestat (1719)
H.225.0 RAS
 RasMessage: gatekeeperRequest (0)
   gatekeeperRequest
     requestSeqNum: 2
     protocolIdentifier: 0.0.8.2250.0.5 (Version 5)
   nonStandardData
     nonStandardIdentifier: object (0)
      data: 3 octets
    Data (3 bytes)
       Data: 850140
       [Length: 3]
   rasAddress: ipAddress (0)
     ipAddress
```

```
)00   00 04 0d e3 e3 d5 00 09   6e 05 cb 11 08 00 45 88    ........ n.....E.
)10   01 52 01 4a 00 00 40 11   d6 60 c0 a8 10 17 c0 a8    .R.J..@. .`......
)20   10 01 c0 95 06 b7 01 3e   85 6c 03 20 00 01 06 00    .......> .l. ....
)30   08 91 4a 00 05 00 0a 60   86 48 01 86 f8 72 04 02    ..J....` .H...r..
)40   01 03 85 01 40 00 c0 a8   10 17 c0 95 02 00 01 03    ....@... ........
)50   00 44 44 44 41 2b 10 80   b1 01 90 00 0a 60 86 48    .DDDA+.. .....`.H
)60   01 86 fc 0b 01 06 02 00   04 00 c5 34 64 5e f9 4a    .........4d^.J
)70   da 22 a0 bc c4 4a e9 1e   0c 3a 0d 1e 2c a8 4a 7c    ."...J.. .:..,.J|
)80   55 40 8a 34 81 8e 4b 5d   f9 86 44 07 82 00 a8 04    U@.4..K] ..D.....
)90   be 7c d9 37 3f d0 34 34   65 f4 ed d0 3f 2d 40 2c    .|.7?.44 e..?-@,
)a0   ab b2 06 b9 db 63 19 42   85 6f bd 1c 2d e5 1d e4    .....c.B .o..-..
)b0   8c 76 c9 a1 3c ef 23 8f   55 b4 3c a8 43 3d 3d 1a    .v..<.#. U.<.C==.
)c0   87 70 5f 70 df c8 c7 81   ea af 7b 60 92 e5 b1 e9    .p_p.... ..{`....
)d0   73 72 5d c7 98 0b ec 37   8c 55 fb dc b6 5e 33 31    sr]....7 .U...^31
)e0   81 f6 60 d0 67 23 2a 0a   1e d6 00 00 00 00 06 20    ..`.g#*. ...... 
)f0   19 02 20 02 00 04 00 00   48 9c 20 01 00 0c 6c 89    .. ..... H. ...l.
100   00 00 10 d2 00 00 08 48   00 00 0f 02 18 10 0b 0a    .......H ........
110   60 86 48 01 86 fc 0b 01   06 02 11 02 05 2b 0e 03    `.H..... .....+..
120   02 06 09 60 86 48 01 86   fc 0b 01 03 33 10 02 48    ...`.H.. ....3..H
130   09 60 86 48 01 86 fc 0b   01 09 00 00 40 00 01 20    .`.H.... ....@.. 
140   01 48 09 60 86 48 01 86   fc 0b 01 0a 00 05 00 00    .H.`.H.. ........
150   01 00 00 03 00 00 05 00   00 07 00 00 0a 00 00 0b    ........ ........
```

Figure 6-12. H.225 RAS beginning

First, even though RAS is part of H.225 signaling, RAS (registration, admission, status) messages are encapsulated in UDP datagrams and use port 1719. Second, the Q.931 and TPKT headers are missing. This is because this portion of the conversation is simply the phone connecting to and communicating with the call server.

H.225 RAS

As was mentioned earlier, the RAS acronym stands for Registration, Admission, and Status. It is a significant part of the H.225 call control, as these processes are responsible for not only the phones connecting to the system but also whether or not endpoints are allowed. Minimally, the H.323 endpoints must find a gatekeeper (Gatekeeper Request—GRQ, Gatekeeper Confirmation—GCF) and request admission (Registration Request—RRQ, Registration Confirmation —RCF) from the gatekeeper. Figure 6-13 depicts a generalized form of autodiscovery and registration events taken from ITU-T

Recommendation H.323. This collection also shows the "unregistration" that occurs when a station disconnects from the system. The messages (particularly the unregistration) do not flow in this precise order.

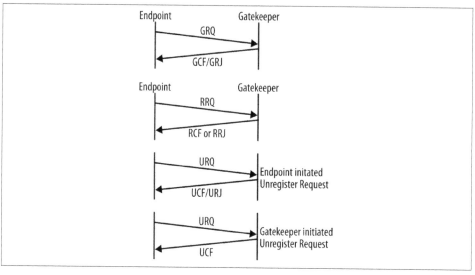

Figure 6-13. RAS message flow

Admission is another important part of this portion of the call. Run between the endpoint and the gatekeeper, a node may request a certain amount of bandwidth from the network using an Admission Request (ARQ) message. Gatekeepers allowing this type of request will respond with an Admission Confirm (ACF) message.

It turns out that there are a bunch of RAS message types and functions listed in section 7.7 of the ITU-T H.225 Recommendation, although the behavior is defined in ITU-T Recommendation H.323. Each type has its own collection of fields. Other examples of H.225 RAS messages are listed here.

- Admissions Confirm (ACF)
- Bandwidth Confirm (BCF)
- Disengage Confirm (DCF)
- Gatekeeper Request (GRQ)
- Information Request Negative Acknowledgment (INAK)

- Information Request Response (IRR)

- Location Reject (LRJ)

- Resource Availability Indication (RAI)

- Request In Progress (RIP)

- Registration Request (RRQ)

- Service Control Response (SCR)

- Unregistration Confirm (UCF)

It should be noted that while all of these messages are defined, not all have to be supported by every node and in every direction. For example, the Gatekeeper Confirm message (GCF) need only be supported by a transmitting gatekeeper. Additionally, some messages are much more common than others. The conversation in Figure 6-14 shows the packets generated in order to satisfy the initial concerns of the endpoints from Figure 6-13: finding a gatekeeper and registering with the same.

No.	Source	Destination	Protocol	Info
568	192.168.16.23	192.168.16.1	H.225.0	RAS: gatekeeperRequest
569	192.168.16.1	192.168.16.23	H.225.0	RAS: gatekeeperConfirm
570	192.168.16.23	192.168.16.1	H.225.0	RAS: registrationRequest
571	192.168.16.1	192.168.16.23	H.225.0	RAS: registrationConfirm

Figure 6-14. RAS messages for phone 1

It is important to remember that on the other side of the topology, the other phone is going through the exact same process, as shown in Figure 6-15.

589	192.168.16.24	192.168.16.1	H.225.0	RAS: gatekeeperRequest
591	192.168.16.1	192.168.16.24	H.225.0	RAS: gatekeeperConfirm
592	192.168.16.24	192.168.16.1	H.225.0	RAS: registrationRequest
593	192.168.16.1	192.168.16.24	H.225.0	RAS: registrationConfirm

Figure 6-15. RAS messages for phone 2

H.225 RAS fields

Updating our topology diagram, the endpoints are working through the initial conversations prior to making a call. These conversations include TFTP and DHCP (Figure 6-16) in addition to H.225 RAS. For clarity, the transactions for one phone are shown, but both complete the operations.

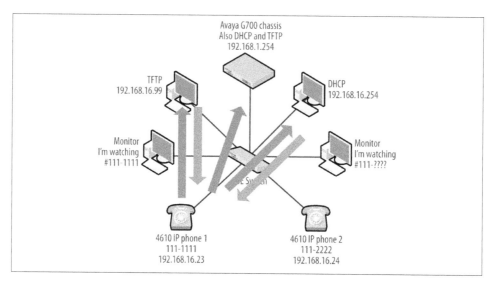

Figure 6-16. Updated topology

Take another look at the packet in Figure 6-12. The hexadecimal portion has been included for reference. The highlighted section is actually the UDP portion of the packet and serves to indicate the starting point of the H.225 RAS message. The little plus sign means that each of the fields shown can be expanded. This is one of the places that the H.323 protocols tend to get complex—there are many fields and subfields to contend with. In fact, this small collection represents 300 bytes of information sent from this endpoint. This RAS message is a gatekeeper request (GRQ), which makes it one of the terminal and gateway discovery messages.

Request Sequence Number (requestSeqNum)
> This value is used to manage multiple requests. The value increases with each message (1 modulo 65536 arithmetic), and any response uses the same sequence number. If we examine the sequence numbers of the calls, we would see that both phones start with a sequence number of 2, and the responses reference the same number.

Protocol Identifier (protocolIdentifier)
> This 6-byte field is used to indicate which version of the recommendation is in use. In this example, the syntax of 0.0.8.2250.0.5 indicates version 5. The values of "0.0.8" refer to the ITU-T (0), the recommendation (0), and the letter H (8).

Nonstandard Data (nonStandardData)

This is an optional field that can be used in the discovery, registration, setup, or connect messages. These elements are vendor specific. There is no requirement for a gatekeeper to forward this message. The 16 bytes are used to reference an Object Identifier (OID) in the Abstract Syntax Notation, or ASN. Per the recommendation, it is usually proprietary information. See Figure 6-17.

RAS Address (rasAddress)

This is the IP address and port number to be used by the VoIP endpoint. The 7 bytes indicate the field descriptor (0), the IP address (192.168.16.23), and the port (49301). The port number is only used for the RAS messages. See Figure 6-17.

```
Internet Protocol Version 4, Src: 192.168.16.23 (192.168.16.23), Dst: 192.168.16.1
User Datagram Protocol, Src Port: 49301 (49301), Dst Port: h323gatestat (1719)
H.225.0 RAS
⊟ RasMessage: gatekeeperRequest (0)
   ⊟ gatekeeperRequest
      requestSeqNum: 2
      protocolIdentifier: 0.0.8.2250.0.5 (version 5)
    ⊟ nonStandardData
       ⊟ nonStandardIdentifier: object (0)
          object: 2.16.840.1.113778.4.2.1 (joint-iso-itu-t.16.840.1.113778.4.2.1)
          data: 2 octets
       ⊞ Data (3 bytes)
    ⊟ rasAddress: ipAddress (0)
       ⊟ ipAddress
          ip: 192.168.16.23 (192.168.16.23)
          port: 49301
    ⊞ endpointType
    ⊞ endpointAlias: 1 item
    ⊞ tokens: 1 item
    ⊞ authenticationCapability: 2 items
    ⊞ algorithmOIDs: 2 items
    ⊞ featureSet
```

Figure 6-17. RAS GRQ object ID, IP address, and port

Endpoint Type (endpointType)

This is the type of endpoint that is registering. Details about this can be found in H.323 Annex F. In this example, a type 2 indicates a simple endpoint type (SET), which is a telephone with an RJ45 jack. This is also an indication of the capabilities of the phone. In this case, the MC bit (multipoint controller function) is also not set, which is understandable, as it is just a phone. See Figure 6-18.

Endpoint Alias (endpointAlias)

This field is a 7-byte value that includes the field name, type of alias, and the name by which other nodes may identify the endpoint. This is also seen in Figure 6-18.

```
Internet Protocol Version 4, Src: 192.168.16.23 (192.168.16.23), Dst: 192.168.16.1
User Datagram Protocol, Src Port: 49301 (49301), Dst Port: h323gatestat (1719)
H.225.0 RAS
⊟ RasMessage: gatekeeperRequest (0)
  ⊟ gatekeeperRequest
      requestSeqNum: 2
      protocolIdentifier: 0.0.8.2250.0.5 (Version 5)
    ⊞ nonStandardData
    ⊞ rasAddress: ipAddress (0)
    ⊟ endpointType
      terminal
        .0.. .... mc: False
        ..0. .... undefinedNode: False
    ⊟ endpointAlias: 1 item
      ⊟ Item 0
        ⊟ AliasAddress: dialledDigits (0)
            dialledDigits: 1111111
    ⊞ tokens: 1 item
    ⊞ authenticationCapability: 2 items
    ⊞ algorithmOIDs: 2 items
    ⊞ featureSet
    [The response to this request is in frame 569]

000  00 04 0d e3 e3 d5 00 09  6e 05 cb 11 08 00 45 88   ........ n.....E.
010  01 52 01 4a 00 00 40 11  d6 6c c0 a8 10 17 c0 a8   .R.J..@. .l......
020  10 01 c0 95 06 b7 01 3e  85 6c 03 20 00 01 06 00   .......> .l......
030  08 91 4a 00 05 00 0a 60  86 48 01 86 f8 73 04 02   ..J....` .H...r..
040  01 03 83 01 40 00 c0 a8  10 17 c0 95 08 00 01 03   ....@... ........
050  00 44 44 44 41 2b 10 80  b1 01 90 00 0a 00 86 48   .DDDA+.. .......H
060  01 86 f8 0b 01 06 02 00  04 00 c5 34 64 5e f9 4a   ........ ...4d^.J
070  da 22 a0 bc c4 4a e9 1e  0c 3a 0d 1e 2c a8 4a 7c   ."...J.. .:..,.J|
```

Figure 6-18. RAS terminal fields

Tokens

This is a collection of items that may or may not be necessary to allow the connection to go forward. They are included here to be complete. The tokens field is of variable length and, as can be seen from Figure 6-19, is a list of the OIDs required. Most of what we see in this connection are Avaya specific, like the OID 2.16.840.1.114187. However, the OID 1.3.14.3.2.6 refers to the Data Encryption Standard (DES) encryption for Electronic Code Book (ECB) mode. This last is specified in Federal Information Processing Standard 81, or FIPS81. Some of the objects listed in this example include Authentication Capability and the Algorithm OID. Each section begins with a numerical value indicating how many items follow.

Feature Set

This is a collection of items supported by the phone. Like most of these fields, the features are referenced by their OIDs, which are Avaya specific. Due to the sheer number of listings, only a portion of this section has been expanded. See Figure 6-20.

There are a number of additional fields that might be required by a particular message type or implementation, such as GateKeeperIdentifier and CallServices. For example, the RegistrationConfirmation message from the gatekeeper to this particular VoIP phone (packet 571) includes the CallSignalAddress (IP address and port) to be used with the H.225 packets. This packet also indicates that the phone is allowed to make calls immediately. See Figure 6-21.

```
⊟ tokens: 1 item
   ⊟ Item 0
      ⊟ ClearToken
         tokenOID: 2.16.840.1.114187.1.6.2 (joint-iso-itu-t.16.840.1.114187.1.6.2)
         ⊟ dhkey
            halfkey: c534645ef94ada22a0bcc44ae91e0c3a0d1e2ca84a7c5540... [bit length 1024]
         ⊟ profileInfo: 2 items
            ⊟ Item 0
               ⊟ ProfileElement
                  elementID: 2
                  ⊟ element: octets (0)
                     octets: 0000489c
            ⊟ Item 1
               ⊟ ProfileElement
                  elementID: 1
                  ⊟ element: octets (0)
                     octets: 6c89000010d2000008480000
⊟ authenticationCapability: 2 items
   ⊟ Item 0
      ⊟ AuthenticationMechanism: pwdSymEnc (1)
         pwdSymEnc: NULL
   ⊟ Item 1
      ⊟ AuthenticationMechanism: keyExch (8)
         keyExch: 2.16.840.1.114187.1.6.2 (joint-iso-itu-t.16.840.1.114187.1.6.2)
⊟ algorithmOIDs: 2 items
   ⊟ Item 0
      algorithmOIDs item: 1.3.14.3.2.6 (desECB)
   ⊟ Item 1
      algorithmOIDs item: 2.16.840.1.114187.1.3 (joint-iso-itu-t.16.840.1.114187.1.3)
⊞ featureSet
```

Figure 6-19. RAS tokens fields

```
⊞ endpointAlias: 1 item
⊞ tokens: 1 item
⊞ authenticationCapability: 2 items
⊞ algorithmOIDs: 2 items
⊟ featureSet
   .... 0... replacementFeatureSet: False
   ⊟ supportedFeatures: 2 items
      ⊟ Item 0
         ⊟ FeatureDescriptor
            ⊟ id: oid (1)
               oid: 2.16.840.1.114187.1.9 (joint-iso-itu-t.16.840.1.114187.1.9)
            ⊟ parameters: 1 item
               ⊟ Item 0
                  ⊟ parameters item
                     ⊟ id: standard (0)
                        standard: 1
                     ⊟ content: number8 (4)
                        number8: 1
      ⊟ Item 1
         ⊟ FeatureDescriptor
            ⊟ id: oid (1)
               oid: 2.16.840.1.114187.1.10 (joint-iso-itu-t.16.840.1.114187.1.10)
            ⊟ parameters: 6 items
               ⊟ Item 0
                  ⊟ parameters item
                     ⊟ id: standard (0)
                        standard: 1
               ⊞ Item 1
               ⊞ Item 2
               ⊞ Item 3
               ⊞ Item 4
               ⊞ Item 5
```

Figure 6-20. RAS feature set fields

```
Internet Protocol Version 4, Src: 192.168.16.1 (192.168.16.1), Dst: 192.168.16.23
User Datagram Protocol, Src Port: h323gatestat (1719), Dst Port: 49301 (49301)
H.225.0 RAS
⊟ RasMessage: registrationConfirm (4)
  ⊟ registrationConfirm
      requestSeqNum: 3
      protocolIdentifier: 0.0.8.2250.0.5 (Version 5)
    ⊞ nonStandardData
    ⊟ callSignalAddress: 1 item
      ⊟ Item 0
        ⊟ TransportAddress: ipAddress (0)
          ⊟ ipAddress
              ip: 192.168.16.1 (192.168.16.1)
              port: 1720
      endpointIdentifier: .n
    ⊞ alternateGatekeeper: 1 item
      0... .... willRespondToIRR: False
    ⊟ preGrantedARQ
      .1.. .... makeCall: True
      ..1. .... useGKCallSignalAddressToMakeCall: True
      ...1 .... answerCall: True
      .... 1... useGKCallSignalAddressToAnswer: True
      1... .... maintainConnection: True
```

Figure 6-21. RAS registration confirmation

H.225 Standard Messages

Now that the phone has located and registered with the gatekeeper (packets 568–571), the conversation moves on to the H.225 messages specific to the call. Recall that 192.168.16.23 (telephone number 111-1111) will be calling to the other side. But at this moment, the call server and the phone are exchanging details. The H.225-Q.931 SETUP message is used to initiate the process. For this portion of the explanation, we will be tearing apart packet 576. Much of the header will be familiar, but because this is a SETUP (type 5) message, the fields have changed a bit. One of the things that makes H.323 and the associated protocols such a pain is the number of message types and fields. Each message type can have a remarkably different set of fields than the next (Figure 6-22).

The basic Q.931 fields were described in a previous section, but as a reminder, they are:

Protocol Discriminator
> This 1-byte field is set to 08 per the ITU-T Rec H.225. This indicates that it is a Q.931 message.

Call Reference Value Length
> This is a 4-bit field and specifies the number of octets used for the call reference value.

```
⊞ Internet Protocol Version 4, Src: 192.168.16.23 (192.168.16.23), Dst: 192.168.16.1
⊞ Transmission Control Protocol, Src Port: 4296 (4296), Dst Port: h323hostcall (1720)
⊞ TPKT, Version: 3, Length: 1367
⊟ Q.931
    Protocol discriminator: Q.931
    Call reference value length: 2
    Call reference flag: Message sent from originating side
    Call reference value: 0001
    Message type: SETUP (0x05)
  ⊟ Bearer capability
     Information element: Bearer capability
     Length: 3
     1... .... = Extension indicator: last octet
     .00. .... = Coding standard: ITU-T standardized coding (0x00)
     ...0 0000 = Information transfer capability: Speech (0x00)
     1... .... = Extension indicator: last octet
     .00. .... = Transfer mode: Circuit mode (0x00)
     ...1 0000 = Information transfer rate: 64 kbit/s (0x10)
     1... .... = Extension indicator: last octet
     .01. .... = Layer identification: Layer 1 identifier (0x01)
     ...0 0010 = User information layer 1 protocol: Recommendation G.711 u-law (0x02)
  ⊞ User-user
⊞ H.225.0 CS
```

Figure 6-22. H.225 SETUP message

Call Reference Flag
This is a single-bit flag indicating the direction of the message.

Call Reference Value
This field identifies the call or request and is valid for the duration of the call.

One difference between the fields of this SETUP packet and the ALERT packet shown earlier is that the Bearer Capability is now included. Expanding this field gives us Figure 6-23.

Some of the values, such as the extension indicators, are predetermined. Other fields, like the information transfer value, are used to provide an indication of connection needs or bandwidth concerns. Note that the possible codec and connection speed (capabilities) are now included (64Kbps based on G.711ulaw) in compliance with ITU-T recommendations, though they may be changed as the connection configuration continues. These also serve to indicate a voice-only versus an H.323 video call. We can also see that the signaling port has changed from the 1719 of the RAS messages to 1720.

Collapsing the Q.931 header allows us to focus on the information exchanged via the H.225 header. From Figure 6-24, some of the important details are that a conference ID has been selected, this is an H.225 FastStart connection, and H.245 tunneling is FALSE. Remember that these are all part of the same packet, 576.

The use of the protocol ID field is consistent with our previous discussion, and the sourceInfo field allows the called party to determine if a gateway is involved. Since this is between the phone endpoint and the local call server, no other gateway is used.

```
Internet Protocol Version 4, Src: 192.168.16.23 (192.168.16.23), Dst: 192.168.16.1
Transmission Control Protocol, Src Port: 4296 (4296), Dst Port: h323hostcall (1720)
TPKT, Version: 3, Length: 1367
Q.931
  Protocol discriminator: Q.931
  Call reference value length: 2
  Call reference flag: Message sent from originating side
  Call reference value: 0001
  Message type: SETUP (0x05)
⊟ Bearer capability
    Information element: Bearer capability
    Length: 3
    1... .... = Extension indicator: last octet
    .00. .... = Coding standard: ITU-T standardized coding (0x00)
    ...0 0000 = Information transfer capability: Speech (0x00)
    1... .... = Extension indicator: last octet
    .00. .... = Transfer mode: Circuit mode (0x00)
    ...1 0000 = Information transfer rate: 64 kbit/s (0x10)
    1... .... = Extension indicator: last octet
    .01. .... = Layer identification: Layer 1 identifier (0x01)
    ...0 0010 = User information layer 1 protocol: Recommendation G.711 u-law (0x02)
⊕ User-user
H.225.0 CS
```

Figure 6-23. H.225 SETUP with capability expanded

```
Internet Protocol Version 4, Src: 192.168.16.23 (192.168.16.23), Dst: 192.168.16.1
Transmission Control Protocol, Src Port: 4296 (4296), Dst Port: h323hostcall (1720)
TPKT, Version: 3, Length: 1367
Q.931
H.225.0 CS
⊟ H323-UserInformation
  ⊟ h323-uu-pdu
    ⊟ h323-message-body: setup (0)
      ⊟ setup
          protocolIdentifier: 0.0.8.2250.0.5 (Version 5)
        ⊕ sourceInfo
          ...0 .... activeMC: False
          conferenceID: 00000000-0000-1000-0000-0000c0a81017
        ⊕ conferenceGoal: callIndependentSupplementaryService (4)
        ⊕ callType: pointToPoint (0)
        ⊕ callIdentifier
        ⊕ fastStart: 36 items
          1... .... mediaWaitForConnect: True
          1... .... canOverlapSend: True
      0... .... h245Tunnelling: False
```

Figure 6-24. H.225 faststart

Conference ID

> This is a 16-byte unique identifier for the conference. This value is used even if it
> is a point-to-point call between two endpoints. All of the messages associated with
> the call will use the same ID.

Conference Goal

> Per H.225, the reasons for the conference can be any of the following: create, invite,
> join, capability negotiation, and callIndependentSupplementaryService, as is the

case with the example in Figure 6-24. During this part of the call, the endpoint and the gateway are communication features and settings. We will see that many of these items are Avaya specific.

Call Type

This field is used to help the gatekeeper or call server determine the actual bandwidth that might be needed or used by the node. In this case, the connection is point-to-point, and the bandwidth consumption can be tied to the codec. Point-to-point is also the default value.

Call Identifier

This 16-byte value is a globally unique value that is set by the originating endpoint.

H.225 Modes

When operating an H.323 topology, it may be desirable to run the protocols in a manner advantageous to the configuration efficiency. This section will cover a couple of operational modes for H.225.

FastStart

The packets shown at the beginning of the chapter came from a Polycom topology and utilize both H.225 and H.245. A closer look at the packets from the current Avaya topology (see Figure 6-25) reveals that H.245 is not being used, because the endpoints and the call gatekeeper support FastStart. This portion of the discussion will be based on the Avaya implementation of FastStart.

```
192.168.16.23    192.168.16.1     H.225.0    RAS: registrationRequest
192.168.16.1     192.168.16.23    H.225.0    RAS: registrationConfirm
192.168.16.23    192.168.16.1     H.225.0    CS: setup OpenLogicalChannel
192.168.16.1     192.168.16.23    H.225.0    CS: callProceeding
192.168.16.1     192.168.16.23    H.225.0    CS: connect OpenLogicalChannel
192.168.16.1     192.168.16.23    H.225.0    CS: empty
192.168.16.1     192.168.16.23    H.225.0    CS: empty
192.168.16.1     192.168.16.23    H.225.0    CS: empty
192.168.16.1     192.168.16.23    H.225.0    CS: empty CS: empty CS: empty
192.168.16.1     192.168.16.23    H.225.0    CS: empty
192.168.16.23    192.168.16.1     H.225.0    CS: empty
192.168.16.1     192.168.16.23    H.225.0    CS: empty
192.168.16.23    192.168.16.1     H.225.0    CS: empty
192.168.16.1     192.168.16.23    H.225.0    CS: empty
192.168.16.1     192.168.16.23    H.225.0    CS: empty
192.168.16.1     192.168.16.23    H.225.0    CS: facility OpenLogicalChannel
192.168.16.4     192.168.16.23    RTP        PT=ITU-T G.711 PCMU, SSRC=0xF5952C7C,
192.168.16.4     192.168.16.23    RTP        PT=ITU-T G.711 PCMU, SSRC=0xF5952C7C,
```

Figure 6-25. Avaya Fast start packet list

The sequence of packets shown in Figure 6-25 demonstrates how the connection can differ using the Fast Connect procedure. With this configuration, the OpenLogical-Channel method from H.245 is utilized when the initiator advertises the modes preferred for transmit and receive. Recalling Figure 6-24, there are 36 options within the packet. Opening some of the subtrees, the desired settings (Figure 6-26) for the connection can be found.

```
⊞ Item 23
⊞ Item 24
⊟ Item 25
   FastStart item: 30 octets
   ⊟ OpenLogicalChannel
      forwardLogicalChannelNumber: 26
      ⊟ forwardLogicalChannelParameters
         ⊞ dataType: nullData (1)
         ⊞ multiplexParameters: none (4)
      ⊟ reverseLogicalChannelParameters
         ⊟ dataType: audioData (3)
            ⊟ audioData: g711Ulaw64k (3)
               g711Ulaw64k: 60
         ⊟ multiplexParameters: h2250LogicalChannelParameters (2)
            ⊟ h2250LogicalChannelParameters
               sessionID: 1
               ⊟ mediaChannel: unicastAddress (0)
                  ⊟ unicastAddress: iPAddress (0)
                     ⊟ iPAddress
                        network: 192.168.16.23 (192.168.16.23)
                        tsapIdentifier: 2742
                     0... .... mediaGuaranteedDelivery: False
               ⊟ mediaControlChannel: unicastAddress (0)
                  ⊟ unicastAddress: iPAddress (0)
                     ⊟ iPAddress
                        network: 192.168.16.23 (192.168.16.23)
                        tsapIdentifier: 2743
                     0... .... mediaControlGuaranteedDelivery: False
                     .1.. .... silenceSuppression: True
⊟ Item 26

Ethernet II, Src: GiantEle_05:cb:11 (00:09:6e:05:cb:11), Dst: Avaya_ef:48:f8 (00:04
Internet Protocol Version 4, Src: 192.168.16.23 (192.168.16.23), Dst: 192.168.16.4
User Datagram Protocol, Src Port: tsb2 (2742) Dst Port: clearvisn (2052)
Real-Time Transport Protocol
```

Figure 6-26. Faststart items

In this case, the logical channel values identify the IP address and port to be used when sending traffic back to the source. Other items included in the FastStart packet are the H.235 (security) options and the codec information. It should be noted that the other end of the connection may refuse the FastStart setup.

H.225 can also tunnel H.245 packets, a technique we'll see in use with Cisco topology in Chapter 7. The reason for tunneling one signaling protocol in another is to save time and resources and for firewall traversal, since the H.245 port changes from call to call. H.245 sessions are set up on another port beyond the H.225 connection. By tunneling this stream, an additional set of ports need not be used, and the connection can move forward with less delay and improved performance metrics.

For this to be used, the H.225 packets indicate support for the tunneling of the desired signaling protocols, and the other end must support the same. If tunneling is to be used, then the H.225 packets will set the H. 245 tunneling bit, or flag, to "1," meaning TRUE. There will also be conversation regarding the support of tunneled protocols, desired protocol, and which is to be used.

Other H.225 Messages

To recap the moderately complex connection we've traced through so far in this chapter, an H.323 endpoint has booted, obtained an IP address, and contacted a TFTP server followed by the call server or gatekeeper. When communicating with the call server, the phone uses H.225 RAS messages followed by H.225-Q.931 signaling. The phone also indicated its desire of a FastStart connection in the SETUP OpenLogicalChannel packet, numbered 576. Examining the exchange between the two nodes shows several other H.225 message types being utilized. Figure 6-25 provides the list, and though there are many messages of the same type (the CS: empty is actually a Q.931 INFORMATION message), others such as the CALL PROCEEDING, CONNECT, and FACILITY messages are also sent between the phone and the call server. These message types are shown in Figure 6-27.

CALL PROCEEDING (Type 2)
   The user or endpoint receives this message in order to indicate that the network has received enough information to allow the call to move forward.

CONNECT (Type 7)
   This message is sent to the caller from the call server and from the called party to the call server. It is used to indicate acceptance of the call by the called party. In this example, the call server 192.168.16.1 sends this message to the phone at 192.168.16.23 to indicate that the other end has accepted the call. This can be seen in the packets from Figure 6-25. The other end can be either the call server or gateway itself or another endpoint such as a phone.

FACILITY (Type 98)
   The facility message is defined in Q.932 and is used to request or acknowledge a "supplementary service." The service and its parameters are described in the facility message body. Opening the Facility OpenLogicalChannel message from the packet

```
⊟ Q.931
    Protocol discriminator: Q.931
    Call reference value length: 2
    Call reference flag: Message sent to originating side
    Call reference value: 0001
    Message type: CALL PROCEEDING (0x02)
  ⊞ User-user
⊞ H.225.0 CS
⊟ Q.931
    Protocol discriminator: Q.931
    Call reference value length: 2
    Call reference flag: Message sent to originating side
    Call reference value: 0001
    Message type: CONNECT (0x07)
  ⊞ User-user
⊞ H.225.0 CS
⊟ Q.931
    Protocol discriminator: Q.931
    Call reference value length: 2
    Call reference flag: Message sent to originating side
    Call reference value: 0001
    Message type: FACILITY (0x62)
  ⊞ User-user
⊞ H.225.0 CS
```

Figure 6-27. H.225 messages expanded

list (Figure 6-28), we can see that the codec, IP address, and port for the reverse channel has been determined. These values are used in the subsequent RTP packet.

```
631      192.168.16.1     192.168.16.23    H.225.0   CS: facility OpenLogicalChannel

⊞ Frame 631: 151 bytes on wire (1208 bits), 151 bytes captured (1208 bits)
              ⊟ reverseLogicalChannelParameters
                ⊟ dataType: audioData (3)
                  ⊟ audioData: g711Ulaw64k (3) ⇐
                    g711Ulaw64k: 20
                ⊟ multiplexParameters: h2250LogicalChannelParameters (2)
                  ⊟ h2250LogicalChannelParameters
                    sessionID: 1
                    ⊟ mediaChannel: unicastAddress (0)
                      ⊟ unicastAddress: iPAddress (0)
                        ⊟ iPAddress
                          network: 192.168.16.4 (192.168.16.4)
                          tsapIdentifier: 2052 ⇐
                    ⊞ mediaControlChannel: unicastAddress (0)
                    0... .... silenceSuppression: False

 Internet Protocol Version 4, Src: 192.168.16.4 (192.168.16.4), Dst: 192.168.16.23
 User Datagram Protocol, Src Port: clearvisn (2052), Dst Port: tsb2 (2742)
 Real-Time Transport Protocol
```

Figure 6-28. FACILITY message

Lastly, there are a whole bunch of "empty" packets in the list from Figure 6-25. Opening one of these, we can see that they are actually INFORMATION messages that point to Avaya-specific parameters via the ASN values. An example is shown in Figure 6-29.

```
Internet Protocol Version 4, Src: 192.168.16.1 (192.168.16.1), Dst: 192.168.16.23 (192.168.16.23)
Transmission Control Protocol, Src Port: h323hostcall (1720), Dst Port: 4296 (4296), Seq: 269, Ac
TPKT, Version: 3, Length: 56
Q.931
  Protocol discriminator: Q.931
  Call reference value length: 2
  Call reference flag: Message sent to originating side
  Call reference value: 0001
  Message type: INFORMATION (0x7b)          <=
⊕ User-user
H.225.0 CS
⊟ H323-UserInformation
  ⊟ h323-uu-pdu
    ⊟ h323-message-body: empty (8)
        empty: NULL
      0... .... h245Tunnelling: False
    ⊟ nonStandardControl: 1 item
      ⊟ Item 0
        ⊟ NonStandardParameter
          ⊟ nonStandardIdentifier: object (0)
              object: 2.16.840.1.113778.4.2.10 (joint-iso-itu-t.16.840.1.113778.4.2.10)
              data: 20 octets
            ⊟ Data (20 bytes)
              Data: 14381120abe31b5b003b00481b5b024ba3830442
              [Length: 20]
```

Figure 6-29. INFORMATION message with Avaya-specifics

 It is important to understand that this is an Avaya-specific topology and that operation here may differ from your implementation.

H.245

With all of this discussion regarding H.225, it is easy to forget that in many topologies, H.225 is only half of the story. While H.225 will be used to register endpoints and set up calls, H.245 is used to describe what can be used for the media and what will be used. From the H.245 recommendation:

> The messages cover receiving and transmitting capabilities as well as mode preference from the receiving end, logical channel signaling and control & indication.

In 2011, version 16 of the recommendation was published, which included several changes regarding the use of dynamic payload types. H.245 provides for the following general services:

Master-slave determination

Many endpoints have the ability to act as both a master or slave. That is, either one can act as the media controller or gatekeeper when setting up a bidirectional connection. In this case, the capabilities of each are compared and a master selected for the call.

Capability exchange

In order to ensure that only those codecs or configurations understood by both sides of the conversation are selected, the capabilities of the endpoints are communicated. This is accomplished via the capability set. The process differentiates between receive and transmit directions. A number of these are considered standard capabilities. Nonstandard values, typically those of a vendor like Avaya, will use the NonStandardParameter structure.

Logical channel signaling

Using the OpenLogicalChannel messages (OLC, OLC ACK, and CLC), H.245 establishes the parameters to be used when encoding and decoding data. Once again, the transmit and receive data flows are separate, so setting up a connection does not necessarily mean that it is automatically configured for the opposite direction. Closing the logical channel occurs from the transmitter side, although it can accept receiver requests for closure.

Audiovisual and data-mode request

Once the capabilities are known and the desired encoding selected, the endpoints signal their desire through this method.

Although H.245 offers other services (e.g., control and indication) as well, the ones in the preceding list might be considered the main components of the protocol. We have seen that during the FastStart or tunneling operations, these methods are used though wrapped in H.225. Figure 6-30 depicts a collection of H.245 messages from the Polycom topology seen earlier in this chapter.

```
25    10.210.200.112    10.210.200.111    H.245    terminalCapabilitySet
27    10.210.200.112    10.210.200.111    H.245    masterSlaveDetermination
31    10.210.200.111    10.210.200.112    H.245    terminalCapabilitySet
33    10.210.200.111    10.210.200.112    H.245    masterSlaveDetermination
38    10.210.200.112    10.210.200.111    H.245    terminalCapabilitySetAck
39    10.210.200.112    10.210.200.111    H.245    masterSlaveDeterminationAck
41    10.210.200.111    10.210.200.112    H.245    terminalCapabilitySetAck
42    10.210.200.111    10.210.200.112    H.245    masterSlaveDeterminationAck
44    10.210.200.112    10.210.200.111    H.245    openLogicalChannel (generic)
46    10.210.200.112    10.210.200.111    H.245    openLogicalChannel (genericVideoCapability)
48    10.210.200.111    10.210.200.112    H.245    openLogicalChannel (generic)
51    10.210.200.112    10.210.200.111    H.245    openLogicalChannelAck
```

Figure 6-30. H.245 messages

A packet-flow diagram (the continuation of the flow seen in Figure 6-5) is shown in Figure 6-31.

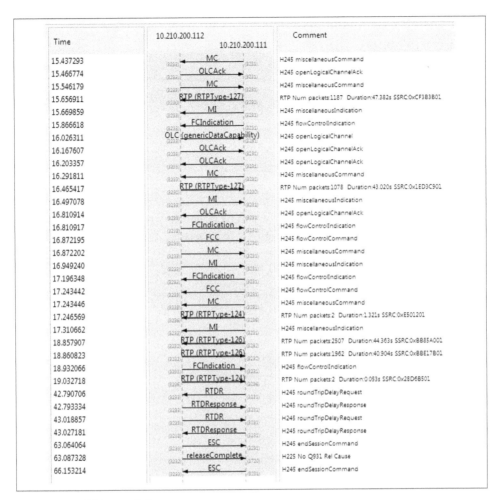

Time	10.210.200.112 10.210.200.111	Comment
15.437293	MC	H245 miscellaneousCommand
15.466774	OLCAck	H245 openLogicalChannelAck
15.546179	MC	H245 miscellaneousCommand
15.656911	RTP (RTPType-127)	RTP Num packets:1187 Duration:47.382s SSRC:0xCF3B3B01
15.669859	MI	H245 miscellaneousIndication
15.866618	FCIndication	H245 flowControlIndication
16.026311	OLC (genericDataCapability)	H245 openLogicalChannel
16.167607	OLCAck	H245 openLogicalChannelAck
16.203357	OLCAck	H245 openLogicalChannelAck
16.291811	MC	H245 miscellaneousCommand
16.465417	RTP (RTPType-127)	RTP Num packets:1078 Duration:43.020s SSRC:0x1ED3C901
16.497078	MI	H245 miscellaneousIndication
16.810914	OLCAck	H245 openLogicalChannelAck
16.810917	FCIndication	H245 flowControlIndication
16.872195	FCC	H245 flowControlCommand
16.872202	MC	H245 miscellaneousCommand
16.949240	MI	H245 miscellaneousIndication
17.196348	FCIndication	H245 flowControlIndication
17.243442	FCC	H245 flowControlCommand
17.243446	MC	H245 miscellaneousCommand
17.246569	RTP (RTPType-124)	RTP Num packets:2 Duration:1.321s SSRC:0xE501201
17.310662	MI	H245 miscellaneousIndication
18.857907	RTP (RTPType-126)	RTP Num packets:2507 Duration:44.363s SSRC:0xBB85A001
18.860823	RTP (RTPType-126)	RTP Num packets:1962 Duration:40.904s SSRC:0xBBE17B01
18.932066	FCIndication	H245 flowControlIndication
19.032718	RTP (RTPType-124)	RTP Num packets:2 Duration:0.053s SSRC:0x28D6B501
42.790706	RTDR	H245 roundTripDelayRequest
42.793334	RTDResponse	H245 roundTripDelayResponse
43.018857	RTDR	H245 roundTripDelayRequest
43.027181	RTDResponse	H245 roundTripDelayResponse
63.064064	ESC	H245 endSessionCommand
63.087328	releaseComplete	H225 No Q931 Rel Cause
66.153214	ESC	H245 endSessionCommand

Figure 6-31. H.245 call flow

As we can see from this list, the master-slave determination flows between the two endpoints, which eventually acknowledge the decision with the MasterSlaveSetAck message. This process begins with the terminalCapabilitySet message. An example of this message is shown in Figure 6-32. We can also see that TCP is used at the transport layer.

```
Transmission Control Protocol, Src Port: whisker (3233), Dst Port: vidigo
TPKT, Version: 3, Length: 1086
H.245
⊟ PDU Type: request (0)
  ⊟ request: terminalCapabilitySet (2)
    ⊟ terminalCapabilitySet
       sequenceNumber: 1
       protocolIdentifier: 0.0.8.245.0.7 (h245 version 7)
     ⊞ multiplexCapability: h2250Capability (4)
     ⊞ capabilityTable: 45 items
     ⊞ capabilityDescriptors: 1 item
```

Figure 6-32. H.245 terminal capability set message

The terminalCapabilitiesSet message is quite large. Figure 6-32 shows that the capability table has 45 items. Thankfully, this table can be boiled down into a single value. The endpoint values are shown in Figure 6-33 for comparison.

```
Internet Protocol Version 4, Src: 10.210.200.112 (10.210.200.112), Dst: 10.210.200.111
Transmission Control Protocol, Src Port: whisker (3233), Dst Port: vidigo (3231), Seq:
TPKT, Version: 3, Length: 11
H.245
⊟ PDU Type: request (0)
  ⊟ request: masterSlaveDetermination (1)
    ⊟ masterSlaveDetermination
       terminalType  50
       statusDeterminationNumber: 1151465
Internet Protocol Version 4, Src: 10.210.200.111 (10.210.200.111), Dst: 10.210.200.112
Transmission Control Protocol, Src Port: vidigo (3231), Dst Port: whisker (3233), Seq:
TPKT, Version: 3, Length: 11
H.245
⊟ PDU Type: request (0)
  ⊟ request: masterSlaveDetermination (1)
    ⊟ masterSlaveDetermination
       terminalType: 50
       statusDeterminationNumber: 10199967
```

Figure 6-33. H.245 master-slave determination message

The circled values are actually used for the final decision. The terminal type is simply a value between 0 and 255, which depends on the unit. The statusDeterminationNumber is a random number in the range of 0 to (224-1). The larger terminal type value will be the master. If these are the same, as in Figure 6-33, the statusDeterminationNumber is compared using modulo arithmetic. Lastly, we come to the messages acknowledging this decision. Figure 6-34 depicts the final results.

```
Internet Protocol Version 4, Src: 10.210.200.112 (10.210.200.112), Dst: 10.210.200.111
Transmission Control Protocol, Src Port: whisker (3233), Dst Port: vidigo (3231), Seq:
TPKT, Version: 3, Length: 6
H.245
⊟ PDU Type: response (1)
  ⊟ response: masterSlaveDeterminationAck (1)
    ⊟ masterSlaveDeterminationAck
      ⊟ decision: master (0)        ⇦
          master: NULL
Internet Protocol Version 4, Src: 10.210.200.111 (10.210.200.111), Dst: 10.210.200.112
Transmission Control Protocol, Src Port: vidigo (3231), Dst Port: whisker (3233), Seq:
TPKT, Version: 3, Length: 6
H.245
⊟ PDU Type: response (1)
  ⊟ response: masterSlaveDeterminationAck (1)
    ⊟ masterSlaveDeterminationAck
      ⊟ decision: slave (1)        ⇦
          slave: NULL
```

Figure 6-34. H.245 master-slave determination ACK

The endpoint with IP address of 10.210.200.112 became the master. Once this has been completed, the parameters for the session itself are negotiated via the OpenLogical-Channel and OpenLogicalChannelAck messages. An example is shown in Figure 6-35.

```
Internet Protocol Version 4, Src: 10.210.200.112 (10.210.200.112), Dst: 10.210.200.111
Transmission Control Protocol, Src Port: whisker (3233), Dst Port: vidigo (3231), Seq:
TPKT, Version: 3, Length: 62
H.245
⊟ PDU Type: request (0)
  ⊟ request: openLogicalChannel (3)
    ⊟ openLogicalChannel
        forwardLogicalChannelNumber: 2
      ⊟ forwardLogicalChannelParameters
        ⊞ dataType: h235Media (7)
        ⊟ multiplexParameters: h2250LogicalChannelParameters (3)
          ⊟ h2250LogicalChannelParameters
              sessionID: 1
            ⊟ mediaControlChannel: unicastAddress (0)
              ⊟ unicastAddress: iPAddress (0)
                ⊟ iPAddress
                    network: 10.210.200.112 (10.210.200.112)
                    tsapIdentifier: 3231                        ⇦
              dynamicRTPPayloadType: 127
```

Figure 6-35. H.245 Open logical channel message

This packet provides some indication of the parameters necessary for the two endpoints to understand each other. With the dynamic payload types, the clients are likely using proprietary or nonstandard codecs. As a reminder, these H.245 packets become fields when using the H.225 FastStart as was seen in Figure 6-26 and Figure 6-28.

Big Picture Reminder

So, let's step back for a moment here, as we have gone through quite a number of packets and a lot of fields. In order to understand what is happening, we do not really need to understand the minutia we've seen here. The phones and the call server go through a number of important steps that are points of interest.

- DHCP
- TFTP
- Gatekeeper discovery and registration via H.225 RAS
- Establishing a connection to the other endpoint via H.225
- Negotiating the communication parameters for the call or session via H.245 or H.245 tunneling
- Transmission of voice data via RTP
- Tracking the performance of the voice data via RTCP
- Termination of the media session via H.245
- Termination of the connection via H.225

If you followed the first five steps and can hang in there for the second half, you are in good shape, especially since we've been going over two topologies to get through all of the messages. Understanding the fields and individual messages will greatly speed up your troubleshooting and in-depth knowledge of the protocol.

Voice Data

Now that we understand much of the call setup and signaling necessary along with the message used in a topology like this, how does the rest work? In order to understand the entirety of the call, there are a couple of other details that we need to be aware of. First, the behavior of RTP in this topology is quite different from the behavior seen in some of the other topologies. For example, in the Skinny topology, the call server sends a message to the VoIP phone indicating what tone is to be played. So, when the user hears dial tone or ringing, it is coming from the phone. In another example, the SIP topologies used RTP only for user voice data, meaning speech.

In this topology, all of the sounds are generated via the RTP stream. In the conversation snippet seen in Figure 6-25, we can see the first RTP packets at the bottom. The IP addresses used indicate that these packets came from one of the call-server addresses and not the other phone. Filtering the Wireshark output for RTP, we can see even more evidence of this. It turns out that on the Avaya, dial tone, ringing, and even dead air when dialing are all sent via RTP packets. If you use the Wireshark player on the capture files from the book website, you can actually hear the tones. This, and the fact that Avaya uses nonstandard items, makes it a little harder to determine the called number via packet captures. Fortunately, the Avaya does use standardized RTCP traffic in order to provide feedback for the call.

Termination

The last part of any phone call is hanging up. The easiest way to understand how the process works is by looking at the Polycom capture and the H.245 messages that start the process. At the beginning of a call, the call manager and possibly the other endpoint are contacted, and then the media session must be set up. These operations occur via the H.225 and H.245 messages. Upon termination, the session must be closed via H.245 and then the call termination finalized by H.225. This short list of packets is shown in Figure 6-36.

```
6946   10.210.200.112   10.210.200.111   H.245     endSessionCommand
6950   10.210.200.112   10.210.200.111   H.225.0   CS: releaseComplete
6978   10.210.200.111   10.210.200.112   H.245     endSessionCommand
```

Figure 6-36. End-of-call packets

The end session message is very straight-forward, informing the opposite end that it is time to disconnect (Figure 6-37).

```
Internet Protocol Version 4, Src: 10.210.200.112 (10.210.200.112)
Transmission Control Protocol, Src Port: whisker (3233), Dst Port
TPKT, Version: 3, Length: 6
H.245
⊟ PDU Type: command (2)
  ⊟ command: endSessionCommand (5)
    ⊟ endSessionCommand: disconnect (1)
        disconnect: NULL
```

Figure 6-37. H.245 End Session message

The message is an example of a command type. It is followed by an H.225 release complete message shown in Figure 6-38.

```
Internet Protocol Version 4, Src: 10.210.200.112 (10.210.200.112)
Transmission Control Protocol, Src Port: mdtp (3232), Dst Port: h
TPKT, Version: 3, Length: 51
Q.931
  Protocol discriminator: Q.931
  Call reference value length: 2
  Call reference flag: Message sent from originating side
  Call reference value: 689f
  Message type: RELEASE COMPLETE (0x5a)
⊕ User-user
H.225.0 CS
⊟ H323-UserInformation
  ⊟ h323-uu-pdu
    ⊟ h323-message-body: releaseComplete (5)
      ⊟ releaseComplete
          protocolIdentifier: 0.0.8.2250.0.4 (Version 4)
        ⊟ reason: undefinedReason (11)
            undefinedReason: NULL
        ⊟ callIdentifier
            guid: 02285a75-300d-9010-1114-e3e0995e3f0d
        ⊟ presentationIndicator: presentationAllowed (0)
            presentationAllowed: NULL
          screeningIndicator: userProvidedVerifiedAndFailed (2)
        0... .... h245Tunnelling: False
```

Figure 6-38. H.225 Release Complete message

If we compare the Call-ID from the messages used earlier in the same conversation (a portion of the ALERTING message from Figure 6-8 has been expanded in Figure 6-39), we can see that the values are the same. This specifies the connection to be torn down.

```
Internet Protocol Version 4, Src: 10.210.200.111 (10.210.200.111)
Transmission Control Protocol, Src Port: h323hostcall (1720), Dst
TPKT, Version: 3, Length: 103
Q.931
H.225.0 CS
⊟ H323-UserInformation
  ⊟ h323-uu-pdu
    ⊟ h323-message-body: alerting (3)
      ⊟ alerting
          protocolIdentifier: 0.0.8.2250.0.4 (Version 4)
        ⊕ destinationInfo
        ⊟ callIdentifier
            guid: 02285a75-300d-9010-1114-e3e0995e3f0d
        0... .... multipleCalls: False
        1... .... maintainConnection: True
        ⊕ presentationIndicator: presentationAllowed (0)
          screeningIndicator: userProvidedVerifiedAndFailed (2)
        0... .... h245Tunnelling: False
```

Figure 6-39. H.225 ALERT message expanded

If we look at the same process from the Avaya topology, we see that not only are the H.245 messages missing, but the H.225 messages used to tunnel the H.245 fields are a little cryptic. The approach uses the same type of Avaya-specific message seen earlier in the chapter. Examples of this approach are depicted in Figure 6-40.

```
H.225.0 CS                                    H.225.0 CS
  H323-UserInformation                          H323-UserInformation
    h323-uu-pdu                                   h323-uu-pdu
      h323-message-body: facility (6)               h323-message-body: empty (8)
        facility                                      empty: NULL
          protocolIdentifier: 0.0.8.2250.0.2 (Version 2)   0... .... h245Tunnelling: False
          reason: undefinedReason (3)               nonStandardControl: 1 item
          callIdentifier                              Item 0
          fastStart: 2 items                            NonStandardParameter
            Item 0                                        nonStandardIdentifier: object (0)
              FastStart item: 7 octets                      object: 2.16.840.1.113778.4.2.10 (joint-iso-itu-t.16.840.1.113778.4.2.10)
              OpenLogicalChannel                          data: 7 octets
                forwardLogicalChannelNumber: 8          Data (7 bytes)
                forwardLogicalChannelParameters           Data: 07381120a28006
                  dataType: nullData (1)                  [Length: 7]
                    nullData: NULL
                  multiplexParameters: none (4)
                    none: NULL
            Item 1
```

Figure 6-40. Avaya termination

Clearly the approaches used by the two systems are different, yet both are valid. Both also have vendorspecific components that must be negotiated during the connection process.

Summary

The H.323 protocol suite is a part of the ITU-T series of recommendations. It is a protocol suite that contains a series of protocols used to set up and tear down connections, negotiate communication parameters, and start and stop media sessions. It falls into the category of signaling protocol and dates from a time when it had little or no competition, becoming the de facto standard for VoIP transmissions. Since that time, both SIP and Skinny carved out market share, with SIP becoming dominant.

As a signaling protocol, H.323 is quite complex, providing messages and fields for every conceivable eventuality. It is supported by a number of other recommendations from the ITU-T, all of them equally complex. This chapter provides the background and operational details for the protocols from the viewpoint of an actual VoIP network. The data captured on the network provides the basis for discussion. Because of the variation in the behavior of H.323, two topologies are explored to provide the reader with a strong understanding of the concepts and performance.

Standards and Reading

ITU-T (http://bit.ly/XnqmrO)
    Recommendations

ITU-T G series (G.701, 703, 711) (http://bit.ly/12JvNsa)
    Recommendations, includes audio codecs

TU-T H series (http://bit.ly/UF1CP3)
> Recommendations, includes H.323, H.225, H.245, and video codecs

TU-T Rec. Q.931 (http://bit.ly/ZezTnq)
> ISDN user-network interface layer 3 specification for basic call control

ITU-T Rec. Q.932 Digital (http://bit.ly/15tfkrM)
> Subscriber Signalling System No. 1— Generic procedures for the control of ISDN supplementary services

ITU-T Rec. X.660 (http://bit.ly/Y7HEe1)
> Information Technology—Procedures for the operation of object identifier registration authorities: General procedures and top arcs of the international object identifier tree

OID Repository
> http://oid-info.com/index.htm

Review Questions

1. What two H.323 subprotocols does this chapter cover?

2. On what two vendors are the topologies in this chapter based?

3. What H.225 type of messages is used when a phone first contacts the call server?

4. What two ports are used by H.225?

5. H.225 uses what recommendation as the basis for its signaling?

6. What is the primary purpose of H245?

7. True or false: all H.323 topologies will deploy H.225 and H.245.

8. What word best describes the purpose of H.235?

9. What H.245 message can be converted to an H.225 field and is also used to select the parameters for a session?

10. True or false: the H.323 suite does not make use of RTP or RTCP.

Review Question Answers

1. H.225 and H.245.

2. Polycom and Avaya.

3. RAS—registration, admission, and status.

4. 1719 and 1720.

5. Q.931.

6. H.245 is the "Control protocol for multimedia communications" and handles capabilities exchange between H.323 endpoints and the configuration of the logical channels between them.

7. False.

8. Security.

9. Open Logical Channel.

10. False.

Lab Activities

This chapter is supported by the book website. So, if the activity lists equipment or software that you do not have, go to the book website for additional content.

Activity 1—Build the Topology Shown

The goal for this topology is to have a couple of VoIP nodes running H.323 (Figure 6-41). Other components include DHCP, TFTP, and a switch. The topology in this chapter utilized an Avaya call server, but this can be replaced with an Asterisk box, as in previous chapters. The topology also has a pair of Avaya VoIP phones. The VoIP endpoints do not have to be desktop phones. They can be softphones. For example, in the smaller topology used in this chapter, Polycom clients were deployed. The TFTP server is only necessary if you wish to support desktop phones or complete the topology.

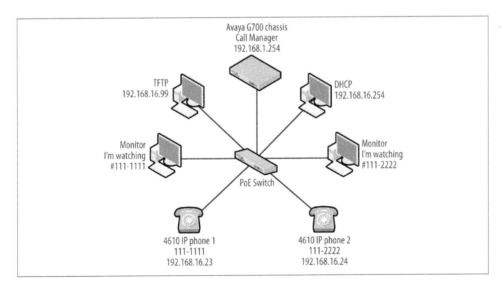

Figure 6-41. Activity 1—Topology

Materials: call server, H.323 endpoints, switch, server nodes

1. Connect all of the nodes to a switch and add a DHCP server. A home gateway can serve as the switch and the DHCP server; however, power over Ethernet (PoE) may be an issue depending on the type of phones used.

2. Configure the call server.

3. Test the phones by making a call.

Activity 2—Capture Setup

The goal of this activity is to understand how H.323 and the phones operate. To this end, at least one capture machine will be required. Depending on the type of VoIP endpoint, the capture may be accomplished on the same node. A mirrored port may also be configured on the switch. Note that the capture files are available on the book website.

Materials: Activity 1 topology, Wireshark

Prepare the nodes for capture. In the following activities, you will be capturing traffic from the phones as they start up, call each other, and then terminate the call.

Activity 3—Packet Capture Analysis

Materials: Activity 1 topology, Wireshark

1. What happens when the phone is powered up?

2. What packets are exchanged, and what protocols are used?

3. Are your DHCP and TFTP services accessed?

4. Are there any other services requested by the phone that are not on the network? Example: NTP

5. Which of the ITU-T recommendations are a part of the exchanges thus far?

Activity 4—Phone-Call Analysis

Materials: Activity 1 topology, Wireshark

1. Start a capture and make a phone call between your endpoints.

2. What H.323 (and H.225 or H.245) messages are involved, and what is the order of operations?

3. What mode of operation has been configured? FastStart? Tunneling?

4. Open the messages pertaining to the logical channel. Analyze the fields. Pay special attention to the final parameters selected.

5. Can you find the response to this packet? Can you identify the codecs, ports, and IP addresses selected?

Activity 5—H.245

Materials: Activity 1 topology, Wireshark

1. Locate the H.245 components in the capture. Note that you may have a tunneled or FastStart configuration, so you might be looking for message types rather than H.245.

2. What are the messages used?

3. Can you follow the terminal capability exchange and the master-slave determination?

4. What happens when the phone is hung up?

CHAPTER 7

Skinny Client Control Protocol

The Skinny Client Control Protocol (SCCP), or Skinny, is a Cisco proprietary signaling protocol for VoIP devices. As a signaling protocol, it is used for registration of endpoints; call messages such as off-hook, on-hook, addressing (dial numbers); and controlling phone display. As the name suggests it is a lightweight protocol and, if you have the right dissector, is straightforward to read and understand. When combined with the light weight Cisco call manger called Call Manager Express (CME), small VoIP deployments supporting a number of features and phones can be set up quickly.

Unlike most of the protocols we study in the Packet Guide series, the Skinny Client Control Protocol (SCCP) is proprietary. So the protocol documentation is not as easy to come by as that for signaling protocols such as H.323 or the Session Initiation Protocol. The massive Cisco website and the complexity of the Cisco IOS can lead to some difficulties in trying to understand even basic operation. It is included in this book because of the large number of installed devices using SCCP and the popularity of Cisco as a platform. To quote from a recent VoIP conference:

> Millions of installed Cisco phones would argue for the continued use of Skinny as a protocol.

Like most VoIP signaling protocols, SCCP has a clearly defined set of messages and behaviors that can be observed and repeated. However, SCCP also implements several methods that are nonstandard. This means that if you are familiar with the operation of both the Session Initialization Protocol (SIP) and H.323 and hope to apply the same knowledge to SCCP, you may be in for some surprises. In order to understand the similarities and differences between these protocols, this chapter will go through the stages of a call (registration, call setup, termination, dial-peer selection, etc.) and explain the steps as we go. The chapter will also examine a scenario in which multiple call servers are deployed.

Protocol Description

Toward the end of 1998, Cisco acquired a company called Selsius, a leading supplier of IP telephony products, and the SCCP story begins there. In fact, several file and product names used in association with Cisco VoIP begin with "SEP," for Selsius Ethernet Phone. As we have said, SCCP (Skinny for short) is a signaling protocol. This means that it has messages used by phones for registering with a call server, establishing a call, teardown of the call, features, interface configuration, and many others. Like other signaling protocols, SCCP is encapsulated in transmission control protocol (TCP) packets. Recall that TCP operates at layer 4 of both the TCP/IP and Open Systems Interconnection networking models.

As a signaling protocol, SCCP is not used to convey voice data and so, like most VoIP architectures, it uses the Real-Time Transport Protocol (RTP) for this purpose. This means that phones register, receive interface information, and make calls using the Skinny protocol and messages, but as soon as voice data is to be transferred from one endpoint to another, RTP is used. Once RTP is in the game, the layer-4 protocol shifts to the user datagram protocol, or UDP.

Structure

SCCP messages are very easy to read, and the names are highly descriptive. It is designed to be used with a call server and communicates on transmission control protocol (TCP) port 2000. An example of a Skinny message is shown in Figure 7-1.

```
Ethernet II, Src: Cisco_61:5f:16 (00:13:c4:61:5f:16), Dst: Cisco_f4:c2:10 (00:1c:58:f4:c2:10)
Internet Protocol Version 4, Src: 192.168.1.2 (192.168.1.2), Dst: 192.168.1.254 (192.168.1.254)
Transmission Control Protocol, Src Port: 50201 (50201), Dst Port: cisco-sccp (2000), Seq: 209,
Skinny Client Control Protocol
   Data length: 56
   Header version: Basic (0x00000000)
   Message ID: RegisterMessage (0x00000001)
   Device name: SEP0013C4615F16
   Station user ID: 0
   Station instance: 1
   IP address: 192.168.1.2 (192.168.1.2)
   Device type: TelecasterMgr (7)
   Max streams: 0

   00 1c 58 f4 c2 10 00 13  c4 61 5f 16 08 00 45 68    ..X..... .a_...Eh
   00 68 04 07 00 00 40 06  f1 d0 c0 a8 01 02 c0 a8    .h....@. ........
   01 fe c4 19 07 d0 40 0e  6e 47 d2 32 5f 70 50 18    ......@. nG.2_pP.
   05 78 88 2b 00 00 38 00  00 00 00 00 00 00 01 00    .x.+..8. ........
   00 00 53 45 50 30 30 31  33 43 34 36 31 35 46 31    ..SEP001 3C4615F1
   36 00 00 00 00 00 01 00  00 00 c0 a8 01 02 07 00    6....... ........
   00 00 00 00 00 00 00 00  00 00 06 00 00 84 00 00    ........ ........
   00 00 00 00 00 00                                   ......
```

Figure 7-1. Skinny registration message

Basic Header Format

Skinny messages begin with the same set of fields but then vary as the Message ID provides an indication of the type of message.

Data length
 4 bytes, this is the amount of information carried in the packet beyond the header-version field.

Header version
 4 bytes, provides the version of the Skinny header. The default value for this field is 0x00000000, meaning basic.

Message ID
 6 bytes, this field provides the hexadecimal value for the type of SCCP packet.

The various packets vary quite a bit in size and purpose. Therefore, after these fields, the header becomes type-specific.

Topology Construction

We'll start off with the basic topology shown in Figure 7-2. While the point of this chapter is not to explain the configuration line by line, some measure of understanding is helpful as we work through this example. At the center of the topology is a Cisco 3550 switch. The 2811 and the monitor machines were connected and given their configurations prior to the phones being plugged in.

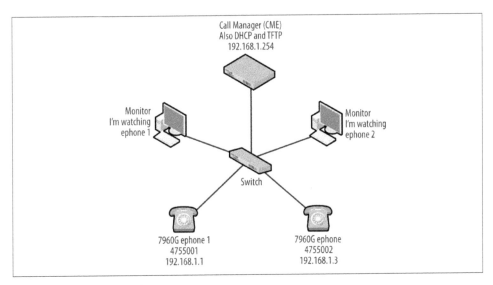

Figure 7-2. Skinny topology

The monitor machines have also been included in the topology in order to observe the traffic generated as we work through the construction of the topology. As can be seen, each of the VoIP endpoints, or *ephones* in Cisco-speak, has its own monitor machine to ensure that all events and messages can be captured.

The router is a Cisco 2811, running version 12.4(3) of IOS and version 3.3 of Call Manager Express. The router will be configured as not only the call server but also the DHCP server. The DHCP configuration on the router is very straightforward in this topology, requiring only the network, gateway, and TFTP server via option 150. Technically, we could probably get away without the default gateway since we are not going off of the network. The 192.168.1.254 address was excluded from the pool in order to prevent it from being assigned to network nodes or phones.

Note that the location of the call server is not part of the DHCP configuration. The call server address is actually read from the files downloaded from the TFTP server. Here is an example of the command used to run the TFTP server on the router.

```
tftp-server P00307020400.bin
```

The file (*P00307020400.bin*) is stored on the router flash card.

Since some of the files we're about to talk about are automatically generated, it is best to use the CME router as the TFTP server accessed by the phones. Like most VoIP phones, Cisco phones have a protocol boot mechanism that ensures they have the latest configuration and firmware. As the phones boot, this mechanism reads files in order to determine what signaling protocol and configuration to load. The TFTP server provides the configuration files for the phone. There are actually seven files (many of them created automatically) in the Cisco hunt algorithm used by the Universal Application Loader that might be touched for this process, though not by a single phone. For example, a single phone would not use different signaling protocols at the same time.

Many of the files are named for the MAC addresses of the phones configured on the call server. From Cisco, these include:

CTLSEP MAC File (ex. CTLSEP0013c4615f16.tlv)
 Optional certificate trust list: supplies a list of trusted servers and certificates.

SEP MAC File (ex. SEP0013c4615f16.cnf.xml)
 Upon reset, tells the phone which image to run when running SCCP (or SIP) along with other important phone configuration items.

MGCP MAC File
 For example, MGC0013c4615f16.cnf—Used when running MGCP.

XML Default File
 For example, *XMLDefault.cnf.xml*.

SIP Default File
 For example, *SIPDefault.cnf*.

MGCP Default File
 For example, *MGCDefault.cnf*.

Older versions may use the *SEPDEFAULT.cnf* file instead of XMLDefault.cnf.xml for the Skinny system information. This file is automatically generated.

After doing a little filtering with Wireshark, we can see in Figure 7-3 a list of files actually requested by the phone. This was obtained after a factory reset of the phone. Remember that the phone may already have some of the files necessary for operation.

```
TFTP    Read Request, File: CTLSEP0013C4615F16.tlv, Transfer type: octet
TFTP    Read Request, File: SEP0013C4615F16.cnf.xml, Transfer type: octet
TFTP    Read Request, File: CTLSEP0013C4615F16.tlv, Transfer type: octet
TFTP    Read Request, File: SEP0013C4615F16.cnf.xml, Transfer type: octet
TFTP    Read Request, File: English_United_States/7960-font.xml, Transfer type: octet
TFTP    Read Request, File: English_United_States/SCCP-dictionary.xml, Transfer type: octet
TFTP    Read Request, File: English_United_States/7960-dictionary.xml, Transfer type: octet
TFTP    Read Request, File: English_United_States/7960-kate.xml, Transfer type: octet
TFTP    Read Request, File: United_States/7960-tones.xml, Transfer type: octet
TFTP    Read Request, File: SEP0013C4615F16.cnf.xml, Transfer type: octet
TFTP    Read Request, File: RINGLIST.XML, Transfer type: octet
TFTP    Read Request, File: DISTINCTIVERINGLIST.XML, Transfer type: octet
```

Figure 7-3. TFTP files

Once the configuration file has been retrieved, next up is a loads file. For example, a file such as term61.default.loads might be used. The loads file contains the application loader and the application image name. The application image files end with "sbn," as in the name *CVM41.2-0-2-26.sbn*.

Thus far, the configuration of the router has only allowed the VoIP phones or ephones to obtain an IP address and access the desired files via TFTP. The next step is to provide the configuration for the phones themselves. The basic VoIP phone configuration consists of two parts: configuring the telephony service and the ephone-specific commands. Working with the Cisco CME is a little different than the Avaya or AsteriskNOW used in other chapters because the commands are all on the router. So, we'll spend a little time on them here. The commands common in the telephony service section include:

```
telephony-service
max-ephones 10
max-dn 10
ip source-address 192.168.1.254 port 2000
system message Packets!
create cnf-files version-stamp 7960 Jun 12 2012 07:59:00
max-conferences 8 gain -6
transfer-system full-consult
```

These commands are not very numerous, but they are important. The ip source-address command not only informs the phones about the call server's IP address and port to be used but also becomes part of the information downloaded by the phones. The system message provides the text seen on the phone interface. This command can be a very simple troubleshooting tool to determine if the phones are reading the call-server configuration. The create command generates some of the other files accessed by the phones.

The ephone portion of the router configuration is required in order to inform the call server about the phone MAC address and assign the phone number. There are two parts to an ephone configuration; an example of the commands used is shown here:

```
ephone-dn 1 dual-line
number 4755001
ephone 1
mac-address 0013.C461.5F16
button 1:1
```

So, each phone gets a directory number (dn), and each is associated with a MAC address. The button command assigns the ephone dial number to a particular interface button on the 7960G phone. In the next section, we will work through the stages of protocol operation by observing all that happens as the phones start up and make calls.

Operational Stages

Generally, VoIP phones have a collection of identifiable stages and operations. Recall that monitor stations are capturing all of the traffic going to and from the VoIP phones. We will use the monitors to record all of the packets resulting from these stages and operations. The connections will proceed as follows:

1. VoIP phones receive DHCP-based addresses.
2. VoIP phones contact the TFTP server for updated files.
3. Phones register with the call server.
4. Phones contact the call server with the number of the destination.
5. Call server contacts the destination phone.
6. Call server informs both phones of the other end and forwards the parameters for the call.
7. Phones communicate directly.
8. One of the phones terminates the call.
9. Call server performs clean up operations.

Startup

As the phone is plugged in, the two conversations that take place first are DHCP and TFTP. The DHCP server also provides the IP address of the TFTP server via option 150. Commands on the router turn it into the TFTP server and point to the particular files necessary to support the phones. Figure 7-3 depicts the TFTP requests made by the phone as it picks up the configuration.

Once the phone is using the appropriate image file and has its configuration, it contacts the call server with a standard TCP three-way handshake. At this point, the phone is ready to begin the registration process. For those not familiar with TCP, all TCP connections begin with the same series of three packets called the handshake. These packets are shown in Figure 7-4. This is sometimes referred to as the SYN, SYN ACK, ACK exchange.

```
TCP     50752 > cisco-sccp [SYN] Seq=0 Win=1400 Len=0 MSS=1400
TCP     cisco-sccp > 50752 [SYN, ACK] Seq=0 Ack=1 Win=4128 Len=0 MSS=1400
TCP     50752 > cisco-sccp [ACK] Seq=1 Ack=1 Win=1400 Len=0
```

Figure 7-4. TCP handshake

Registration

The first Skinny messages appear as the phone begins the registration process. The first message is actually an alarm message addressing the last-known status of the phone. However, we will begin our examination with a Skinny packet called the RegisterMessage, as seen in Figure 7-5.

```
Ethernet II, Src: Cisco_61:5f:16 (00:13:c4:61:5f:16), Dst: Cisco_f4:c2:10 (00:1c:58:f4:c2:10)
Internet Protocol Version 4, Src: 192.168.1.1 (192.168.1.1), Dst: 192.168.1.254 (192.168.1.254)
Transmission Control Protocol, Src Port: 50752 (50752), Dst Port: cisco-sccp (2000), Seq: 209,
Skinny Client Control Protocol
  Data length: 56
  Header version: Basic (0x00000000)
  Message ID: RegisterMessage (0x00000001)
  Device name: SEP0013C4615F16
  Station user ID: 0
  Station instance: 1
  IP address: 192.168.1.1 (192.168.1.1)
  Device type: TelecasterMgr (7)
  Max streams: 0
```

Figure 7-5. Skinny register message

From this image, we can see that the message is unicast from the phone directly to the call server (192.168.1.254) and that the messages use TCP port 2000. The RegisterMessage has a message ID of one, and the device name used in this message (SEP0013c4615F16) includes the MAC address of the phone. The call server responds with a RegisterACKMessage (Figure 7-6).

```
Internet Protocol Version 4, Src: 192.168.1.254 (192.168.1.254), Dst: 192.168.1.1 (192.168.1.1)
Transmission Control Protocol, Src Port: cisco-sccp (2000), Dst Port: 50752 (50752), Seq: 1, Ack: 273
Skinny Client Control Protocol
  Data length: 24
  Header version: Basic (0x00000000)
  Message ID: RegisterAckMessage (0x00000081)
  Keep-alive interval: 30
  Date template: M/D/YA
  Secondary keep-alive interval: 60
```

Figure 7-6. Skinny register ACK message

This message also contains the keepalive value. The keepalive is there to provide a registration "heartbeat" to the phone in order to ensure that the phone is still alive and well. Following the successful registration, the phone and call server exchange information about the interface setup and supported features. This is done via the Capability and Template messages. For example, the server asks the phone for its capabilities, and the phone responds as shown in Figure 7-7.

```
No.     Source                  Destination              Protocol    Info
   222 192.168.1.254            192.168.1.1              SKINNY      CapabilitiesReqMessage
   226 192.168.1.1              192.168.1.254            SKINNY      CapabilitiesResMessage

Frame 222: 66 bytes on wire (528 bits), 66 bytes captured (528 bits)
Ethernet II, Src: Cisco_f4:c2:10 (00:1c:58:f4:c2:10), Dst: Cisco_61:5f:16 (00:13:c4:61:5f:16)
Internet Protocol Version 4, Src: 192.168.1.254 (192.168.1.254), Dst: 192.168.1.1 (192.168.1.1)
Transmission Control Protocol, Src Port: cisco-sccp (2000), Dst Port: 50752 (50752), Seq: 33, Ack: 273
Skinny Client Control Protocol
  Data length: 4
  Header version: Basic (0x00000000)
  Message ID: CapabilitiesReqMessage (0x0000009b)

Frame 226: 182 bytes on wire (1456 bits), 182 bytes captured (1456 bits)
Ethernet II, Src: Cisco_61:5f:16 (00:13:c4:61:5f:16), Dst: Cisco_f4:c2:10 (00:1c:58:f4:c2:10)
Internet Protocol Version 4, Src: 192.168.1.1 (192.168.1.1), Dst: 192.168.1.254 (192.168.1.254)
Transmission Control Protocol, Src Port: 50752 (50752), Dst Port: cisco-sccp (2000), Seq: 289, Ack: 45.
Skinny Client Control Protocol
  Data length: 120
  Header version: Basic (0x00000000)
  Message ID: CapabilitiesResMessage (0x00000010)
  Capabilities count: 7
  Payload capability: wideband 256k (25)
  Max frames per packet: 120
  Payload capability: G.711 u-law 64k (4)
  Max frames per packet: 40
  Payload capability: G.711 A-law 64k (2)
  Max frames per packet: 40
  Payload capability: G.729 Annex B (15)
  Max frames per packet: 60
  Payload capability: G.729 Annex A+Annex B (16)
  Max frames per packet: 60
  Payload capability: G.729 (11)
  Max frames per packet: 60
  Payload capability: G.729 Annex A (12)
  Max frames per packet: 60
```

Figure 7-7. Skinny capabilities exchange

The information contained in Frame 226 indicates that the phone can support a collection of codecs from the ITU-T G series. Once the phone has gone through the entire registration process, the interface on the phone looks something like the one shown in Figure 7-8.

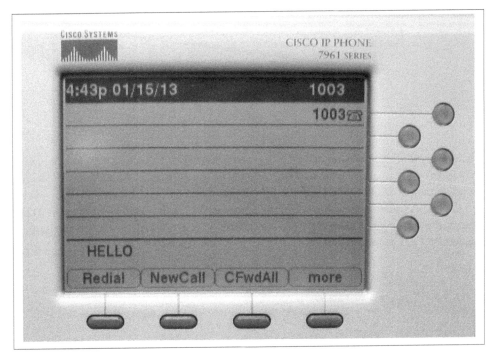

Figure 7-8. Registered phone

But how does this information get to the phone? Several of the Skinny messages are used to populate the interface. From the router and call manager configuration lines listed previously in the chapter, we know that the phone number for ephone 1 is 475-5001. A Skinny LineStatMessage is used to tell the phone that this dial number should be placed on line number 1 (Figure 7-9).

```
Skinny Client Control Protocol
    Data length: 116
    Header version: Basic (0x00000000)
    Message ID: LineStatMessage (0x00000092)
    Line number: 1
    Line directory number: 4755001
    Fully qualified display name: 4755001
    Display name:
```

Figure 7-9. Skinny line stat message

And a Skinny DisplayPromptStatusMessage provides the system message "Packets!" This can also be found in the decoded Figure 7-10.

```
Skinny Client Control Protocol
    Data length: 48
    Header version: Basic (0x00000000)
    Message ID: DisplayPromptStatusMessage (0x00000112)
    Message time-out: 0
    Display message: Packets!
    Line instance: 0
    Call identifier: 0
```

Figure 7-10. Skinny display prompt message

The messages are far too numerous for us to look at each of them individually; however, we can get a sense of them by looking at some of the exchange. As we can see, Skinny message names are very descriptive and easy to read. Toward the end of Figure 7-11, the KeepAliveMessage type makes an appearance. When all is said and done, the keep-alive is the only Skinny message that continues to be produced, at a rate described by the RegisterAckMessage.

```
Filter:  skinny && ip.src==192.168.1.1                    ▼  Expression...  Clear  Apply
No.      Source                  Destination           Protocol   Info
217 192.168.1.1            192.168.1.254          SKINNY   AlarmMessage
218 192.168.1.1            192.168.1.254          SKINNY   AlarmMessage
219 192.168.1.1            192.168.1.254          SKINNY   RegisterMessage
224 192.168.1.1            192.168.1.254          SKINNY   HeadsetStatusMessage
226 192.168.1.1            192.168.1.254          SKINNY   CapabilitiesResMessage
227 192.168.1.1            192.168.1.254          SKINNY   HeadsetStatusMessage
228 192.168.1.1            192.168.1.254          SKINNY   ButtonTemplateReqMessage
231 192.168.1.1            192.168.1.254          SKINNY   SoftKeyTemplateReqMessage
234 192.168.1.1            192.168.1.254          SKINNY   SoftKeySetReqMessage
243 192.168.1.1            192.168.1.254          SKINNY   LineStatReqMessage
248 192.168.1.1            192.168.1.254          SKINNY   LineStatReqMessage
251 192.168.1.1            192.168.1.254          SKINNY   LineStatReqMessage
255 192.168.1.1            192.168.1.254          SKINNY   LineStatReqMessage
259 192.168.1.1            192.168.1.254          SKINNY   LineStatReqMessage
264 192.168.1.1            192.168.1.254          SKINNY   LineStatReqMessage
272 192.168.1.1            192.168.1.254          SKINNY   RegisterAvailableLinesMessage
274 192.168.1.1            192.168.1.254          SKINNY   TimeDateReqMessage
291 192.168.1.1            192.168.1.254          SKINNY   KeepAliveMessage
```

Figure 7-11. Skinny message list

After the initial conversations (DHCP, TFTP, and Registration) have been completed, the topology in Figure 7-2 can be updated with the phone numbers and the addresses (Figure 7-12).

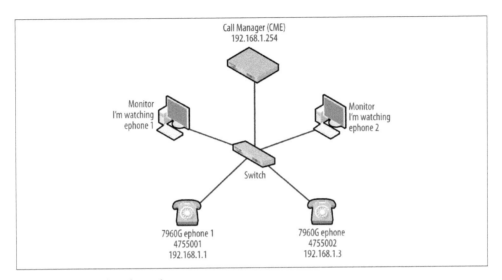

Figure 7-12. Updated topology

Examining the messages actually transmitted rather than simply looking for a successful registration can often help in the troubleshooting process. For example, in building the topology for this particular chapter, Skinny alarm messages were seen on the monitor machine. Opening these alarm messages indicates that there was a software mismatch. Even though the phones register and operate just fine, it may be that the configuration may be suboptimal. An example of this message can be seen in Figure 7-13.

```
Skinny Client Control Protocol
    Data length: 96
    Header version: Basic (0x00000000)
    Message ID: AlarmMessage (0x00000020)
    Alarm severity: Warning (1)
    Display message: 3: Name=SEP0013C4615F16 Load=7.2(2.0)Version Error
    Alarm param 1: 0x00000900
    Alarm param 2: 192.168.1.1 (192.168.1.1)
```

Figure 7-13. Skinny alarm message

Watching the packets and the phone display can provide a lot of information about the current condition of the device. But what can we see from the call manager end? Using a combination of debug and show commands (such as in Figure 7-14), we can follow the registration process from a different perspective.

```
Router#show ephone registered

ephone-1 Mac:0013.C461.5F16 TCP socket:[2] activeLine:0 REGISTERED in SCCP ver 6 and Server in ver 5
mediaActive:0 offhook:0 ringing:0 reset:0 reset_sent:0 paging 0 debug:0
IP:192.168.1.1 50201 Telecaster 7960  keepalive 2781 max_line 6
button 1: dn 1  number 4755001 CH1    IDLE        CH2    IDLE
```

Figure 7-14. Show ephone registered

The show ephone registered command can tell the administrator not only the state of the VoIP unit (REGISTERED) but also the MAC address, IP address, type of endpoint (7960), phone number (4755001), and the port (50201) being used by the device.

Picking up the Handset—Going Off-Hook

There are several points of interest when making a call, and knowledge of these events can facilitate not only an understanding of the call process but also some of the other aspects of telephony. For this reason, we will be following the call from both sides of the connection.

In a Skinny conversation, many of the normal procedures used in other protocols are not followed. For example, what happens when a user performs the simple action of picking up the handset (Figure 7-15)?

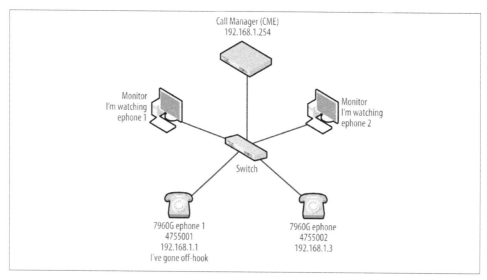

Figure 7-15. Off-hook topology

Packet captures in Figure 7-16 show that a number of events are triggered, beginning with a Skinny message informing the call manager that the phone has gone off-hook.

This is followed by a call-state message from the server, acknowledging the off-hook state.

```
Internet Protocol Version 4, Src: 192.168.1.1 (192.168.1.1), Dst: 192.168.1.254 (192.168.1.254)
Transmission Control Protocol, Src Port: 50202 (50202), Dst Port: cisco-sccp (2000), Seq: 13, A
Skinny Client Control Protocol
  Data length: 12
  Header version: Basic (0x00000000)
  Message ID: OffHookMessage (0x00000006)
  Line instance: 0
  Call identifier: 0
Internet Protocol Version 4, Src: 192.168.1.254 (192.168.1.254), Dst: 192.168.1.1 (192.168.1.1)
Transmission Control Protocol, Src Port: cisco-sccp (2000), Dst Port: 50202 (50202), Seq: 13, A
Skinny Client Control Protocol
  Data length: 28
  Header version: Basic (0x00000000)
  Message ID: CallStateMessage (0x00000111)
  Call state: OffHook (1)
  Line instance: 1
  Call identifier: 13
```

Figure 7-16. Skinny messages from off-hook event

Additional messages are used to set the display of the phone and one other important operation. In traditional analog telephony systems, dial tone arrives from the central office or the PBX. In VoIP systems, dial tone must arrive in some other way. For a Skinny-based system with these phones, the tone is generated by the device itself after the receipt of the correct Skinny message such as the one shown in Figure 7-17. In other systems, tones can arrive at the VoIP endpoint via RTP messages sent from the call server.

```
Skinny Client Control Protocol
  Data length: 20
  Header version: Basic (0x00000000)
  Message ID: StartToneMessage (0x00000082)
  Tone: InsideDialTone (0x00000021)
  Line instance: 1
  Call identifier: 1
```

Figure 7-17. Skinny start-tone message

Dialing a Number

Once the phone generates dial tone (mostly for the user), the destination number can be dialed. In the case of this small topology, the phone numbers are 475-5001 and 475-5002. Ephone 1 (192.168.1.1) will be calling ephone 2 (192.168.1.3). So the next thing to do is dial the number as indicated in Figure 7-18.

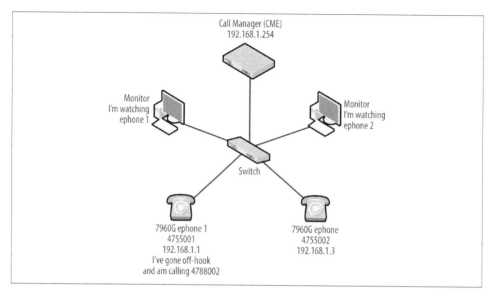

Figure 7-18. Dialing topology

Again, a traditional telephony system would send the tones or frequencies matching the dialpad number along the wire to the PBX. The VoIP phone in this topology actually sends the numerical digits to the call server in a series of packets called KeypadButton-Messages, samples of which are shown in Figure 7-19.

```
Skinny Client Control Protocol      Skinny Client Control Protocol       Skinny Client Control Protocol
  Data length: 16                     Data length: 16                      Data length: 16
  Header version: Basic               Header version: Basic                Header version: Basic
  Message ID: KeypadButtonMessage     Message ID: KeypadButtonMessage      Message ID: KeypadButtonMessage
  Keypad button: Four (0x00000004)    Keypad button: Seven (0x00000007)    Keypad button: Five (0x00000005)
  Line instance: 1                    Line instance: 1                     Line instance: 1
  Call identifier: 2                  Call identifier: 2                   Call identifier: 2
```

Figure 7-19. Skinny keypad button messages

These three messages show that the first three digits (475) of the destination have been sent. Once the entire number has been sent, the call server responds with a Dialed-NumberMessage (Figure 7-20).

```
Internet Protocol Version 4, Src: 192.168.1.254 (192.168.1.254), Dst: 192.168.1.1 (192.168.1.1)
Transmission Control Protocol, Src Port: cisco-sccp (2000), Dst Port: 50202 (50202), Seq: 225,
Skinny Client Control Protocol
  Data length: 36
  Header version: Basic (0x00000000)
  Message ID: DialedNumberMessage (0x0000011d)
  Called party number: 4755002
  Line instance: 1
  Call identifier: 13
```

Figure 7-20. Skinny dialed-number message

This message is generated immediately upon completion of the last digit. Remember that the call server is configured with the numbers of the other ephones and so is aware of the number patterns. An additional packet, called the CallInfoMessage, contains a more complete collection of data about the parties involved in the call. In the case where the destination is not directly managed by the call server, a dial peer will have been configured with an associated dial pattern. This will be covered a little later in the chapter.

An additional StartToneMessage is sent to the source phone, informing it that it is time to generate a different sound—ringing or ring back (Figure 7-21). To be accurate, the ring back is started after we ring the receiver.

```
Skinny Client Control Protocol
    Data length: 20
    Header version: Basic (0x00000000)
    Message ID: StartToneMessage (0x00000082)
    Tone: AlertingTone (0x00000024)
    Line instance: 1
    Call identifier: 2
```

Figure 7-21. Skinny start tone message—ringing

At the Receiver

The call server must notify the other phone that a call is incoming. It does this with a CallStateMessage. A second Skinny packet is used to provide an indication of the calling number (Figure 7-22).

```
Internet Protocol Version 4, Src: 192.168.1.254 (192.168.1.254), Dst: 192.168.1.3 (192.168.1.3)
Transmission Control Protocol, Src Port: cisco-sccp (2000), Dst Port: 51052 (51052), Seq: 13, A
Skinny Client Control Protocol
    Data length: 28
    Header version: Basic (0x00000000)
    Message ID: CallStateMessage (0x00000111)
    Call state: RingIn (4)
    Line instance: 1
    Call identifier: 14
Internet Protocol Version 4, Src: 192.168.1.254 (192.168.1.254), Dst: 192.168.1.3 (192.168.1.3)
Transmission Control Protocol, Src Port: cisco-sccp (2000), Dst Port: 51052 (51052), Seq: 49, A
Skinny Client Control Protocol
    Data length: 48
    Header version: Basic (0x00000000)
    Message ID: DisplayPromptStatusMessage (0x00000112)
    Message time-out: 0
    Display message: \200\027: 4755001
    Line instance: 1
    Call identifier: 14
```

Figure 7-22. Skinny call-state and display-prompt messages

Another message sent at this time tells the phone that it is time to ring (Figure 7-23). The phone generates the sound. This message also tells the phone how long to ring. As we can see, it is set for a long time. Note that all of these messages come from the call server (192.168.1.254) to the destination phone at 192.168.1.3.

```
Internet Protocol Version 4, Src: 192.168.1.254 (192.168.1.254), Dst: 192.168.1.3 (192.168.1.3)
Transmission Control Protocol, Src Port: cisco-sccp (2000), Dst Port: 51052 (51052), Seq: 581,
Skinny Client Control Protocol
  Data length: 20
  Header version: Basic (0x00000000)
  Message ID: SetRingerMessage (0x00000085)
  Ring type: InsideRing (0x00000002)
  Ring mode: RingForever (0x00000001)
  Line instance: 1
  Call identifier: 12
```

Figure 7-23. Skinny set-ringer message

Of course, the ringer is silenced when the handset is picked up. This causes the off-hook message to be sent to the call server (Figure 7-24).

```
Internet Protocol Version 4, Src: 192.168.1.3 (192.168.1.3), Dst: 192.168.1.254 (192.168.1.254)
Transmission Control Protocol, Src Port: 51052 (51052), Dst Port: cisco-sccp (2000), Seq: 13, Ack
Skinny Client Control Protocol
  Data length: 12
  Header version: Basic (0x00000000)
  Message ID: OffHookMessage (0x00000006)
  Line instance: 1
  Call identifier: 12
```

Figure 7-24. Skinny off-hook message

The topology can now be updated to show the physical state of the phones (Figure 7-25).

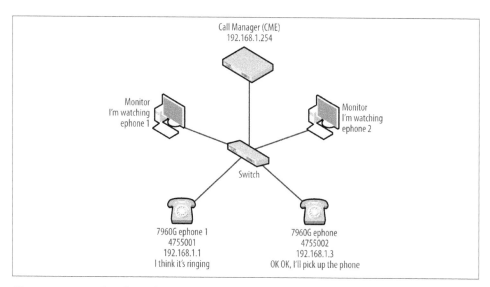

Figure 7-25. Updated topology

In order to start the transmission of voice packets, a logical channel must be set up between the two phones. This is accomplished via the call server's OpenReceiveChannel message and the corresponding ACK from the answering phone (Figure 7-26).

```
Internet Protocol Version 4, Src: 192.168.1.254 (192.168.1.254), Dst: 192.168.1.3 (192.168.1.3)
Transmission Control Protocol, Src Port: cisco-sccp (2000), Dst Port: 51052 (51052), Seq: 885,
Skinny Client Control Protocol
  Data length: 72
  Header version: Basic (0x00000000)
  Message ID: OpenReceiveChannel (0x00000105)
  Conference ID: 4
  Pass-thru party ID: 0
  MS/packet: 20
  Payload capability: G.711 u-law 64k (4)
  Echo-cancel type: Media_EchoCancellation_On (1)
  G723 bitrate: Media_G723BRate_6_4 (2)

Internet Protocol Version 4, Src: 192.168.1.3 (192.168.1.3), Dst: 192.168.1.254 (192.168.1.254)
Transmission Control Protocol, Src Port: 51052 (51052), Dst Port: cisco-sccp (2000), Seq: 105,
Skinny Client Control Protocol
  Data length: 24
  Header version: Basic (0x00000000)
  Message ID: OpenReceiveChannelAck (0x00000022)
  Opened receive-channel status: orcOk (0)
  IP address: 192.168.1.3 (192.168.1.3)
  Port number: 27368
  Pass-thru party ID: 0
```

Figure 7-26. Skinny open-receive channel messages

Finally, the call server sends the StartMediaTransmission message with the final parameters for the call (Figure 7-27).

```
Internet Protocol Version 4, Src: 192.168.1.254 (192.168.1.254), Dst: 192.168.1.3 (192.168.1.3)
Transmission Control Protocol, Src Port: cisco-sccp (2000), Dst Port: 51052 (51052), Seq: 985,
Skinny Client Control Protocol
  Data length: 88
  Header version: Basic (0x00000000)
  Message ID: StartMediaTransmission (0x0000008a)
  Conference ID: 4
  Pass-thru party ID: 0
  Remote IP address: 192.168.1.1 (192.168.1.1)
  Remote port: 25438
  MS/packet: 20
  Payload capability: G.711 u-law 64k (4)
  Precedence: 0
  Silence suppression: Media_SilenceSuppression_Off (0x00000000)
  Max frames per packet: 0
  G723 bitrate: Media_G723BRate_6_4 (2)
```

Figure 7-27. Skinny start-media transmission

Together, these messages establish the codec to be used, the IP addresses of the two endpoints, and the port to be used during the transmission of voice data. Now the topology can be represented as seen in Figure 7-28.

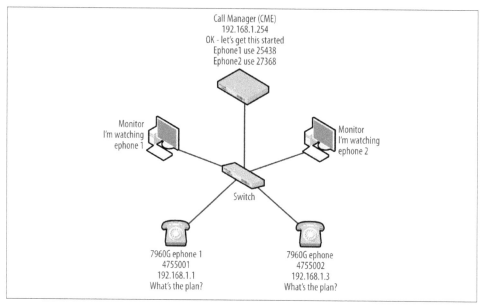

Figure 7-28. Start-media transmission topology

Back at the Source Phone

Once the destination has been reached and is available, the call server informs the source phone that the voice-data transmission can begin. Just like the receiver side, the call server and the phone exchange OpenReceiveChannel messages in order to exchange capability and communication parameters (Figure 7-29).

```
Internet Protocol Version 4, Src: 192.168.1.254 (192.168.1.254), Dst: 192.168.1.1 (192.168.1.1)
Transmission Control Protocol, Src Port: cisco-sccp (2000), Dst Port: 50202 (50202), Seq: 1105,
Skinny Client Control Protocol
  Data length: 72
  Header version: Basic (0x00000000)
  Message ID: OpenReceiveChannel (0x00000105)
  Conference ID: 2
  Pass-thru party ID: 0
  MS/packet: 20
  Payload capability: G.711 u-law 64k (4)
  Echo-cancel type: Media_EchoCancellation_On (1)
  G723 bitrate: Media_G723BRate_6_4 (2)
Internet Protocol Version 4, Src: 192.168.1.1 (192.168.1.1), Dst: 192.168.1.254 (192.168.1.254)
Transmission Control Protocol, Src Port: 50202 (50202), Dst Port: cisco-sccp (2000), Seq: 273,
Skinny Client Control Protocol
  Data length: 24
  Header version: Basic (0x00000000)
  Message ID: OpenReceiveChannelAck (0x00000022)
  Opened receive-channel status: orcOk (0)
  IP address: 192.168.1.1 (192.168.1.1)
  Port number: 25438
  Pass-thru party ID: 0
```

Figure 7-29. Skinny open-receiver channel at the source

The call server finalizes the settings for the channel with another StartMediaTransmission message (Figure 7-30). Remember that this message also includes the port used by the other end of the call, in the "Remote port" field.

```
Internet Protocol Version 4, Src: 192.168.1.254 (192.168.1.254), Dst: 192.168.1.1 (192.168.1.1)
Transmission Control Protocol, Src Port: cisco-sccp (2000), Dst Port: 50202 (50202), Seq: 1205,
Skinny Client Control Protocol
  Data length: 88
  Header version: Basic (0x00000000)
  Message ID: StartMediaTransmission (0x0000008a)
  Conference ID: 2
  Pass-thru party ID: 0
  Remote IP address: 192.168.1.3 (192.168.1.3)
  Remote port: 27368
  MS/packet: 20
  Payload capability: G.711 u-law 64k (4)
  Precedence: 0
  Silence suppression: Media_SilenceSuppression_Off (0x00000000)
  Max frames per packet: 0
  G723 bitrate: Media_G723BRate_6_4 (2)
```

Figure 7-30. Skinny start-media transmission at source

Examining Figure 7-29 and Figure 7-30 closely, we can see that the port selected by the receiver in the OpenReceiveChannelAck message (27368) is the same one reported to the source phone in StartMediaTransmission message. The reverse is also true, as the source phone (192.168.1.1) selected port 25438, and this was reported to the destination phone (192.168.1.3) in the other StartMediaTransmission message shown in Figure 7-30. Thus, the two phones now know each other's IP addresses, port numbers to be used and the payload type for the voice data.

Voice Data

Once actual voice packets start to flow, it is typical for the call server to be removed from the conversation until it is time to disconnect. Updating, we have the events shown in Figure 7-31.

Recall that the destination port is a UDP port because the transport protocol is RTP. Packet captures once again show the flow of traffic as the two ends begin to communicate directly. Beginning with the ARP requests from the two endpoints, the two phones begin to send RTP packets directly to each other (Figure 7-32).

While RTP is the subject of another chapter in this book, it is instructive to examine one of these packets in order to see if the settings exchanged are actually used. The packet list indicates that the G.711 codec was used to encode the data, and we can see that the IP addresses show that the exchange is directly between the phones. This is a little different from some of the topologies used elsewhere in this book, where the call manager was more involved.

As we can see in Figure 7-33, the ports used in this particular packet are the same ones exchanged in the previous Skinny messages.

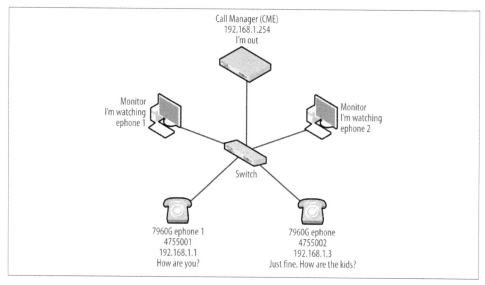

Figure 7-31. *Topology with media transmissions*

```
63 192.168.1.254      192.168.1.1        SKINNY  StartMediaTransmission
64 192.168.1.1        192.168.1.254      TCP     50202 > cisco-sccp [ACK] Seq=305 Ack=1301 win=1400 Len=0
65 Cisco_61:5f:16     Broadcast          ARP     who has 192.168.1.3? Tell 192.168.1.1
66 Cisco_7f:32:97     Cisco_61:5f:16     ARP     192.168.1.3 is at 00:19:2f:7f:32:97
67 192.168.1.1        192.168.1.3        RTP     PT=ITU-T G.711 PCMU, SSRC=0x165F61CD, Seq=1093, Time=169872
68 192.168.1.1        192.168.1.3        RTP     PT=ITU-T G.711 PCMU, SSRC=0x165F61CD, Seq=1094, Time=170032
32 192.168.1.254      192.168.1.3        SKINNY  StartMediaTransmission
33 Cisco_61:5f:16     Broadcast          ARP     who has 192.168.1.3? Tell 192.168.1.1
34 Cisco_7f:32:97     Cisco_61:5f:16     ARP     192.168.1.3 is at 00:19:2f:7f:32:97
35 192.168.1.3        192.168.1.254      TCP     51052 > cisco-sccp [ACK] Seq=137 Ack=1081 win=8076 Len=0
36 192.168.1.1        192.168.1.3        RTP     PT=ITU-T G.711 PCMU, SSRC=0x165F61CD, Seq=1093, Time=169872,
37 192.168.1.1        192.168.1.3        RTP     PT=ITU-T G.711 PCMU, SSRC=0x165F61CD, Seq=1094, Time=170032
```

Figure 7-32. *Transport packets*

```
Ethernet II, Src: Cisco_61:5f:16 (00:13:c4:61:5f:16), Dst: Cisco_7f:32:97 (00:19:2f:7f:32:97)
Internet Protocol Version 4, Src: 192.168.1.1 (192.168.1.1), Dst: 192.168.1.3 (192.168.1.3)
User Datagram Protocol, Src Port: 25438 (25438), Dst Port: 27368 (27368)
Real-Time Transport Protocol
```

Figure 7-33. *RTP packet*

Teardown of the Call

The teardown or closing of the call circuit on a Skinnybased deployment is straightforward and begins with the aptly named OnHookMessage (Figure 7-34).

```
Internet Protocol Version 4, Src: 192.168.1.3 (192.168.1.3), Dst: 192.168.1.254 (192.168.1.254)
Transmission Control Protocol, Src Port: 51052 (51052), Dst Port: cisco-sccp (2000), Seq: 209,
Skinny Client Control Protocol
  Data length: 12
  Header version: Basic (0x00000000)
  Message ID: OnHookMessage (0x00000007)
  Line instance: 0
  Call identifier: 0
```

Figure 7-34. Skinny on-hook message

At the start of the call, we saw the OpenReceiveChannel and StartMediaTransmission messages. At the close of the call, we have the corresponding CloseReceiveChannel and StopMediaTransmission messages (Figure 7-35).

```
Internet Protocol Version 4, Src: 192.168.1.254 (192.168.1.254), Dst: 192.168.1.3 (192.168.1.3)
Transmission Control Protocol, Src Port: cisco-sccp (2000), Dst Port: 51052 (51052), Seq: 1245,
Skinny Client Control Protocol
  Data length: 16
  Header version: Basic (0x00000000)
  Message ID: CloseReceiveChannel (0x00000106)
  Conference ID: 4
  Pass-thru party ID: 0
Internet Protocol Version 4, Src: 192.168.1.254 (192.168.1.254), Dst: 192.168.1.3 (192.168.1.3)
Transmission Control Protocol, Src Port: cisco-sccp (2000), Dst Port: 51052 (51052), Seq: 1269,
Skinny Client Control Protocol
  Data length: 16
  Header version: Basic (0x00000000)
  Message ID: StopMediaTransmission (0x0000008b)
  Conference ID: 4
  Pass-thru party ID: 0
```

Figure 7-35. Skinny stop-media transmission

In our example, we can see that ephone 2 (192.168.1.3) initiated the connection shutdown by placing the handset in the cradle (Figure 7-36).

This generated the on-hook message as well as the CloseReceiveChannel and StopMediaTransmission messages. It is important to note that these last two messages were also sent to ephone 1 (192.168.1.1) at the other end in order to inform it that the channel is no longer necessary. Lastly, the conference ID numbers used in these messages, 4 for ephone 2 and 2 for ephone 1, are consistent throughout the messages and prevent confusion regarding which connection to tear down.

An examination of some of the other Skinny messages sent at this time displays the additional exchanges between the call server and the VoIP endpoints (Figure 7-37). The purpose of these is to return the ephones and the displays back to a precall state.

Performance Measuring

Performance monitoring of a VoIP call is an important component in controlling and troubleshooting the behavior. The critical metrics are latency, packet loss, and jitter, but other measurements, such as the number of packets and the number of bytes

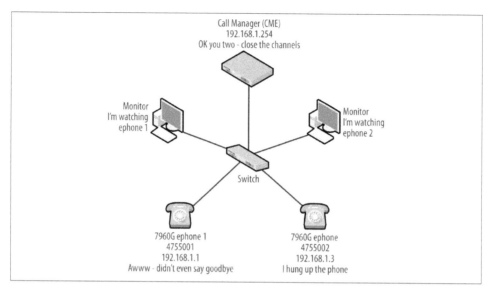

Figure 7-36. Topology shutting down

```
849 192.168.1.254        192.168.1.1           SKINNY   ConnectionStatisticsReq
850 192.168.1.254        192.168.1.1           SKINNY   CloseReceiveChannel
851 192.168.1.254        192.168.1.1           SKINNY   StopMediaTransmission
852 192.168.1.254        192.168.1.1           SKINNY   ConnectionStatisticsReq
853 192.168.1.254        192.168.1.1           SKINNY   CallStateMessage
854 192.168.1.254        192.168.1.1           SKINNY   ClearPromptStatusMessage
855 192.168.1.254        192.168.1.1           SKINNY   SelectSoftKeysMessage
856 192.168.1.254        192.168.1.1           SKINNY   SetSpeakerModeMessage
857 192.168.1.254        192.168.1.1           SKINNY   StopToneMessage
858 192.168.1.1          192.168.1.254         SKINNY   ConnectionStatisticsRes
859 192.168.1.254        192.168.1.1           SKINNY   SetLampMessage
860 192.168.1.254        192.168.1.1           SKINNY   DisplayPromptStatusMessage
861 192.168.1.254        192.168.1.1           SKINNY   ClearPromptStatusMessage
862 192.168.1.254        192.168.1.1           SKINNY   SelectSoftKeysMessage
863 192.168.1.254        192.168.1.1           SKINNY   DisplayPromptStatusMessage
```

Figure 7-37. Skinny teardown messages

transmitted, are often part of the picture. RFC 3550 (which obsoletes 1889) provides the specifications for the Real-Time Transport Protocol, or RTP. The main function of RTP provides for the conveyance of real-time (voice) data between the nodes involved in the voice or video conversation. The RFC also describes the Real-Time Control Protocol (RTCP), which is used monitor the real-time stream and provides some of the performance data mentioned here. From the RFC:

> The primary function is to provide feedback on the quality of the data distribution.

There are several scenarios for the deployment of the protocol, but most of them require the use of RTCP. RTCP packets are interspersed within the RTP stream. Also from the RFC:

> The first two functions require that all participants send RTCP packets, therefore the rate must be controlled in order for RTP to scale up to a large number of participants. Functions 1-3 SHOULD be used in all environments, but particularly in the IP multicast environment.

So, it is clear that RTCP is intended to be used for this purpose. However, when we take a look at the RTP stream generated by the Cisco phones, we can see that there is not a single RTCP packet to be found. It turns out that Cisco Skinny deployments use their own packets to capture this information. At the beginning of the conversation, two messages are exchanged: ConnectionStatisticsReq (request) and ConnectionStatisticsRes (response), and these contain information about the connection up to the current point (Figure 7-38). This is true for both ends of the connection.

```
Internet Protocol Version 4, Src: 192.168.1.254 (192.168.1.254), Dst: 192.168.1.3 (192.168.1.3)
Transmission Control Protocol, Src Port: cisco-sccp (2000), Dst Port: 51052 (51052), Seq: 841,
Skinny Client Control Protocol
  Data length: 36
  Header version: Basic (0x00000000)
  Message ID: ConnectionStatisticsReq (0x00000107)
  Directory number: 4755002
  Call identifier: 14
  Stats processing type: clearStats (0)
Internet Protocol Version 4, Src: 192.168.1.3 (192.168.1.3), Dst: 192.168.1.254 (192.168.1.254)
Transmission Control Protocol, Src Port: 51052 (51052), Dst Port: cisco-sccp (2000), Seq: 33, A
Skinny Client Control Protocol
  Data length: 64
  Header version: Basic (0x00000000)
  Message ID: ConnectionStatisticsRes (0x00000023)
  Directory number: 4755002
  Call identifier: 14
  Stats processing type: clearStats (0)
  Packets sent: 244
  Octets sent: 41968
  Packets Received: 250
  Octets received: 43000
  Packets lost: 0
  Jitter: 0
  Latency(ms): 13
```

Figure 7-38. Skinny connection statistics request, ephone 1

These two packets were caught by the monitor station watching ephone 2. Midway through the stream, another set of these messages report the statistics up to that point (Figure 7-39).

```
Internet Protocol Version 4, Src: 192.168.1.254 (192.168.1.254), Dst: 192.168.1.1 (192.168.1.1)
Transmission Control Protocol, Src Port: cisco-sccp (2000), Dst Port: 50202 (50202), Seq: 1697,
Skinny Client Control Protocol
  Data length: 36
  Header version: Basic (0x00000000)
  Message ID: ConnectionStatisticsReq (0x00000107)
  Directory number: 4755001
  Call identifier: 13
  Stats processing type: doNotClearStats (1)
Internet Protocol Version 4, Src: 192.168.1.1 (192.168.1.1), Dst: 192.168.1.254 (192.168.1.254)
Transmission Control Protocol, Src Port: 50202 (50202), Dst Port: cisco-sccp (2000), Seq: 305, .
Skinny Client Control Protocol
  Data length: 64
  Header version: Basic (0x00000000)
  Message ID: ConnectionStatisticsRes (0x00000023)
  Directory number: 4755001
  Call identifier: 13
  Stats processing type: doNotClearStats (1)
  Packets sent: 238
  Octets sent: 40936
  Packets Received: 229
  Octets received: 39388
  Packets lost: 0
  Jitter: 0
  Latency(ms): 0
```

Figure 7-39. Skinny connection statistics request, ephone 2

At the end of the stream, as the connection closes, another set of these messages crosses the network (Figure 7-40).

```
Internet Protocol Version 4, Src: 192.168.1.254 (192.168.1.254), Dst: 192.168.1.1 (192.168.1.1)
Transmission Control Protocol, Src Port: cisco-sccp (2000), Dst Port: 50202 (50202), Seq: 1741,
Skinny Client Control Protocol
  Data length: 36
  Header version: Basic (0x00000000)
  Message ID: ConnectionStatisticsReq (0x00000107)
  Directory number: 4755001
  Call identifier: 13
  Stats processing type: doNotClearStats (1)
Internet Protocol Version 4, Src: 192.168.1.254 (192.168.1.254), Dst: 192.168.1.1 (192.168.1.1)
Transmission Control Protocol, Src Port: cisco-sccp (2000), Dst Port: 50202 (50202), Seq: 1833,
Skinny Client Control Protocol
  Data length: 36
  Header version: Basic (0x00000000)
  Message ID: ConnectionStatisticsReq (0x00000107)
  Directory number: 4755001
  Call identifier: 13
  Stats processing type: clearStats (0)
Internet Protocol Version 4, Src: 192.168.1.1 (192.168.1.1), Dst: 192.168.1.254 (192.168.1.254)
Transmission Control Protocol, Src Port: 50202 (50202), Dst Port: cisco-sccp (2000), Seq: 377,
Skinny Client Control Protocol
  Data length: 64
  Header version: Basic (0x00000000)
  Message ID: ConnectionStatisticsRes (0x00000023)
  Directory number: 4755001
  Call identifier: 13
  Stats processing type: doNotClearStats (1)
  Packets sent: 389
  Octets sent: 66908
  Packets Received: 380
  Octets received: 65360
  Packets lost: 0
  Jitter: 0
  Latency(ms): 0
```

Figure 7-40. Closing the statistics for the connection

This series of packets also shows that as the connection is to be closed, the statistics will be cleared. As this example was a very short call, there are not that many Connection-Statistics messages and the number of packets between messages is pretty close. Given the size of the network (the ephones are connected to the same switch), we would expect that the performance numbers would be well within acceptable levels. This is borne out by the numbers seen in these packets. Latency is extremely low,` as is the jitter, and no packets were lost. This information is used by the VoIP endpoints and can be viewed from the VoIP phones' screen interface.

Off-Site Calling

So far, we've been working with a topology that has a single call manager. The VoIP phones all register with this one call manager, and as we saw in the earlier packet captures, phones communicate with the call manager for registration and call setup but then communicate directly with each other. So, there is no way to call to another site or phone numbers that do not have the same dial pattern as the local phones.

This section will examine a topology that has multiple call managers and requires routing between the VoIP endpoints. The topology is shown in Figure 7-41. This discussion is similar to the SIP trunking in Chapter 3.

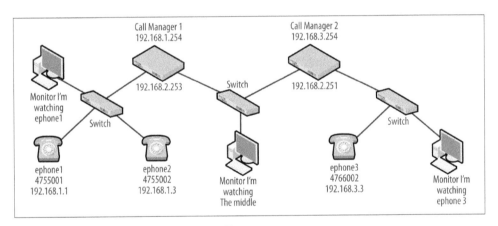

Figure 7-41. Topology with multiple call managers

From the topology diagram, we can see that a second call manager has been added and that there is a new dial pattern for the associated phones. Ephone3 has a phone number of 476-6002. The original phones (ephone2 and ephone3) retain their phone numbers. The two call managers are separated by the 192.168.2.0/24 network and an additional monitor station has been added in order to watch the exchange between the call servers.

In building this topology, there are a couple of problems that have to be solved:

1. End-to-end routing

2. Configuration of the second call manager (DHCP, TFTP, telephony service, ephones)

3. Contacting the call server and VoIP phones on other networks

The routing is straightforward, as the *ip route* command established the static routes necessary. The second call manager was also straightforward, differing very little from the previous configuration. Since the phone models are the same, the only notable changes were to the DHCP parameters, the dial pattern, and the ephone MAC addresses.

From an initial operations perspective, the behavior is nearly a carbon copy with ephones 1 and 2 obtaining IP addresses from the router, pulling the necessary files via TFTP, and then registering with the call manager. Ephone3 goes through the same operations, except that it is communicating with the other router at 192.168.3.354. Packet captures show us that everything is proceeding according to plan.

In order to solve the last problem, we have to modify the configuration of the call manager to tell it how to contact phones on the other network or server. This is done with the dial-peer command. This section also allows us to tell the call manager the IP address of the other server. To be complete, this must be done on the other end as well.

```
dial-peer voice 1

voip destination-pattern 475....

session target ipv4:192.168.2.253

incoming called-number .
```

The period or dot is a wildcard character.

Let's examine a call made from ephone3 (476-6002) to ephone1 (475-5001). The basic process requires that ephone3 contact its call manager 2 (192.168.3.254) with the number to be dialed. Call manager 2 consults its configuration to see if it knows how to forward this call. The dial-peer lines provide the information necessary. Call manager 2 now contacts call manager 1 with the destination number. But what does the transmission between the call managers look like? Based on the chapter so far, we might expect to see Skinny messages, but since there is no indication that the receiving call manager is a Cisco device, it is wise to use a nonproprietary standard. It turns out that for both the topologies tested (Call Manager versions 3.3 and 8.5), the call managers both default to the H.225 protocol defined by H.323, as we discussed in Chapter 6. These packets are displayed in Figure 7-42. However, they can be told to use SIP.

```
 5 192.168.2.254          192.168.2.253          H.225.0 CS: setup OpenLogicalChannel
 6 192.168.2.253          192.168.2.254          H.225.0 CS: callProceeding OpenLogicalChannel
 7 192.168.2.253          192.168.2.254          H.225.0 CS: alerting
 8 192.168.2.254          192.168.2.253          TCP      63780 > h323hostcall [ACK] Seq=312 Ack=190 Win=2974 Len=0
10 192.168.2.253          192.168.2.254          H.225.0 CS: connect
11 192.168.2.253          192.168.2.254          H.225.0 CS: notify
12 192.168.2.254          192.168.2.253          TCP      63780 > h323hostcall [ACK] Seq=312 Ack=351 Win=2813 Len=0
13 192.168.2.253          192.168.2.254          RTP      PT=ITU-T G.729, SSRC=0x7E402FD, Seq=2627, Time=407040, Mark
```

Figure 7-42. H.225 messages between call managers

This packet list is short, although we know from the previous chapters that protocol messages in the H.323 suite are much more complex than Skinny messages. The first RTP packet has been included in order to depict the point at which voice data begins to flow. Opening packet number 5, we can see that the call managers are exchanging the endpoint phone numbers (Figure 7-43).

```
Internet Protocol Version 4, Src: 192.168.2.254 (192.168.2.254), Dst: 192.168.2.253 (192.168.2.253)
Transmission Control Protocol, Src Port: 63780 (63780), Dst Port: h323hostcall (1720), Seq: 1, Ack:
TPKT, Version: 3, Length: 311
Q.931
   Protocol discriminator: Q.931
   Call reference value length: 2
   Call reference flag: Message sent from originating side
   Call reference value: 0004
   Message type: SETUP (0x05)
 ⊕ Bearer capability
 ⊕ Calling party number: '4766002'
 ⊕ Called party number: '4755001'
 ⊕ User-user
   H.225.0 CS
```

Figure 7-43. Phone number exchange

Another critical piece of information is the codec to be used. The previous conversation between ephones on the same call manager and network used G.711. In fact, opening all of the fields in packet 5 we would see that the recommendation from call manager 2 would be G.711. However, in packet 6 the negotiated codec ends up as G.729 (Figure 7-44). This packet also reveals the other parameters to be used for the logical channel, such as the ports to be used for RTP and RTCP.

The codec and parameters for the reverse channel are also identified in this packet (Figure 7-45).

When H.323 is deployed, it is common to see both H.225 and H.245. H.225 is for connection setup, and H.245 handles the media session. In this case, H.245 is notably absent because tunneling is used. This means that the H.245 message content is encapsulated within the H.225 messages. Figure 7-45 depicts the flags set when this is true.

Following this connection setup to its conclusion, we can see another difference in the connection between the call managers. Recall that a Skinny deployment does not make use of RTCP. From the packets above, we can see that ports have been assigned to the media stream. Examining the captures between the call managers proves that RTCP is

```
⊟ Item 0
    FastStart item: 26 octets
  ⊟ OpenLogicalChannel
      forwardLogicalChannelNumber: 1
    ⊟ forwardLogicalChannelParameters
      ⊟ dataType: audioData (3)
        ⊟ audioData: g729 (10)
            g729: 2
      ⊟ multiplexParameters: h2250LogicalChannelParameters (3)
        ⊟ h2250LogicalChannelParameters
            sessionID: 1
          ⊟ mediaChannel: unicastAddress (0)
            ⊟ unicastAddress: iPAddress (0)
              ⊟ iPAddress
                  network: 192.168.2.253 (192.168.2.253)
                  tsapIdentifier: 18964
          ⊟ mediaControlChannel: unicastAddress (0)
            ⊟ unicastAddress: iPAddress (0)
              ⊟ iPAddress
                  network: 192.168.2.253 (192.168.2.253)
                  tsapIdentifier: 18965
            1... .... silenceSuppression: True
```

Figure 7-44. Channel parameters

alive and well and that the ports used are those specified in the channel control messages (Figure 7-46).

What is interesting about the use of RTCP between the call managers (in addition to the return to standardized operation) is that RTCP is not used by the end nodes. This means that the data contained is generated by the call managers forwarding the RTP stream.

Summary

The Skinny Client Control Protocol (SCCP) is a versatile and easy-to-read protocol. With the vast number of installed Cisco VoIP endpoints, understanding the operation and messaging of this proprietary protocol can be very helpful in supporting, trouble-shooting, and securing Cisco-based deployments. However, as a nonstandard protocol, finding the desired protocol specifications is not always as straightforward as the protocol itself. This chapter covered the basic operation of Skinny in both single and dual call manager topologies, explained the message types used, and touched on the integration with H.323.

Reading

The following documents were useful in building the topologies used in this chapter. The links to the documents were valid at the time of this writing.

```
⊟ Item 1
    FastStart item: 30 octets
  ⊟ OpenLogicalChannel
      forwardLogicalChannelNumber: 1
    ⊞ forwardLogicalChannelParameters
    ⊟ reverseLogicalChannelParameters
      ⊟ dataType: audioData (3)
        ⊟ audioData: g729 (10)
            g729: 2
      ⊟ multiplexParameters: h2250LogicalChannelParameters (2)
        ⊟ h2250LogicalChannelParameters
            sessionID: 1
          ⊟ mediaChannel: unicastAddress (0)
            ⊟ unicastAddress: iPAddress (0)
              ⊟ iPAddress
                  network: 192.168.2.254 (192.168.2.254)
                  tsapIdentifier: 17546
          ⊟ mediaControlChannel: unicastAddress (0)
            ⊟ unicastAddress: iPAddress (0)
              ⊟ iPAddress
                  network: 192.168.2.253 (192.168.2.253)
                  tsapIdentifier: 18965
            1... .... silenceSuppression: True
      1... .... multipleCalls: True
      1... .... maintainConnection: True
      1... .... h245Tunnelling: True
```

Figure 7-45. Reverse channel parameters

```
Ethernet II, Src: Cisco_f6:aa:90 (00:1c:58:f6:aa:90), Dst: Cisco_f4:c2:11 (00:1c:58:f4:c2:11)
Internet Protocol Version 4, Src: 192.168.2.254 (192.168.2.254), Dst: 192.168.2.253 (192.168.2.253)
User Datagram Protocol, Src Port: 17546 (17546), Dst Port: 18964 (18964)
Real-Time Transport Protocol
Ethernet II, Src: Cisco_f4:c2:11 (00:1c:58:f4:c2:11), Dst: Cisco_f6:aa:90 (00:1c:58:f6:aa:90)
Internet Protocol Version 4, Src: 192.168.2.253 (192.168.2.253), Dst: 192.168.2.254 (192.168.2.254)
User Datagram Protocol, Src Port: 18964 (18964), Dst Port: 17546 (17546)
Real-Time Transport Protocol
Ethernet II, Src: Cisco_f6:aa:90 (00:1c:58:f6:aa:90), Dst: Cisco_f4:c2:11 (00:1c:58:f4:c2:11)
Internet Protocol Version 4, Src: 192.168.2.254 (192.168.2.254), Dst: 192.168.2.253 (192.168.2.253)
User Datagram Protocol, Src Port: 17547 (17547), Dst Port: 18965 (18965)
Real-time Transport Control Protocol (Receiver Report)
Real-time Transport Control Protocol (Source description)
Ethernet II, Src: Cisco_f4:c2:11 (00:1c:58:f4:c2:11), Dst: Cisco_f6:aa:90 (00:1c:58:f6:aa:90)
Internet Protocol Version 4, Src: 192.168.2.253 (192.168.2.253), Dst: 192.168.2.254 (192.168.2.254)
User Datagram Protocol, Src Port: 18965 (18965), Dst Port: 17547 (17547)
Real-time Transport Control Protocol (Receiver Report)
Real-time Transport Control Protocol (Source description)
```

Figure 7-46. RTP and RTCP between call managers

- Cisco Unified Cisco Unified IP Phone 7960G and 7940G Link Page (*http://bit.ly/XtbrhU*)
- Cisco 7940 and 7960 IP Phones Firmware Upgrade Matrix (*http://bit.ly/WNz98o*)
- Cisco UCME Administration Guide (*http://bit.ly/Yli96N*)
- CallManager System Guide, Release 8.5.1 (*http://bit.ly/Yli9Ui*)
- CallManager System Guide, Release 3 (*http://bit.ly/11TOGcr*)
- Cisco TFTP (part of the much larger CallManager System Guide), available here (*http://bit.ly/153WSEN*)

Review Questions

1. What is the name of the VoIP company credited with Skinny that was purchased by Cisco?
2. What is the TCP port number used by Skinny?
3. True or False: Skinny VoIP streams do not use the Real-Time Control Protocol.
4. True or false: all of the audible tones associated with an SCCP phone call are generated from the VoIP endpoint or phone itself.
5. True or false: all Skinny messages follow the same header format, changing based on the type code.
6. What is the DHCP option for TFTP?
7. True or false: the call server address comes to the phone via the DHCP server.
8. True or false: in a topology with multiple call servers, Skinny messages flow from call to server to call server in order to control the flow of voice data packets.
9. What Cisco command begins the configuration allowing multiple call servers to communicate?
10. What Skinny messages are responsible for establishing the ports to be used and the codec for the transmission?

Review Answers

1. Selsius.
2. 2000.
3. True.
4. True.

5. True.

6. 150.

7. False.

8. False.

9. dial-peer.

10. OpenReceiveChannel, OpenReceiveChannelACK, StartMediaTransmission.

Lab Activities

This chapter is supported by the book website. So, if the activity lists equipment or software that you do not have, go to the book website for additional content.

Activity 1—Basic Topology Build

Materials: Cisco router with Call Manager Express, 7960 VoIP phones, computer with Wireshark, mirror/monitor capable switch

1. Complete the topology shown (Figure 7-47).

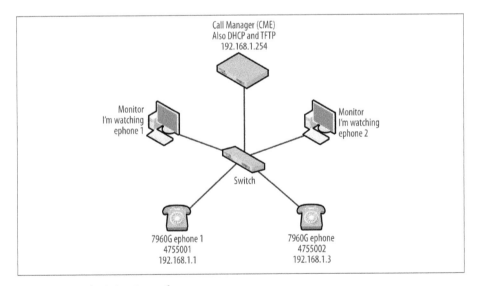

Figure 7-47. Activity 1 topology

Working through the configuration shown at the beginning of this chapter, add the following:

Switch: spanning-tree PortFast, set up a monitor port to capture traffic to and from one of the phones.

Router: build a DHCP pool with options for the network, default gateway, and TFTP server. Give the router an IP address on the same network, and add the tftp-server lines, telephony service, and ephones—copy the lines shown for the chapter configuration.

2. On the monitor machine, start a capture.

3. Add the phones to the topology, ensuring that one of them will be monitored.

4. Stop the capture.

5. Analyze the capture, looking for the events outlined in this chapter. Can you find the stages of the connection: DHCP, TFTP, registering, display configuration?

6. Can you match the messages to the nodes?

Activity 2—Going Off-Hook

Materials: Activity 1 topology

1. Start a new capture on the monitor machine.

2. Remove the handset from the cradle and dial the destination number.

3. Answer the call and allow for about five seconds of voice data and then hang up.

4. Stop the capture.

5. Analyze the capture for the following information: Skinny messages providing the setup information for the call, packets containing the dialed number and codec selection.

6. Do the values found in the packets match the information contained in the RTP stream?

Activity 3—Show and Debug

Materials: Activity 1 topology

1. Experiment with the show and debug commands specific to the phones and the calls.

Examples:

```
show ephone
show telephony-service
debug call detail
debug call events
```

2. Perform the same analysis done in Activity 2, but using the show and debug command output as the source.

Activity 4—Call-Flow Diagram

Materials: Captures from the previous activities.

1. Create a call-flow diagram such as the one shown in the image for this activity (Figure 7-48).

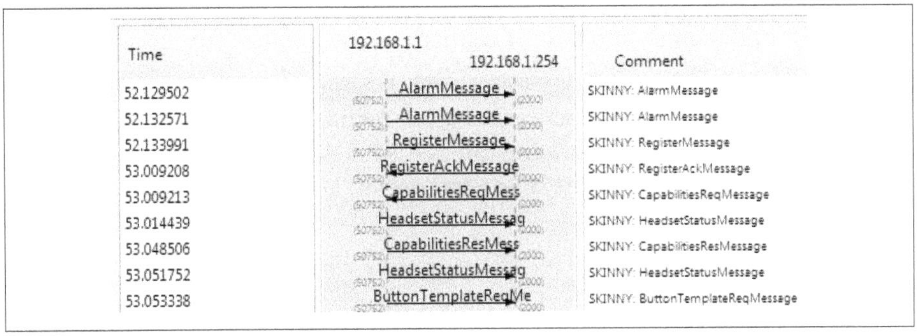

Time	192.168.1.1 / 192.168.1.254	Comment
52.129502	AlarmMessage	SKINNY: AlarmMessage
52.132571	AlarmMessage	SKINNY: AlarmMessage
52.133991	RegisterMessage	SKINNY: RegisterMessage
53.009208	RegisterAckMessage	SKINNY: RegisterAckMessage
53.009213	CapabilitiesReqMess	SKINNY: CapabilitiesReqMessage
53.014439	HeadsetStatusMessag	SKINNY: HeadsetStatusMessage
53.048506	CapabilitiesResMess	SKINNY: CapabilitiesResMessage
53.051752	HeadsetStatusMessag	SKINNY: HeadsetStatusMessage
53.053338	ButtonTemplateReqMe	SKINNY: ButtonTemplateReqMessage

Figure 7-48. Activity 4 call-flow diagram

Activity 5—Multiple Call Managers

Build the topology shown above, adding the second call manager and adjusting the routing as necessary. Add the dial-peer commands to the two call servers. Add the additional phone and monitor stations (Figure 7-49).

Additional materials: router with Call Manager Express, switch with similar configuration as the first (VLANs may also be used), VoIP phone, monitor stations

1. Start captures on all of the monitor machines.

2. Place a call from one end to the other, ensuring that all of the monitors are capturing call data.

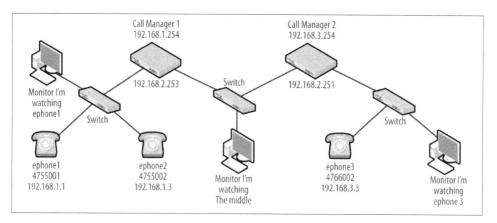

Figure 7-49. Activity 5 topology

3. After hanging up, stop the capture.

4. Analyze the capture from the start of the call to the finish. Can you follow the call packets and identify the flow of traffic? Can match the setup packets to the RTP packets?

5. Analyze the packets sent between the call managers. How do these integrate into the call flow. Can you follow the call as easily? What protocols or codecs are used here? Compare them to the ones seen earlier. Does the communication between routers have to be H.323?

About the Author

Bruce Hartpence is a faculty member in the Golisano College of Computing and Information Science (GCCIS) at Rochester Institute of Technology (RIT) in Rochester, New York. He currently teaches in the areas of wireless communication, Voice over IP, and network design. He also runs an industrial training program in networking.

Current research projects include protocol design based on meshed trees, virtualization, and software-defined networks.

Bruce is the author of two other O'Reilly books: the Packet Guide to Core Network Protocols (*http://oreil.ly/Packet_Guide_CNP*) and the Packet Guide to Routing and Switching (*http://oreil.ly/Packet_Guide_RS*). He runs a website (*http://www.brucehart pence.com*) and a Youtube channel (*http://www.youtube.com/brucehartpence*) in support of all three books. A veteran of the US Navy, he served on the USS Enterprise and loves a good sea story.

Colophon

The animal on the cover of *Packet Guide to Voice over IP* is the Green woodpecker (*Picus viridis*).

The cover image is a loose plate engraving, origin unknown. The cover font is Adobe ITC Garamond. The text font is Adobe Minion Pro; the heading font is Adobe Myriad Condensed; and the code font is Dalton Maag's Ubuntu Mono.

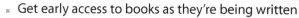

Get even more for your money.

Join the O'Reilly Community, and register the O'Reilly books you own. It's free, and you'll get:

- $4.99 ebook upgrade offer
- 40% upgrade offer on O'Reilly print books
- Membership discounts on books and events
- Free lifetime updates to ebooks and videos
- Multiple ebook formats, DRM FREE
- Participation in the O'Reilly community
- Newsletters
- Account management
- 100% Satisfaction Guarantee

Signing up is easy:

1. **Go to: oreilly.com/go/register**
2. **Create an O'Reilly login.**
3. **Provide your address.**
4. **Register your books.**

Note: English-language books only

To order books online:
oreilly.com/store

For questions about products or an order:
orders@oreilly.com

To sign up to get topic-specific email announcements and/or news about upcoming books, conferences, special offers, and new technologies:
elists@oreilly.com

For technical questions about book content:
booktech@oreilly.com

To submit new book proposals to our editors:
proposals@oreilly.com

O'Reilly books are available in multiple DRM-free ebook formats. For more information:
oreilly.com/ebooks

O'REILLY®

9 781449 339678